# Living as Equals

# Living as Equals

*How Three White Communities*
*Struggled to Make*
*Interracial Connections*
*During the Civil Rights Era*

**Phyllis Palmer**

**Vanderbilt University Press**

NASHVILLE

© 2008 by Vanderbilt University Press
Nashville, Tennessee 37235
All rights reserved

12  11  10  09  08   1  2  3  4  5

This book is printed on acid-free paper.
Manufactured in the United States of America

Frontispiece: Neighbors Inc. annual report, 1964 (courtesy
of D.C. Public Library, Washingtoniana Division, D.C. Com-
munity Archives, Collection 110); NCCJ Brotherhood Youth
Institute, Camp Kittatinny, New York, August 1962 (courtesy of
Walter Chambers); striking workers at Friedrich Refrigeration
Inc., San Antonio, Texas, 1964 (courtesy of Paul Javior).

Library of Congress Cataloging-in-Publication Data

Palmer, Phyllis M.
Living as equals : how three white communities struggled
to make interracial connections during the civil rights era /
Phyllis Palmer.
    p. cm.
Includes bibliographical references and index.
ISBN 978-0-8265-1596-4 (cloth : alk. paper)
ISBN 978-0-8265-1597-1 (pbk. : alk. paper)
    1. United States—Race relations—History—20th century.
2. United States—Ethnic relations—History—20th century.
3. Racism—United States—History—20th century.  4. Race
discrimination—United States—History—20th century.
I. Title.
E185.615.P35 2008
305.800973—dc22
2007051877

*To Elizabeth Johnson*

*and, in memoriam,*

*to Marcus Falkner Cunliffe,*

*Ruth Barnes Marynick,*

*and Joe Lee Stubblefield*

# Contents

# Acknowledgments

This project was completed over many years with advice, encouragement, and assistance from many friends, colleagues, and others who offered insights, information, and inspiration. I am certain to miss some of you in these acknowledgments, but I appreciated your help.

I thank the American Council of Learned Societies for its tangible aid of a year's sabbatical research in 1993–1994 and the George Washington University's Faculty Facilitating Fund and the Center for Washington Area Studies for grants to cover research expenses in 1999 and 2000 respectively.

Although the project relied primary on oral history interviews, a number of archivists gave assistance and useful advice: David Klaassen of the Social Welfare History Archives at the University of Minnesota; Faye Haskins and Ryan Semmes at the Washingtoniana Collection of the District of Columbia Public Library; and Brother Edward Loch at the Catholic Archives of San Antonio, Roman Catholic Archdiocese of San Antonio.

Colleagues in the American Studies Department and the Women's Studies Program at the George Washington University unfailingly supported my work. Especially helpful were early comments by James Miller and Melani McAlister and faculty and graduate students in the Americanist seminar. James Horton cotaught an early course about race in America with me and was one of the project's inspirations. Char Miller of Trinity University, San Antonio, sponsored me for a year's affiliation and introduced me to his wide-ranging scholarly network and knowledge about San Antonio politics. I was fortunate to learn about the power and practice of group dynamics through Dee Hahn-Rollins and Al Rollins, who was leading the Mid-Atlantic Training and Consulting group during the 1980s. A constant inspiration were GW faculty colleagues and outside advisors who participated in the curriculum workshops that group dynamics training helped me lead titled "Integrating Materials about Women of Color into the Undergraduate Curriculum," funded by the Ford Foundation between 1989 and 1992. Many San Antonio friends and experts gave useful guidance, especially Ben Aguirre, Mariscela Aguirre, Herschel Bernard, Linda Hardberger, Phillip Hardberger, Gail Raney, Marc Raney, Raul Rodriguez, Jan Jarboe Russell, Helen Worsham, and John Worsham.

A number of colleagues, academic and otherwise, read portions of the book and offered critiques, information, and resolve; my thanks to Marjorie Baer, Cece Box, Janet Brown, Sr. Pearl Ceasar, Howard Gillette, Avery Gordon, Vivien Hart, Ruth Jordan, Marie Tyler McGraw, Char Miller, Terry Odendahl, Carol Rose, and Josephine Woll. My constant and supportive writing group, Ann Romines and Susan Strasser, finished important books of their own during this project and inspired and prodded me to complete mine. The readers at Vanderbilt University Press gave generous and helpful suggestions. Vanderbilt University Press director Michael Ames pushed and pulled to get me to make my manuscript better, and this book owes much to his wisdom and interest. Portions of Chapter 1 were published in earlier form in "Recognizing Racial Privilege: White Boys and Girls at National Conference of Christians and Jews Summer Camps, 1959–1974," *Oral History Review* 27 (Summer/Fall 2000).

The book would not exist without the brave, sensible, self-reflective, cheerful, dedicated lives of the people I interviewed and their willingness to tell me about them. They gave wise, loving, and canny assessments of their interracial aspirations and activities. My central concern throughout the project was to give adequate voice to what I learned from them.

My mother died in the last month of my finishing this book and made me conscious again of thankfulness for my birth family of Marynicks and my Southern ancestors, the Barneses and the Lawlers. In many years living outside the South I have accumulated a friendship family that expanded my world, taught me the value of heterogeneous connections, and directly and indirectly gave me the hopefulness to write the book. I have been gifted with two marital families of Cunliffes and Stubblefields, another enlargement of association. My deepest gratitude is to one husband, Marcus Cunliffe, who died as the project was being born; to my dear husband Joe Stubblefield, who lived with it for many years and died as the book was completed; and to my darling goddaughter, Elizabeth Johnson, who never stopped asking about "the book" and cheering me on.

# Living as Equals

# Introduction

I grew up in a postwar America devoted to church attendance, house pride, and celebration of the nation's generosity. All these came together each Sunday, first at the neighborhood Methodist church, and then at a lavish midday meal. We dressed carefully in fresh clothes for Sunday school and worship service, where the minister led us in thanks for America's blessings. Afterward we drove home to a big Sunday supper of fried chicken, biscuits, cream gravy, green beans, and mashed potatoes, proofs of the nation's prosperity and the modest comforts of my middle-class neighborhood.

We white Methodists took up a special collection on World Mission Sunday, and we children brought the dimes and nickels and pennies we had saved to help other little children. In Sunday school class, we enthusiastically sang:

> Jesus loves the little children, all the children of the world.
> Red or yellow, black or white, they are precious in his sight.
> Jesus loves the little children of the world.

Following Jesus' example, we sent our child-size savings out to the needy places of Asia and Africa, learning also a lesson of white responsibility for less fortunate children whose parents couldn't provide nice homes and good food to eat.

Caring at a distance was familiar. At home, in Dallas, Texas, I learned benevolence for worthwhile inferiors who lived around us, even as I gained a sense of why those people, as a group, were not quite up to the standards of my people. The Indians my family had known in Oklahoma; the Negroes, in polite parlance, who worked for us; the Mexicans, whatever their citizenship status, we saw when we visited the Rio Grande Valley—all these fit into a mental constellation with white Americans at its center.

Simultaneously, I learned a fear of racial others, transmitted indirectly through casual admonitions or unexplained warnings. "Chinese restaurants catch stray cats and pass the meat off as chicken." "It's not safe for a girl"—implicitly, a *white* girl—"to be out at night with all these colored men around." Jesus might love dark-skinned people who lived far away and expect us to help them. Closer to home we whites still needed to maintain the separation that asserted white competence and authority over the Indians, Mexicans, Negroes, and Chinese who lived on the margins of white life and bounded white consciousness.

In the postwar era, the white majority in the United States enforced racial segregation; accepted racial discrimination in jobs, housing, and schooling; and applauded a popular culture starring admirable whites. We took the preeminence of white people so much for granted that, except when enacting segregation practices, we didn't identify our families, our neighbors, and ourselves as white.[1] In Texas, the segregation signs on the local streetcars, placing my family in the "White" section and our housekeeper in the "Colored," seemed only a benign sorting device, an affirmation, almost, of personal preferences. I did not think of my family and neighborhood as "white," as segregationist, and as upholders of a three-centuries-old system of white supremacy.

At eighteen, in 1962, I left Texas for college in Ohio and discovered many black people whose intelligence, ambition, talent, energy, and moral concern equaled my own. At Oberlin, an institution that advertised its historic position as the first U.S. college to admit black students and women students (adding them to the assumed student population of white men), I found classmates I had not imagined in my racially segregated upbringing. Down the hall lived an African American classical pianist from Chicago, and across the hall, the bookish daughter of African American librarians in Ohio. The sophisticated, widely traveled African diplomat's son majoring in chemistry tore apart my mental picture of rural, underdeveloped Africa. Africans and African Americans, once remote, were now friends, classmates, dance partners, and smoking chums at the campus hangout. "Negro," in polite early 1960s speech, no longer evoked servant or shadowy threat but an interesting peer.

The disruption of my childhood complacency led to an adolescent rejection of my family's "racism," a new term for me, and hostility to my white Southern roots. But the North quickly showed that racism was not a Southern monopoly. Some black students were townies, and they alerted the campus's budding civil rights activists to discrimination in the town of Oberlin itself, which had a substantial black population from its nineteenth-century days as a haven for escaping slaves. Leading employers followed racial codes designed for white comfort that banished black employees to janitorial and cleaning jobs behind the scenes. Northern protocol enforced segregation and white authority as effectively as did Southern law. Oberlin College students responded by picketing the recalcitrant local telephone company, urging it to hire black women as operators and black men as installers. We picketed in front of the snobbish local drugstore, demanding it give black workers some of the salesclerk jobs in the front of the store.

I threw myself into these activities to end racism, drawing on a well-established tradition of white women's aiding the downtrodden and needy. I felt courageous in debates with my Texas family, even though I shared few of the risks of my classmates, black and white, who joined voter registration drives in the Deep South, or the hardships of visiting South African students, black and white, forced into exile by hardening apartheid policies. With classmates, I raised money for civil rights workers and South African antiapartheid campaigners.

During the next decade the civil rights movement sparked racial power assertions and a women's liberation movement. From these, I learned to search for the institutions and political patterns that sustained racial separation and inequality—to see racism as not just personal antipathy but as an entire social order in need of change. Simultaneously, I began to examine the ways my white girlhood had trained me in racial confidence and female self-constriction. The nicer books, pleasanter surroundings, and better-outfitted science laboratories of the white schools in Dallas's segregated system gave me confidence in my intellectual superiority and ability to achieve. The oppressive Southern disapproval of smart girls—loud-mouthed tomboys all—drove me to find a college outside the South. By the early 1970s, the social movements of the 1960s seemed to me to be making some headway in breaking down the old structures that enforced social distance, unequal opportunities, and gender and race conformity. As a white woman, I knew that my personal well-being required changing the institutions and policies that enforced systematic inequalities, and one step was making interracial connections in graduate school, at work, and in everyday life.

## The White Response to Civil Rights

As an adult and a professor of history, I came to understand that the civil rights movement and its attractive promise of interracial connection had emerged from large changes in the postwar nation. Nazi racial practices had discredited race-based laws; the Cold War had emphasized U.S. commitments to pluralism and equality; and African American activists had modeled a world free from deference to white authority. Fortuitously, my personal life had intersected a moment of great national change, and I had embraced its possibilities.

My confidence that many white Americans of my generation had responded with the same joyous hope for racial interconnection was shaken in the early 1990s. In 1992, an all-white jury excused police officers who had pulled a black man, Rodney King, from his car and beaten him, sparking violent unrest in Los Angeles; in 1995, a racially mixed jury found the black former athlete O. J. Simpson innocent of killing his white wife, setting off hostile comments from white citizens. The national print and broadcast media revived a public discourse of "natural" racial animosities. Even though survey numbers after both events showed that a substantial minority of white Americans held opinions similar to those of black Americans, the media reported on a nation divided along racial, specifically white and black, lines.[2] Why, thirty years after the passage of the landmark civil rights legislation, was it so easy for journalists to depict a nation characterized by little cross-race understanding?

The media's use of polarizing racial language raised questions I had rarely considered since the late 1960s: How did white Americans change during the civil rights era? How did some white Americans learn to see race's effects in ways not too dissimilar from how black Americans perceived them? And how did other white Americans give up formal segregation and discrimination, yet remain suspicious of black and other people of color as a problem for the country? Why did the media go on assuming natural racial disagreements outside any historical context? The question about media depictions was one for social scientists. The question about how white Americans created new conceptions of race in response to civil rights demands for full human equality was one for a historian.

The parameters of white people's reactions were easy to draw: Some white Southerners and Northerners vehemently, and sometimes violently, opposed any loss of white power; another and much smaller group of white Americans dedicated their lives to the movement for racial justice. On the one side, some Southern political authorities mounted massive resistance to school desegregation and unleashed police dogs on black residents who were demanding voting rights, while some Northerners firebombed black home buyers moving into white areas, rioted over forced school busing for integration, and litigated against mixing urban schools with nonwhite majorities with suburban ones with white majorities.[3] On the other side, heroic white activists marched alongside black civil rights demonstrators, raised funds to finance the movement, and brought publicity to long-hidden Southern violence, while sympathetic officials used governmental power to force unsympathetic whites to accept new rules.[4]

Between these poles lay the stories of the great majority of white Americans, who joined neither mobs nor the movement for equality. Many hoped to ride out the social change without losing, or changing, much. Some white Southerners acquiesced to the necessity of giving up official segregation, and a few even described the end of the system as "liberation" for themselves. They did not become supporters of integration or interracial connections, but they felt freed from the compulsions of a system that overrode individual judgment and enforced behaviors both monstrous and prosaic.[5]

Many other white Americans eluded responsibility for racial change through a couple of distinctive, though related, strategies. Postsegregationist white Southerners moved to new suburbs but kept intact much of the apparatus of white racial advantage as they supported private, religious-oriented schools and opposed government action to improve public education, support affordable housing, offer job training, or perform any other public service that might benefit those impoverished by Jim Crow. These white Southerners and suburban white families in other regions of the country presented their beliefs as antigovernment political conservatism instead of antiblack or anti–Mexican American racial discrimination.[6] White ethnics, born into families from southern and eastern Europe who had joined the great immigration at the start of the twentieth century, formed an overlapping group that aligned with the antigovernment, individualistic ethos that left peoples of color to fend for themselves. Although Italians, Poles, Slavs, and especially Russian Jews had backed interracial labor unions since the New Deal era, the civil rights gains for racial equality coincided with the loss of labor union influence and the replacement of class interests by ethnic consciousness. By the early 1970s, white ethnic members of the working class, instead of lamenting lost union bargaining power, asserted claims to public attention and power through a revival of ethnic identity and heritage—disguised expressions of white pride.

The working class of southern and eastern European immigrants who had moved into the middle class with unionized wages, GI Bill education, and suburban homes after World War II claimed in the 1970s to stand as the representative hard-working, self-made white Americans—now, because of their recent arrival, exempt from responsibility for the racial past of slavery and Jim Crow.[7] The intertwined white reactions of acceptance of desegregation and withdrawal from racial debate laid the basis for 1980s conservatism's professions of racial fairness and its complete disinterest in persistent inequalities.

The focus of this book is white Americans who responded hopefully to the civil rights era's promise of a freer and more equitable nation. They were inspired by the movement to cross old racial boundaries and to place themselves in settings where they had to consider their responsibilities as Americans who had enjoyed benefits from being white.[8] Initially, during the 1950s, many embraced the idea of a nation liberated from racial barriers and social norms that violated ideals of individual worth and reduced freedom of association. Generally middle class, often affiliated with labor unions and other organizations associated with New Deal principles, inspired by religious affiliations, and trained in social science theories of human relations, these white Americans sought ways to break down segregation and suspicion. Following the lead of Gunnar Myrdal's wartime classic *American Dilemma* (1944), these optimistic white Americans sought to reduce prejudice through personal, though organized, connections with nonwhite Americans. If enough white Americans came to know their nonwhite neighbors, then the animosity of ignorance would metamorphose into the recognition of human sameness under the skin. Unwittingly, and sometimes arrogantly, well-intentioned advocates assumed that integration meant white people's welcoming previously marginalized peoples of color into normative white America, unaware that African Americans, Mexican Americans, or Asian Americans might have their own ideas about American ideals.

By the mid-1960s, racial power movements (black power, Chicano power, red power, third world power) claimed cultural and political representation for their communities' distinct viewpoints and challenged white

Americans to understand that personal friendliness was not sufficient to overcome centuries-old systems of white advantage. White Americans who wanted to build a genuinely egalitarian nation needed to confront the images and structures that assigned Americans to set racial categories, distributed opportunities according to racial assignments, explained away inequalities with mythologies of racial natures, and maintained whiteness as the nation's preferred and normative identity; they had to transform their behavior to withdraw their support from the institutional authority of white persons over those labeled, by contrast, nonwhite. Humans might all be the same under the skin, but the histories, circumstances, social positions, and cultural valences attached to different skin colors were not. To care for each other as equal humans required organizing political systems that enabled participants to explain and to negotiate these differences.

To study these hopeful, welcoming white responders, I asked, how did some white Americans set out to seize the moment of racial disruption for connections across the boundaries of race? In what ways, in the words of psychologist Paul L. Wachtel, did some white Americans create interracial connections that required them to ask, "Is this someone I should care about?" and then allowed them to answer yes.[9] In what ways did some white Americans change themselves, their gender expectations, and their social institutions to erode white privilege and embrace egalitarian interracial connection?

## Three Interracial Communities

Interracial connections necessarily took place in specific times and spaces. What follows are stories of three physical and organizational locations where white Americans sought out interracial connection—distinct sites of interracialism: teen summer camps, a residential neighborhood, and a city. The diversity of sites allows me to consider how racial existence was organized at the scale of the individual, the neighborhood, and the municipal polity and to probe more closely the quality of individual and institutional resistance to interracialism.

In a time and place accustomed to segregation and social distance, bringing together people defined as racially different required conscious organization. The stories I uncovered revolve around three kinds of communities—a human relations group; a neighborhood group in a desegregating city; and a citywide community-organizing group—each of which had significant religious connections. Each of these sympathized with civil rights goals, but none was directly involved in the movement. In the first instance, a longtime human relations organization, the National Conference of Christians and Jews (NCCJ), recruited a racially diverse group of teenagers to attend summer camps in the New York City and Los Angeles regions. In the second, a neighborhood group, Neighbors Inc. (NI), formed to solidify a middle-class urban neighborhood in Washington, D.C., that could offer white home buyers an interracial alternative to the highly publicized and subsidized white suburbs. In the third, the Industrial Areas Foundation (IAF) trained organizers to work with Mexican American citizens in San Antonio to claim participation in governance and then aided the organizing of Anglo citizens willing to join a cross-racial alliance to break up the white monopoly of city government.

The book investigates a spectrum of encounters to examine how white Americans came to understand different instruments of white racial privilege—social distance, segregated housing, and undemocratic definitions of the "public." In the camps, young people questioned social distance and its implicit ideals of superior white worth. In the neighborhood, adult homeowners refused residential segregation and its ostensible guarantee of real estate security and superior schools. In San Antonio, adult citizens confronted white political dominance and its assumptions of beneficent white competence. In each instance, playing, living, or working across color lines in unprecedented closeness eroded ideas of exclusively white intelligence, material comfort, and political authority, some of what Peggy McIntosh has called the "invisible package of unearned assets" that white Americans take for granted.[10]

These stories also allow consideration of a variety of racial identifications beyond the black and white designations that still limit much writing about race. Though the Washington, D.C., housing market did segregate by black and white, at the summer camps, Asian and Mexican American teens joined white and black peers. In San Antonio, the Anglo demographic minority worried much more about the Mexican American majority's voting than about the much smaller African American community, whose largest turnout would still have minimal impact.

Finally, the three stories extend the typical chronology for assessing the racial reordering stimulated by the civil rights revolution into the early 1980s. As in many recent histories, I conceive the racial power movements of the late 1960s and early 1970s not as an unfortunate diversion of civil rights activism, but as an integral unfolding of the civil rights effort. Moreover, since the 1965 Voting Rights Act was extended to protect Mexican Americans in the Southwest only in 1975, civil rights successes for Mexican Americans in the Southwest came later than black civil rights gains in other regions.[11]

## Brotherhood (and Sisterhood) Camps

Chapters 1 and 2 tell the story of the National Conference of Christians and Jews' (NCCJ) Brotherhood Camps from the mid-1950s to the mid-1970s. Inspired by Protestant Christian ideals of the equal value of God's children, NCCJ camp leaders put a multiracial and multireligious mix of high school students in an environment that afforded every young person protection and praise. Chapter 1 examines the integration years from the late 1950s to 1967. During this era, the directors and counselors organized daily living to bring young people into friendly association—sharing cabins, meals, intense discussions, dancing, singing, and hand-holding—that defied patterns of racial social distance outside the camps' realm.

Chapter 2 moves to the years from 1968 through the mid-1970s, when African American, Mexican American, American Indian, and various groups of Asian American campers more forcefully asserted the importance of their particular racial histories within the larger American story. Now the camps began each morning with race group meetings, where young people examined the situations of African Americans, Mexican Americans, or Asian Americans before reconvening to present their conclusions to the whole camp.

## Neighbors Inc.

Chapters 3 and 4 are about one Washington, D.C., group that countered the residential segregation that institutionalized social distance. In 1958, Neighbors Inc., as a set of white families and black families named their group, vowed to stake out ground that would not succumb to the emerging pattern of residential segregation: white families spreading out to exclusive new suburbs and black families confined in older center cities.[12] Instead, the group advanced a vision of living in a "democratic," necessarily heterogeneous neighborhood.

Chapter 3 describes the organization's work in the euphoric years between 1958 and 1965, when it saw neighborliness as fulfilling the newly expressed national commitment to racial desegregation. By choosing integrated housing, the NI white families gave up the white privilege of ignoring the racial inequities created by segregated housing markets; they experienced what could happen in black neighborhoods: city agencies cutting services and public schools declining. NI presumed its families would not sacrifice middle-class benefits and created a family-oriented, politically adept neighborhood to counter the allure of suburban homogeneity.

By 1965, the Neighbors Inc. area had a black majority, raising questions for its white families about what integrated living meant. These families learned about living as a minority, even if they retained some of the privileges of whiteness, especially the option to move out. Chapter 4 focuses on some of the reasons white families stayed and how organizational anchors for some families, white and black, helped them share space and negotiate disagreements—a Conservative Jewish synagogue whose members voted not to leave the city, and nearby Howard University, the premier African American establishment of higher education. Maintaining an interracial neighborhood now required facing some unpleasant, hard issues: first, recruiting white families, who had lots of housing options, and not black families, who had few; and second, moving their children into private schools and abandoning the public schools essential to the well-being of working-class and poor black families.

## Multiracial Community Organizing

Chapters 5 and 6 examine the political struggle by Mexican Americans to gain inclusion as full citizens and legitimate participants in the city government of San Antonio, Texas. After World War II, Mexican American and African American political groups tried to crack Anglo political domination, stimulating the local business leadership to reassert its control over city governance.[13]

Chapter 5 focuses on the limited interracialism of the city's Roman Catholic diocese during the 1950s and 1960s, when Archbishop Robert Lucey and his young activist white priests advocated for government funds to improve housing, job training, and wages for their poor Mexican American parishioners. Church-supported protests to gain poverty program funds, to register voters, to aid farmworkers through a state minimum wage, and to back labor union organizing of low-wage workers made only minimal gains by the late 1960s. Among the small number of middle-class Mexican Americans who had seen assimilation as the path to racial equality, white obstinacy turned many toward racial power politics.

Chapter 6 opens with the battle of the local Chicano movement for political power for the Mexican American demographic majority.[14] In the mid-1970s the Communities Organized for Public Service (COPS), affiliated with Saul Alinsky's Industrial Areas Foundation, presented a new kind of group to assert the interests of its long-ignored constituents—neighborhood and Catholic parish based, Mexican American identified, and bilingual, with strong women's leadership. The Metropolitan Congregational Alliance, a group of predominantly Anglo church congregations, collaborated with COPS to put human development on the city's agenda. Anglos who participated in an interracial political alliance learned to argue and work in appreciative relationships to build a coalition that made clear that public goods were an interracial goal.[15]

## Emotional Learning

Each of the book's three stories has a foundation in the usual historical sources of organizational archives, newspaper reports, public documents, and related scholarship. These, however, often provide little information about processes of personal change, the shifts in feeling and emotion that encourage a person to risk new relationships and behaviors. To investigate how some white Americans put themselves in new situations that might reveal white privilege and provoke new responses, I relied heavily on oral interviews. Each of the almost one hundred interviews asked for a racial autobiography: where the person grew up; what family, teachers, neighbors, ministers, priests, or rabbis told him or her about race; when she or he first became aware of racial inequality; how she or he began to unlearn old, and to formulate new, understandings of race; how the camp, neighborhood, or political work affected perceptions of racial difference; what new behaviors followed; and how she or he thought about race today, at the turn of the twenty-first century. The questions probed differences among girls' expectations of boys, and women's of men, in terms of friendships, family roles, community responsibility, and leadership. Women's and men's changing racial behaviors were simultaneously upsetting gender norms, and these witnesses reflected on how interracial choices changed them and their environments.

Although the book focuses on the hard work required of white Americans to give up white racial benefits, it also significantly depends on interviews with nonwhite campmates and camp leaders, neighbors, and political organizers. I used a similar protocol with these witnesses and found, of course, a very different set of racial autobiographies than those recounted by their white peers. Their stories gave me a good idea of what my white witnesses had heard when they put themselves into an interracial location. They also gave me new respect for the complex experiences of race in the United States—the rich specifics of Mexican American history, the profound depth and variety of African American presence, the American-enforced unity on diverse Asian immigrations, and the mix of many of these groups and of white Americans, too, in the neighborhoods of postwar cities on the eve of white flight. Multiracial urban life in the 1940s and 1950s offered an alternative to integration driven by a singular white norm, though it was an option more often recognized by nonwhite than by white Americans.

I located the first participants through fortuitous meetings, then asked for names and contacts for others they had known—at camps, in Neighbors Inc., and among San Antonio's rare interracial alliances. Starting with this snowball sample, I sought out people who emerged as centrally memorable or institutionally significant: NCCJ camp directors, for instance; Neighbors Inc., officers or oft-mentioned volunteers; Catholic Anglo priests identified with interracial projects and Anglo leaders in the COPS/Metro organization.

Since my primary goal is to tell not the institutional histories of these organizations but the stories of how the organizations enabled new moments of confrontation, caring, and change, I did not seek a random sample of participants. Rather, I examine processes of how some white Americans put themselves into new associations, developed new relationships, and underwent intellectual and emotional shifts.[16] Since each experience was unique, these descriptions might be infinite. Certainly, each person I talked with remains a distinct voice and character for me. But each person also came into the interracial setting with expectations and ideas developed from within a shared national history and culture. Following the lead of sociologist Ruth Frankenberg, I have analyzed a set of racial autobiographies "to map out and situate in sociocultural terms some patterns in . . . which whiteness [was] lived" and revised in the civil rights era; to explore sources of white people's aspirations for freer connections with nonwhites; and to identify the helps and hindrances to racially egalitarian relationships.[17]

# Whiteness

Unlike studies of race relations, which ask how white people changed their attitudes toward black people, Mexican people, or others perceived as not white while assuming that "white" remains unchanged, this book argues that civil rights inspired some white Americans to become new kinds of white people. I rely on the insights of the massive scholarship on the social construction of race produced during the past two decades. In this view, race is a system of categorizing humans and awarding resources accordingly. Race is not something a person has, in a biological sense; rather, race is a social location that a person inhabits as a consequence of the place assigned to a person's birth family, skin color, or both. To make the relations of racial groups different, in this view, requires changing the systems that define racial groups as mutually exclusive, incommensurable entities and that allot and determine racial identities.

A significant element of the new racial scholarship has been devoted to investigating how white became the privileged race, holding cultural, economic, political, and social supremacy during the past five centuries or so. By the mid-twentieth century population geneticists and cultural anthropologists had concluded that race was neither genetically based nor culturally determined. Europeans, some scholars argued, had formulated the categories of African, Asian, Indian, and mestizo in order to justify white colonial and imperial authority by the presumed Asian deviance, African laziness, indigenous backwardness, and mestizo ineffectualness in contrast to European intelligence.[18] Instead of the social positions of various races being naturally derived, humans have constructed them through the application of substantial resources to create a rich cultural fabric of stories and pictures of racial differences and to enforce laws and social regulations that keep doubters in their assigned places.

To indicate the actions required to make race, many scholars use the neologism "racialize" to indicate that active choices (or benign inaction) make race. Philosopher K. Anthony Appiah defines "racializing" as an ongoing historical process that divided humanity "into a small number of groups, called 'races,' in such a way that members of these groups shared fundamental, heritable, physical, moral, intellectual, and cultural characteristics with one another that they did not share with members of any other race."[19] Throughout this book, the term "racialize" indicates any behavior intended to define human groups as basically bounded and unlike in some significant elements. Racializing, then, is not the same as what is usually called exhibiting racism—hostility to another group. It is both subtler and harsher. A racialist may claim to value all racial groups equally and at the same time hold a person of a different race to be absolutely unlike himself, which precludes empathy and a shared hold on humanity.

Some scholars and activists object to the idea of social construction as implying that if race is created, then it's not real and so its consequences are minimal. Cultural studies thinkers, such as Stuart Hall, have responded that just because something is a cultural creation and constituted through language, historical images, and cultural definitions doesn't mean that it doesn't also have " 'real' social, economic, and political conditions of existence and 'real' material and symbolic effects."[20] Philosopher Judith Butler adds that just because race is constructed does not mean that "it is artificial." Especially for groups fighting against the fictions of white superiority and seeking political mass, "it is a mobilizing fiction" for unified assertion.[21]

By the mid-1970s, feminist theorists applied a social construction approach to gender and posited that reproductive organs, like skin color, had been used to categorize fundamentally similar humans as having mutually exclusive natures (popularly expressed by the concept of "the opposite sex").[22] Feminists of color then pointed out that a combination of race and gender had programmed quite different lives across the panoply of racialized women.[23] Divisions into female and male tracked across racial distinctions and determined appropriate roles and relationships, within any racial group and across racial groups. Like those of race, the constructions of gender historically worked to create and to rationalize systems of male power and authority, proliferated through the hierarchies of race. Humanly designed and enforced systems racialized and gendered people simultaneously and did so in similar relational ways. If one was male, one could not be female; if one was white or Anglo, one could not be black or Mexican American.

One example reveals the relational quality of gendered racializing as I experienced it in 1950s Texas. As a youngster, I visited my aunt and uncle in the Rio Grande Valley and loved Maria, the young woman who cooked and cleaned for my relatives, and from the evidence of an old photo, hugged and fussed over me. Maria was a Mexican national who crossed the border illegally (without the requisite visa) to earn money to care for her children, lived in my aunt's garage during the week, and snuck across the border on weekends to see her family. As a child, I considered my aunt kind and generous for fixing up the garage bedroom and my uncle clever for helping Maria come and go in defiance of the border patrol.

Only while doing the research for this book did I learn how U.S. immigration law had been designed to control Mexican labor for the benefit of U.S. employers. In the early twentieth century, when U.S. agriculture needed a pliable labor force, the United States began requiring visas for the movement of workers across the southern border. The federal government issued hundreds of thousands of visas to low-wage Mexican workers, and it also ignored thousands more workers who crossed the border without papers, leaving them legally unprotected and easy for U.S. employers to hire or fire. This immigrant workforce displaced long-settled Mexican American families as workers and encouraged a "migratory agricultural workforce" that historian Mae Ngai calls "the central element in the . . . process of modern Mexican racial formation in the United States."[24] This system of border regulation produced racialized/gendered persons. It enabled my uncle to show off a white man's earning power. It allowed my aunt to employ Maria for basic housework and at the same time appear benevolent for paying her wages she could not earn in Mexico. And it required Maria to fulfill the stereotype of a Mexican domestic in the United States: one who accepts a domestic's job, stifles her anger at the border guards and her employers, and leaves her own children behind in Reynosa—proof that she was a less civilized woman than my aunt—in order to earn money to feed them.

Disrupting the social divisions of race upset gender norms and vice-versa. White girls had been trained to accept white women's responsibility to maintain the social distance that prevented casual cross-race friendship from leading to race mixing and miscegenation. White boys had been taught to be protectors of females, though usually only of *white* girls. In the utopian setting of NCCJ camps, young people experienced the excitement of pursuing newly allowed adolescent curiosity, competition, and affection, even as they negotiated sexual attractions in the shadow of longtime racial divides that had protected white women's purity through threats of violence to nonwhite men and debasement of nonwhite women. In the Cold War setting of the 1950s and 1960s, white women's domesticity in new suburbs, supported by white men's hard and disciplined work, epitomized U.S. prosperity and freedom. When white husbands and wives chose instead to live in cities, they transformed the white family from one with rigid gender roles into one closer in character to the black and interracial families they found as allies: wives who contributed to the family income and shared adult responsibilities for the whole community's well-being.

The white priests and nuns who applied Roman Catholic concern to public issues in San Antonio and the white women and men who joined Metro Alliance upset different kinds of racialized gender. Priests moved from paternal protectiveness to assisting organizers, and nuns asserted interest in social injustice as well as social work. The white men who joined Metro Alliance gave up reliance on their professional authority, and the white women, on their civic expertise; each group learned about realities of power that had been invisible in the cocoon of white, middle-class comfort.

To be a different sort of white person inevitably required being a different kind of man or woman. In the last two decades, scholars in the field of whiteness studies have written rich explanations of how white Europeans and their offspring came to dominate the rest of the world and to perpetuate institutions that sustained white power in a postcolonial era.[25] This scholarship equates whiteness with dominance and oppression. A question for this book was how to conceive a white person's ability to transform herself as a means to transform the institutions of whiteness. What could a white person do to rectify an inheritance of privilege and dominance and to reduce its ongoing consequences? Was the solution to abolish whiteness, as the nation abolished slavery?[26] How could a white person appreciate her ancestors and celebrate her childhood, yet not perpetuate many of the historical stories, cultural images, and social advantages that came along with that history and location?

The stories in this book show white people who entered new interracial relationships based on mutual respect and care, daily neighborliness, and constructive bargaining in scenarios that revealed new possibilities for white existence. These race-mixing communities upset the expected patterns of everyday life where, historian Thomas C. Holt argues, "racist ideas and practices are naturalized, made self-evident, and thus seemingly beyond audible challenge."[27] Only as they interacted in new ways with African Americans, Mexican Americans, Filipinos, and Asian Americans could they enact different relationships of race that undermined and negated white as authoritative and dominant.

Even with good intentions, however, many found it difficult to give up the unreflective benefits and comfort of whiteness. One of the most insidious elements of post–civil rights whiteness was its assumption of white innocence. If a particular white person did not behave in overtly hostile, violent, derogatory ways toward nonwhites, then he could assume the mantle of nonracism, affecting friendly impartiality while evading any recognition of or responsibility for the persistence of white advantage. Some manifested innocence by moving to middle-class suburbs and embracing an ideology of class segregation that disguised inherent racial inequality, as Matthew Lassiter describes.[28] Others, even so bold an antiracist as writer Wendell Berry, might apologize for past racism even while overlooking its persistent effects—a hazard, theorist Debian Marty argues, of seeing ourselves according to "our antiracist ideals" and not "as others know us." Her remedy— "caring about our interracial relationships more than we care for our antiracist self-image"—became a possibility in the three communities in this book, but it was not always and never easily achieved.[29]

## Inspiration for Change

What ideas inspired white people to cross old lines? What institutions supported them as they put themselves into places to develop new relationships? The left-liberal tradition in U.S. culture and politics sees positive social gains as resulting from conflict between the powerless and the powerful. Social change occurs through contests with winners and losers, hard power struggles, and so scholars search for the roots of anger. Processes of changing hearts, by contrast, look soft, defy easy measurement, and sound sappy. This book presumes, by contrast with the conflict model, that cultivating new kinds of relationships can transform people and the way they live everyday forms of race and gender sufficiently to bring substantial change. To move from existences firmly defined by the gendered, racialized practices of the past and the comfortable habits of privilege required what theorist Avery Gordon calls "utopian" inspiration: not an "ideal future world," but a new "standpoint for comprehending and living in the here and now."[30] For many of my witnesses, the motivation to take risks came out of the three predominant U.S faiths—Protestant Christianity, Roman Catholic Christianity, and the Conservative and Reform branches of American Judaism—and from a secular-based professional rethinking of approaches to building better human relations.

For religious groups and for the visionaries who changed older ideas of human relations into the new field of group dynamics, empowerment was a liberatory process of coming into a fuller expression of being, stretching out of old roles, and living in relationships without either fearfully holding onto dominance or resentfully abasing oneself. Religious groups invoked God, while human relations professionals did not, but both emphasized social change as a process of developing into the mutual care and reconciliation that provided security and freedom for each person's full human expression. Conflict was inevitable as people argued through diverse interests, but it was enfolded by a commitment to existing within a mutually respectful relationship.

The professional study of group processes and the development of the field of human relations in the immediate postwar era owed much to German émigré psychologist Kurt Lewin, who arrived in the United States in 1934 fleeing Nazi hostility. Lewin and others theorized about the effects on human feeling and relationships of consciously organizing central social groups—families, classrooms, schools, workplaces, and neighborhoods—in democratic patterns.[31] Perhaps because of Lewin's untimely death in 1947, or perhaps because of the difficulties historians face in documenting the evanescent human interactions of groups, the phenomenon of training in group dynamics has rarely been linked with civil rights activities.

Historians have certainly credited religion as a central element in black civil rights struggles.[32] Fewer studies have focused on religion's role in challenging and encouraging white Americans to seek new kinds of racial existence, perhaps because many of the most prominent whites in the movement came out of secular, though Jewish-identified, left-liberal politics. Religious Judaism and Roman Catholic social justice impulses have often been overlooked, and Roman Catholicism has been implicated in white opposition to civil rights, as upwardly mobile communities of Italian and Polish Catholics opposed residential integration.[33] Despite its early twentieth-century social gospel imperative to reform the world, white Protestant Christianity split on the issue of supporting civil rights. Studies of white Protestantism's institutional support of civil rights focus on national federations, such as the National Council of Churches or the Christian Student Movement, and not on the kinds of congregation-level, neighborhood commitments that black Protestant churches nurtured.[34]

My interviews reveal that convictions of human connectedness, taught by local ministers and rabbis in a variety of community-based institutions, inspired a sense of possibility and responsibility and, at the same time, provided communal support for risk taking. Similar to the white people whose Protestant and Jewish faith carried them into civil rights activism, many of the white people in this book, including Roman Catholics, attribute their impetus to seek out interracial relationships to religious teachings, often learned when they were young.[35] Indeed, white suburban churches that backed civil rights lost members by the tens of thousands to evangelical churches that valued personal piety over social activism.

Protestant, Catholic, and Jew, the quasi-official religious affiliations of the postwar United States, drew on different traditions and different positions in U.S. society. Mainstream white Christian churches, with very few exceptions, had refused nonwhite members into the 1930s. By the late 1940s, however, worldwide protest against Christian involvement with colonialism and local demands for desegregation of all-white urban congregations forced U.S. Christians to confront the hypocrisy of preaching brotherhood while practicing racial separation. Although segregation seemed more understandable in a faith grounded in ancestry and not conversion, Jewish congregations still had to decide what position to take in a civil rights struggle against racist social injustice.

Among white Protestants who responded to the civil rights challenge, the predominant vision was an expansive beloved community of love and justice uniting all peoples. In theological and practical terms, Protestants interpreted "beloved community" in two distinct ways. For those schooled in a nineteenth-century liberal Protestantism bent on the inevitable improvement of the world, ending racial segregation and injustice was a significant natural step to human perfectibility and progress. In the more pessimistic strain of Protestantism that continued to stress human sinfulness, though often modernized or intellectualized as alienation from God's purpose for human community, civil rights challenged believers to struggle but to prepare to receive a divine gift of human reconciliation across the rift of racism.[36] Held within the magnetic field of these powerful impulses for racial change, Protestant ministers and staff leading the National Conference of Christians and Jews, ministers in Washington, D.C., and advocates for Metro Alliance in San Antonio had an image of a just world—integrated and just—that they could, and should, help bring into being.

Roman Catholicism had no similar traditions of perfectionism or of individual salvation. By the 1950s, however, an American Catholicism that had primarily served the needs of blue-collar immigrants began to feel the effects of its parishioners' upward mobility and of the Church's rapidly evolving human rights orientation. The Church had earlier advocated some social interventions, beginning with Pope Leo XIII's 1893 encyclical, *Rerum Novarum*, which approved labor union organizing to balance the overweening power of great industrialists. By the early 1940s, San Antonio's archbishop, Robert Lucey, was invoking Leo XIII to support labor unions as a means to raise the low wages of Mexican Americans and African Americans.

In the 1930s, the Church formulated alternatives to state/corporate fascism and its promises to aid the working class. European Catholic thinkers, notably Jacques Maritain, claimed that democratic government and citizen participation were an "inspiration of the Gospel."[37] A few U.S. Catholics began denouncing racial segregation after a Jesuit priest, John LaFarge, published *Interracial Justice* in 1937, and in the 1940s and early 1950s, many Catholic archbishops, like Lucey, led the way in desegregating schools in their parishes.[38] After World War II, as once-colonized peoples demanded independence and new standing for the world's peoples of color, the Church moved away from tacitly condoning prevailing political authorities. Pope John XXIII convened the Second Vatican Council and in 1963 issued *Pacem in Terris*, an encyclical that called for governments to recognize "that all men are equal by reason of their natural dignity" and required to participate in self-governance.[39] For young white priests and nuns, as well as for many U.S. laity, Vatican II's call to personal responsibility to empower citizens and end poverty was an incentive to join the civil rights movement. Although Vatican II led to divisions among laity and religious authorities about issues of hierarchical order, a more democratically oriented Church allowed for the ecumenical connections that brought some young people to NCCJ camps and supported the local organizing that built community solidarity in San Antonio.[40]

In the 1950s, Judaism, the demographically smallest of the three religions, spoke from the stance of a people singled out for destruction in the Holocaust. Earlier generations of secularized Jewish labor organizers had joined African Americans to battle social and racial discrimination.[41] With the postwar confidence of successful assimilation, religiously engaged Jews emerged as activists. Rabbi Abraham Heschel, a Holocaust refugee who taught at the Jewish Theological Seminary in New York, embraced civil rights as another moment when humans had to act against the evil of racism—the treatment of one class of humans as less than God's creation.[42] Heschel argued that Jews must act, even Jews who were still the target of prevailing prejudices. Good deeds preceded good thoughts, Heschel wrote; when humans acted in kinder, braver, more generous and helpful ways, then feelings gradually came into line with actions.[43]

In the highly religious postwar U.S. environment, Rabbi Heschel advocated ecumenical joint action to advance the realm of God through political decisions. He and Rev. Martin Luther King Jr. shared theological interests, and, according to historian Jonathan Sarna, each saw the other as an heir to the Old Testament prophets who warned against violating God's principles of justice. The American Jewish Congress sponsored postwar interracial projects to advance U.S. democracy. The NCCJ, though directed by Protestants, included a high percentage of Jewish teens among its campers. One of Heschel's students became a leading rabbi in the Neighbors Inc. area.

Historian James J. Farrell expansively applies the term "personalism," a theological premise that all "people were created in God's image, [and] the dignity of human beings was God-given," to claim an affinity among religious and secular political activists during the 1960s. Describing personalism as "a combination of Catholic social thought, communitarian anarchism, radical pacifism, and humanistic psychology," Farrell ideologically unites secularist humanistic psychologists with theologically grounded Catholics and some Protestants and Jews.[44] Farrell's eclecticism captures the easy optimism of 1960s dreams of a revolution toward egalitarian, peaceful caring. But it obscures the difficult processes of changing long-term behaviors.

Religiously based and humanistic conceptions of democracy and equality required building new communities in which to live as a new kind of person; changing laws was not sufficient. For Roman Catholics of the social justice and Protestants of any beloved community persuasion, the fulfillment of one's humanity came through enacting relationships of mutual respect. Although these principles sounded like the secularized version of participatory democracy advocated by the New Left, their source was "Christian conviction," Charles Marsh argues, and not the "desacralized" affirmations of individuality in documents like the Students for Democratic Society's Port Huron Statement.[45] The well-intentioned white communities this book describes did not generally hold the intense religious faith that Marsh and David Chappell define as central to the courageous work of civil rights activists, black and white, in the South. But they shared a set of theological imperatives and often belonged to churches struggling to align their professions of God's care for all with the realities of segregation and discrimination. And religious and human relations training both stressed that humans changed only through placing themselves in egalitarian environments that affirmed each person. Creating spaces of crude equality was a means to reduce the self-satisfied assurance of the powerful, to arouse the self-assertion of the less powerful, and to build relationships more in accord with God's care for every person. One of Martin Luther King Jr.'s Boston University teachers, Paul Tillich, had argued that the connection between love and justice always flowed through power. Without some equality of power, love acted sentimentally on its good impulses, producing not justice but patronizing charity. Absent social connections between the more powerful and the less powerful, those in authority cynically held on to power, unable to imagine why they should help those who couldn't stand up for themselves.[46]

Motivated by the possibility of living without the inhibitions and barriers of race, many of this book's white witnesses chose to put themselves into settings that enabled greater equality and to keep their minds and feelings open to their new associates. Though they certainly faced conflicts—within the groups, with the housing industry, with politically and economically dominant Anglos—their vision was advanced not by opposition, but by engagement. Without losing sight of the envisioned future, group work firmly anchored people in the present, their new relationships acting as means that embodied their utopian ends. As theologians and psychologists warned, building a new self was not comfortable, and individuals often sought and found excuses to give up the task, but such hopeful interracial encounters deserve historical attention and offer lessons for our time.

## The Choice

Fannie Lou Hamer, one of the prophetic leaders of the civil rights movement and a canny politician, used parables to present lessons to ponder. In a 1971 speech, she shifted the onus for civil rights success from legislators and demonstrators to ordinary people. There was an old, wise man, "and he could answer questions that was almost impossible for people to answer," she said. One day, two young people decided they could trick the old man. They would catch a bird, carry it to the old man, and ask, "This what we hold in our hands today, is it alive or is it dead?" If he answered, "Dead," they would release the bird; if he replied, "Alive," they would crush it to death. "They walked up to the old man and asked, 'This that we hold in our hands today, is it alive or is it dead?' He looked at the young people and he smiled. And he said, 'It's in your hands.' "[47]

The white Americans spotlighted in this book saw the civil rights era as putting new choices in their hands. They put themselves into new relationships and into locations where being white was no guarantee of privilege. In these riskier, more egalitarian environments, they found other ways of being white. Our own historical moment raises different challenges for those of us uncomfortable with white advantage still only partly diminished. In the spirit of my own religious heritage, I offer these stories as inspiration—to remind us that we constantly construct gendered race in our daily lives and that the choice between stultifying self-protection and power or vivifying relationship and love is in our hands.

# 1

# Camping for Democracy

## *Brotherhood Camps, 1957–1967*

This [camp] showed that brotherhood isn't just a word, but
rather a way of life. It proves that something can be done.
—*Brotherhood camper, 1960*

In the summer of 1959, a bright, almost fifteen-year-old blond rode from
Long Island into Manhattan. Her parents dropped her at a rank of buses
waiting to transport a couple hundred of the region's teenagers to a rural campsite. An academic leader and school newspaper editor, Gail Kern
had volunteered to attend a week-long National Conference of Christians
and Jews (NCCJ) camp focused on the issues of prejudice and democracy.
She calculated that this "citizenship-type activity" would contribute to her
"standing out" at school.[1]

Gail's family conceived itself as not racist. Her German-Irish Catholic
American father and Swedish Lutheran American mother had both expressed disapproval of racial discrimination, even though they lived in a
segregated town. By the end of her week at camp, Gail had become aware
of unspoken constraints, especially the objections that she believed her
parents would have to her dating a black boy. In the afternoon discussion
groups assigned to campers to argue through the morning lectures, she
met an "African American boy from Brooklyn whom [she became] really
fond of." She remembers that when the campers bussed back into New
York City and said their good-byes in front of their waiting parents,

I hugged and kissed [him]. I don't know whether that was the first
time we had kissed or the only time we had kissed. My memory is
I would have felt perfectly comfortable walking around that camp,

may well have done, holding hands with him—out of friendship, a sense of real closeness.

Filled with a sense of companionship, this dutiful eldest daughter could ignore her parents' presumed disapproval as they witnessed what she had learned at camp. But she knew that the social intimacy between a white girl and a black boy that had been comfortable and unremarkable in the camp's realm could become a spectacle in the everyday outside world.

In recounting her teenage experiences, Gail expressed a distinction between two meanings of whiteness available to well-intentioned white Americans during the 1950s. The good-citizen form of whiteness required displays of fair-mindedness and disapproval of race prejudice—all consistent with living in a segregated neighborhood. But the social association model that Gail had lived at camp asked for actual engagement with other races and opened possibilities of disrupting presumptions of natural white authority. The NCCJ camps that Gail and thousands of other teens would attend during the 1950s and 1960s came out of citizenship traditions, but they created learning spaces that authorized young people to try out unprecedented behaviors not generally allowed in their families, schools, and neighborhoods.

Regional offices of the NCCJ chose whether to make human relations camps part of the local program. From the early 1950s on, starting in Los Angeles, regional directors authorized one-week, residential sessions of camps intended to teach a diverse group of young people how to live in more democratic ways, accepting heterogeneity as an essential component of democracy. Depending on the camp director's vision, the camps recruited between 125 and 300 students for each session, usually at the start and the end of the summer school break when NCCJ could rent facilities from church, community, or college groups. Over the period covered by this chapter, between the mid-1950s and the mid-1960s, about 5,000 young people attended Los Angeles region camps; about 4,000 went to New York City camps; about 1,500 attended the Newark, New Jersey, camps; and a few thousand more joined NCCJ discussion groups at their high schools. Although the overall numbers were small, the emphasis on recruiting school leaders, working with sympathetic teachers and organizations, and offering a practical response to the cultural vision of inclusive democracy made the NCCJ camps, and others organized by church and community groups, visible experiments in the willingness of some white Americans to replace racial dominance with friendship.

## Cultural Pluralism in Practice

The camps emerged within a prevalent, post–World War II liberal ideal of cultural pluralism, which promised that the United States would never fall into the disastrous racism so recently defeated in Nazi Germany and Imperial Japan. Moreover, the image of white Americans as accepting of heterogeneous groups was essential to the nation's claim to lead the free world in the Cold War against the authoritarian Communists of the USSR and China. For the United States to compete for the allegiance of newly independent or soon-to-be independent nations of Asia and Africa, white Americans had to prove that theirs was a country able to respect myriad racial, religious, and cultural differences. The inspirational language of cultural pluralism never made clear, however, whether pluralism implied only toleration of minorities by a benevolent, white- and Protestant-dominant majority or recognition of varied races and communities as fully American.[2]

Prewar practices of intergroup relations, such as those the National Conference of Christians and Jews developed, focused on teaching dominant white Protestants to accept Roman Catholic and Jewish immigrants from the eastern and southern margins of Europe. The NCCJ formed from a committee in the Protestant-only Federal Council of Churches, triggered by virulent anti-Catholic attacks on Democratic candidate Al Smith during the 1928 presidential campaign. Led from its founding into the 1960s by a Presbyterian minister and educator, Everett Clinchy, the organization had affiliated a few leading Catholic and Jewish proponents of ecumenicalism; a succession of prominent businessmen, always one from each of the three religions, had routinely served as cochairs. NCCJ began by circulating information pamphlets about diverse religious beliefs, and in early 1934, as fascist appeals spread in the United States, began the observance of Brotherhood Day (expanded to Brotherhood Week in 1939). The national imperative to reduce social conflict was clear when President Franklin Roosevelt accepted the position of the event's honorary chair (a tradition all U.S. presidents followed into the 1960s). After 1933, NCCJ's Trio Tours featured a rabbi, a Catholic priest, and a Protestant minister debating in front of large audiences in various cities, and local newspapers and national newsreels reported favorably their friendly verbal sparring matches. The U.S. Army asked NCCJ to continue Trio visits to U.S. military bases during World War II to help defuse religious friction among the newly enlisted troops.[3]

Brotherhood events advocated respect for different peoples but avoided questions about the existing distribution of economic, political, and social power. Throughout most of its first two decades, NCCJ confined its universalistic appeals to the "brotherhood of man under the fatherhood of God" within socially and politically acceptable boundaries set by white racial segregation. The Brotherhood campaigners did not, for instance, endorse the call by African American intellectuals and the black press for the wartime Double-V campaign of victory against fascism abroad and racism at home. The Brotherhood Week ads, even in Southern cities, advocated generalized goodwill among people of different religious and racial groups, without challenging ongoing practices of racial segregation and discrimination.

American Protestantism's usual prewar default in favor of social order over social justice was changing, however, in favor of a more expansive conception of brotherhood. An international Christian (excepting the Roman Catholic Church) conference on church, community, and the state, meeting in Oxford, England, in 1937, had asserted as a fundamental Christian principle "the right of every person, whatever his race, color or present status, to the conditions essential for life as a person." A prelude to founding the World Council of Churches in 1948, the Oxford meeting also inspired new thinking among U.S. Protestants. In 1946, the Federal Council of Churches (soon to be the National Council of Churches) adopted a resolution against racial segregation and encouraged member denominations to do the same. During the next few years, Northern Baptists, Episcopalians, Lutherans, and Methodists debated internally and, over the next decade, issued pronouncements that "gave expression for the first time to the theological concern for the total man [sic], man as a creature of God living in society."[4]

Social conflicts during and after the war pushed human relations groups like NCCJ to expand their activities to include more direct education and mediation and to recruit a wider array of Americans. In 1943, when anti-Mexican race riots occurred in Los Angeles and antiblack riots in Detroit, NCCJ started a pilot project in the Springfield, Massachusetts, public schools to teach racial tolerance. Postwar racial confrontations—over wartime internment of Japanese Americans, abuse of imported Mexican laborers, discrimination against Puerto Ricans and African Americans working in defense plants, recognition of poverty on Indian reservations and among southwestern Mexican Americans, and resentment against Jewish refugees in the United States—demanded new responses. NCCJ extended its intergroup relations programs, cosponsoring a Parent-Teacher Association program, Rearing Children of Good Will; organizing labor-management relations workshops; and establishing police-community training programs to reduce the conflicts caused by predominantly white police units enjoying officially sanctioned power and force as they patrolled predominantly nonwhite neighborhoods. Even after the New York City headquarters office widely distributed copies of *To Secure These Rights* (the 1947 report of President Truman's Committee on civil rights) and appointed "Negroes, Orientals, and people of Mexican origin" to its committees, however, regional offices in the South and Southwest (especially the large offices in Atlanta, Dallas, and San Antonio) were careful not to alienate their local business supporters by taking up issues raised by local civil rights groups.[5]

Teaching tolerance could serve as a device to avoid direct commentary on controversial public issues. And a new postwar emphasis on teaching tolerance to the young moved the spotlight onto young people and off adult authorities. The young, experts speculated, held ideas less hardened than their parents' and were more able to learn acceptance of peoples from different communities and backgrounds. As one guidebook to programs advised: "Youth and teenage years, when the individual is widening his horizons beyond neighborhood and home . . . are times when significant personal growth through [inter]group experience is possible."[6] In public schools and in summer programs often run by church groups like the American Friends Service Committee and the Ethical Culture Society, adults organized classroom and experiential lessons to open young people to new encounters with previously segregated groups.[7]

The earliest NCCJ camps taught tolerance as civics. Concerned about Mexican American young people's social isolation and reports of juvenile delinquency in Los Angeles's Mexican American neighborhoods, in 1951 the City Welfare Commission put funds into NCCJ's Anytown, USA, summer camps designed and led by intergroup relations expert Stewart Cole. In a one-week session, the teens elected a mayor, vice mayor, and town council to direct camp activities for the week; the council continued to meet during the winter months to plan the next summer's camp. The LA camps recruited primarily from public schools that were de facto segregated and worked on the principle that if young people were brought together to work on a civics project, even an artificial one, they would internalize new attitudes of mutual acceptance. Cole had a falling-out with NCCJ and moved Anytown, USA, to Phoenix in the late 1950s, after which the camps began a transition to a human relations orientation under the name Brotherhood, USA. When the New York City camps got underway in the mid-1950s, their leaders came out of new academic programs in human relations, so the region's camps began with that approach.

Simultaneously, the NCCJ confronted the organization's timidity about aligning itself with the civil rights revolution in opposition to white dominance. Split over whether to advocate for the Supreme Court's *Brown v. Board of Education* decision to end legal segregation or to limit the organization's mandate to religious tolerance, in 1958 NCCJ hired a prominent sociologist to advise about whether to add racial issues to its primary mission of religious tolerance. Professor J. Milton Yinger concluded:

> Brotherhood is indivisible. Attacks on the rights of Negroes easily spill over into anti-semitic and anti-Catholic activity [and] since there are 500,000 Negro Catholics, seven or eight million Negro Protestants, and even a few non-Caucasian Jews, the NCCJ is almost inevitably interracial. . . . For a National Conference of Christians and Jews in 1958 to fail to say forthrightly and clearly that it stands for desegregation "with all deliberate speed," that it supports the law [enunciated in *Brown v. Board*], seems to me to be unthinkable.[8]

NCCJ staff could now pay attention to race as a part of the organization's official purpose, and racial differences became a regular topic for youth camps.

With a stronger emphasis on race, NCCJ camps began to form democratic groups using new human relations techniques developed by psychologists to build cooperation and civilian morale during World War II. By contrast with intergroup relations methods that stressed information and contact theory that promised benefits simply from cross-racial meetings, German émigré psychologist Kurt Lewin had theorized the social formation of identities. Lewin argued that in democratic group interactions, humans could confront challenges from others, glean new insights, break out of old responses and habits, and receive encouragement and affirmation to adopt new ideas and behavior. One gained the ability to be self-governing through mutually respectful interdependence with people alike and unlike oneself.[9]

The developing field of human relations emphasized that individuals needed to engage their emotions in order to change their views of self and of others. Without confronting emotional attachments, a person was un-likely to shift from long-held, socially approved patterns of avoidance and dominance that sustained U.S. racial norms.[10] In a new group formed just after Lewin's death in 1947 and based on his new theory, group dynam-ics, the National Training Laboratories developed techniques that distin-guished training from teaching. Teaching relied on the cognitive trans-mission of information and assumed that behavior changed in response to new data. Training, by contrast, organized people in small groups to accomplish tasks, imparted skills to examine the feelings and self-conceptions participants experienced in working together, and assumed that participants could undergo a process of self-transformation through consciously analyzing the emotions, ideas of self, and behavior they en-acted within the group.[11] By the early 1950s, human relations programs developing in universities drew on group dynamics techniques that distin-guished their work from the older human or intergroup relations practice of teaching tolerance.

## Making White Visible

To encourage the candid discussions that developed knowledge of self and others, camps had to undo the reality that, as Encampment for Democracy founder Algernon Black put it, "American social structure tends to con-dition youth toward homogeneity rather than heterogeneity."[12] Since the homogeneous dominant culture glorified white children as the standard of U.S. humanity, to challenge homogeneity meant exposing young white people to realities outside their daily experiences, realities that young people of color knew firsthand. But polite young white people had learned to avoid the public mention of difference—a diplomatic way, perhaps, to avoid embarrassing another young person who didn't fit the standard. The effect, however, was to leave the white ideal intact, the nonwhite young person a minority, and assumptions of white predominance invisible and unexamined.

In various ways, NCCJ camp directors learned the new human rela-tions/group dynamics techniques, and white directors cheerfully used them to upset the expectations of the United States as a homogeneous and white-normative country. The New York camp director, Margaret Gillmore, aided by human relations experts at Teachers College, Colum-bia University, explicitly set out to disrupt the comfort of tacit white self-segregation. When she began to direct the camp in the mid-1950s, she decided to hold the camps at Briarcliff College during the school's vacant summer months to demonstrate the reality of white aloofness in that setting. "We took the students there, and it was quite a shock in Briarcliff, since we had no black families, to see those kids walk down the village [streets]. Everybody talked about integration, but when they saw black faces like that, it really [shook them up]."[13] The setting itself triggered discussions about the freedom of various people to move through all U.S. spaces. Gillmore herself, after her husband died, had followed a somewhat similar trajectory from white suburban housewife and Junior League volunteer to staff member in NCCJ's Westchester County. Vivacious, energetic, and young, Margaret was invited to direct the teen camp and began a process of interracial collaboration that lasted until her retirement in the late 1990s.

Gillmore recruited campers from varied high schools and neighborhoods to create a diverse community among the campers themselves. The result, as she remembers, was that the camps

> were wild. They were wild in the sense they were held in wild territory. . . . Because in those days you didn't really associate with each other, [and] for the first time you truly were getting involved with Hispanics, or Puerto Ricans, Latinos, Latin Americans, and blacks, or African Americans.

White youngsters accustomed to seeing themselves as benign people tolerant of marginal groups found that others did not have the same worldview. In a setting where white campers couldn't assume their neighborhoods and families to be the norm, they had to listen carefully to how others talked, look for signals about appropriate behavior, and examine how they responded to people unlike themselves and to being out of control. Breaking down expectations, violating norms of polite evasiveness, and opening space for students to explain themselves, Gillmore's camps provided the spaces where young people like Gail Kern and an African American boy from Brooklyn could become friends and not just racial emissaries.

In order to lead a heterogeneous set of campers, white camp leaders had to recognize the informal and official power of white homogeneity and to reject its restrictiveness. Nancy Trask, who took over the Los Angeles camps in 1961, had grown up in the clear racial orderliness of prewar Southern California.

I was brought up in the town of Anaheim in a Presbyterian church that had no concern for anything. It was a town where they let the Mexicans swim on one day and cleaned the pool the next day [to be fresh on all the succeeding days for its regular white swimmers]. . . . We segregated our schools in Anaheim. I never went to school with a Mexican because they were segregated. I was brought up in the days when we left the Japanese to be put in internment camps and I did nothing about it. . . . I went to Scripps [College] in Claremont. And it even had a limitation on Jews that were allowed to go, and I didn't fight it. I'd accepted it, and that was what people did in those days. Just one of those situations that happen.[14]

Perhaps only in memory did Trask feel embarrassed about the varied ways she had been expected to acquiesce in myriad forms of racial discrimination—not asking questions about who swam when or who went to school where. As a child and young person, she had simply accepted the world given to her by adults.

Trask's acceptance of social norms that sustained white comfort had only gradually changed. Like Gillmore, through volunteering for community projects she crossed long-enforced social boundaries and gained confidence in breaching them. In the late 1950s Trask signed up with the American Field Service (AFS) to host students invited to live and study in the United States. When a host family "found out that this young man was coming from France and was a Catholic, this Protestant family wouldn't have a Catholic in the house. And my young children said, 'Heavens, we'll take him.'" After a successful year's sponsorship, Trask was inspired by the new African states to confront another of the polite exclusions practiced in the United States. She informed the local AFS committee that she would "only take somebody if they were black, because I felt the community needed to see a black person. And so I took a young man from Uganda." Trask interpreted her actions as "the kind of thing I've sort of had basic Christian concerns for," even though her childhood church had not. As an adult, she finally had the authority to redefine situations instead of ignoring them. By 1961, Nancy Trask had succeeded Stewart Cole as director of the Los Angeles camp and advertised Brotherhood, USA, as a leadership conference for "living and learning good human relations."[15] Instead of having students hold offices in a pseudogovernment, she designed exercises that engaged them in some of the straight talk she had been denied during her own youth.

White camp leaders, especially the skilled women who moved beyond a housewife role into public activity, learned from human relations courses and perhaps from their own liberating encounters to seek out heterogeneous staff who would disrupt white expectations. Working with Margaret Gillmore for two years before becoming director of the Newark camps, Walter Chambers demonstrated how African American staff shifted the tenor of camp discussions from an assumption of white northern tolerance to a recognition that civil rights issues existed in states like New Jersey.

A Newark native, Chambers had attended segregated black schools in the 1940s, then worked for the Newark Mayor's Commission on Group Relations in the 1950s as the Newark schools desegregated and earned an MA in human relations from a new program at New York University. Chambers saw in his human relations skills and the NCCJ camp format a way to advance the process of social change the civil rights movements were pushing through "the Montgomery bus boycott, the freedom rides, and all of the confrontational approaches."[16] To create a new postprotest nation, he believed, "there were other techniques and approaches that could be used, and education was one of them. . . . This was an approach that could lead to bettering a group understanding."

As a black man, Chambers wanted to transform the nation's conception of the "Negro," as he put it in the early 1960s, into something besides "a statistic and a problem." That opinion shift would occur, Chambers declared in his platform for the Newark NCCJ's Brotherhood Institutes, through "appeal to their [teens'] intellect, but at the same time [through] appeal to their emotional involvement of understanding people." Young white people who learned to care for young peers of color could begin to see that that the "Negro" was not the nation's "problem"; the problem was white discrimination, practiced almost unwittingly by a complacent "majority." Chambers's leadership rebutted the image of the black person as "problem," and his concern for young people allowed them to feel the error of that personification.

## A World of Difference

The camps operated on two fundamental premises: Every salient racial and religious group needed to be present, but mere contact was not sufficient to change minds. Sociologists such as Gordon Allport had analyzed the hopeful 1940s contact theory, which had posited that simply having individuals of different groups meet each other would result in positive reassessments. By the 1950s Allport qualified that if contact were not simply to harden old prejudices, it "must embody equal status and a common objective, and it must enjoy official approval."[17] The camp directors shaped an environment that diminished the privileges white youngsters held outside the camps and that authorized the sometimes controversial speech of young people of color. Camp leaders designed a consciously egalitarian space that did not stress reducing white prejudice so much as rethinking assumptions about oneself and others.

The camps had to undo the prevalent white idea that integration was a white-controlled process to admit nonwhites into membership in the nation. Intensifying segregation in white-exclusive suburbs removed whites from contact with African American, Filipino, Mexican American, and Asian American peers who might put forward their own ideas and histories as equally American, and solidified the situation of white Americans as representatives and arbiters of national life.[18] The popular antiracist message that "we're all the same under the skin" conveyed that nonwhites had the ability to comport themselves like white people, if given the opportunity. But just as the early religious versions of intergroup relations assumed that dominant white Protestants would be gracious and civil to minority religions, new integration efforts pushed white Americans to behave more politely to groups that would remain, nevertheless, "minorities."[19]

Camp leaders had a more radically democratic ideal in mind than opening up a white world to a few nonwhites who could assimilate. First, the camps created an unprecedented interracial space where young people could put flesh onto the intangible hope of integration. Second, the white, black, Latino, and Asian American camp leaders organized daily existence so that students acted as equal participants. Third, the leaders created discussions that engaged students' intellects and emotions, encouraging disagreements and conflicts that would help students recognize old habits of ignorance and animosity and experience new feelings of curiosity and friendship. The camps offered a moment to try out behaviors outside the existing racial hierarchies of white power and black subordination or of white centrality and Mexican American and Asian American marginality, and the gender roles integral to the racial ordering. In the artificial, temporary world of Brotherhood Camp, students tried out behaviors and relationships outside the prevailing racial hierarchies and gender divisions that popular culture and social norms associated with their particular bodies. Camp activities designed to support the expressiveness of teens of color enabled these young people to disrupt the expectations that white campers had of them. Minority students, no matter how able and attractive, occupied a place at the nation's social margins; their usual representation was as "problems," as Walt Chambers said. The camps, however, nurtured all kids, providing the sort of space that some feminist theorists have labeled "public homeplaces."[20] Usually marginalized voices, now authorized to speak up, challenged the white students, who came to camp with assumptions that they would be gracious, polite, and in charge. Discussions shifted from vaguely defined prejudice to presentations about how racism affected people previously unknown to white campers.

Instead of passing along information to change white attitudes, the camps freed young people to act outside the scripts usually assigned according to the race and the gender of the player, and to experiment with the attractions and affections, disagreements and negotiations possible among any array of equals. In describing another camp for white Southern girls, where campers imagined integration only through role-playing and dramatic performances, Jay Watson argues that even this limited escape from racial conformity gave "back their bodies" to the campers.[21] In the Brotherhood Camp setting, young people felt their diverse physical selves as attractive and admired. White campers usually felt these new freedoms as expanding the territories they could enter and the relationships they could form. Extraordinarily vivid and fond memories reveal how precious and exciting such opportunities were for both campers and counselors.

### Living Democratically

Young people got the first unsettling hint that this camp week would be different when they gathered to catch the Brotherhood Camp bus. Meeting at Newark's City Hall or Los Angeles's Exposition Park, they found an assortment of about 150 teens from across their region, a group of new faces with no reassuring (or limiting) high school cliques and rules. There would be "strange looks and attention and 'Who are *they*?'" Walt Chambers remembers. Campers could not predict what they were in for. The bus ride gave them a chance to discover some shared interests, with campers singing rock 'n' roll songs in the late 1950s, folk songs in the early 1960s, and Beatles songs by the mid-1960s.

NCCJ staff directors operated on the premise that racial understanding came through negotiating new relationships. Organizers worked hard to assemble a group that looked like a microcosm of the region's residentially segregated racial and religious groups. Staff publicized the camps and made contacts at schools, churches, synagogues, community organizations, and religious- or racial-identified groups like the American Jewish Congress; the Leaguers Inc., a New Jersey club for middle-class African Americans; and a Korean-language newspaper in Los Angeles. Many of these groups, eager to have their young people participate in this civic event, raised funds for camp scholarships. NCCJ staff also solicited donations and used some organizational funds to make certain that lack of money did not exclude interested students likely to thicken the mix. Throughout the era, the staff worked to get a boy-girl balance, which certainly helped attract many of the adolescent campers.

Although not a representative sample of the general population, white campers, with slightly more girls than boys, made up the majority in the camps into the mid-1960s. While many Protestant and Catholic white teens attended, young people identifying as Jewish made up a large, and sometimes the largest, component of the white campers. A regular witticism about NCCJ, one New Jersey boy recalled, was that "all the whites were Jewish and all the Christians were black." A rare race/religion chart from the 1964 New Jersey session lists forty-eight of the campers as white Jewish, thirty-five as white Protestant, and twelve as white Catholic, with girls predominant among white Jewish and Protestant campers and comprising the entire Catholic group. The twenty-seven black campers, all Protestant, were almost evenly divided into boys and girls.[22] Among the nonwhite campers at East Coast camps, African Americans predominated, joined by young people of Filipino and Puerto Rican, usually Christian, backgrounds. The visual evidence in photos of the camps indicates about one quarter of the campers were nonwhite on the East Coast. In Los Angeles, white campers, also with a large Jewish contingent, predominated, with a more diverse nonwhite representation from Southern California's Chinese, Japanese, Korean, Filipino, Mexican, and African American populations.

The directors' commitment to democratic work necessitated recruiting young people capable of meeting on relatively even ground. Rough equality did not require that every student come from a middle-class or higher-income household, but that the young people have the confidence to speak up and to participate in the verbal and emotional give-and-take of scheduled discussions and informal cabin talk. Either through self-selection or nomination by adults in regularly participating schools and associations, the young people who came to camp were intellectually curious, willing to test their existing ideas and to listen to new ones.

For white youngsters, being outstanding students equated with leadership. Campus intellectual leaders such as Gail Kern came because the camp offered the kind of innovative work appropriate for a school newspaper editor and academic achiever. A California camper from a liberal Jewish family, Nina Asher, who worked on an alternative student newspaper, describes herself as "sort of on a track of being a little different, but not excessively different."[23] Some of the nonwhite kids, and especially boys not pushed in school, had not always been top academic performers. After their camp experience, however, many saw themselves as different from their less intellectually ambitious classmates. Jim Horton, an African American camper whose mother taught school and whose father was a skilled workman suspects the aspiring Leaguers picked him because he had a lot of white friends in his Newark high school and functioned comfortably in a white setting. He recalls that his new cohort of NCCJ friends distanced him from some of his high school cronies,

> because [NCCJ kids] had very intellectual conversations . . .
> [and] at that time [in the late 1950s and early 1960s], in our peer
> group, people didn't have conversations, except in school classes,
> about ideas and about books. And we talked about prejudice as a
> *construction*. We had read Gordon Allport's *On Prejudice* as a result
> of camp. We read Charles Silberman's *Crisis in Black and White*. We
> were reading all these things that our peers were not reading. And
> we were sure that we were changing the world.[24]

The NCCJ young people had the capacity to reflect about what they heard and the self-assurance to follow up on new ideas, even if these violated some high school norms. When they arrived at camp, they received cabin assignments and went to meet the new people they would live with during the week. In a repeat of their unsettling meetings at the buses, they found an unusually diverse group in the cabin, selected to maximize the differences among campers' backgrounds. Walt Chambers remembers: "I, personally, did the cabin assignments. I used to put every student's name on a three-by-five card and what school and city they were from, and, to my knowledge, what racial/religious background, and so on, and then I would lay those out on my dining room table or somewhere and line up the cabins." He mixed suburban and city, too, and for some, this was "the first time, absolutely the first time they had ever had this kind of living experience," he recalls.

Many of the East Coast and Southern California white youngsters had not thought much about the racial segregation of their home neighborhoods. The experiences of "a white [person] living with people who have different backgrounds than ourselves" made the segregation of daily lives apparent, mused one unidentified camper in the September 1960 *Peacemaker,* the Los Angeles camps' newsletter.[25] For many white adolescents, living in an interracial cabin revealed the disconnection between affirmations of integration and realities of daily segregation. When Nina Asher came to the Los Angeles camp in 1967: "We didn't know any other kids of any other races. . . . What I felt noticeable is that as much as my parents believed in all this stuff [about integration], we didn't know any black kids, we didn't know any Hispanic kids." At camp, she "crossed into a new, different territory, . . . where you were physically locked onto people who were different races than you were. [It] was really very odd, [since] when you left home you didn't know anyone of a different race." Once white young people did know someone of a different race, the apparatus of segregation became more apparent.

The racially inclusive camp spaces tested the unspoken rationales for social distance, especially ideas that different skin colors or hair textures reflected differences in character or ability. Bodies usually segregated spatially or socially were now intimate: sharing a cabin and shower, using the same latrines, eating meals together, swimming in the same pool in the same water, dancing, and holding hands. In the intimate cabin space, Jacqui Norris, an African American girl with café au lait skin whose family contained a spectrum of skin colors, remembered that cabin discussions showed teens that they didn't have "any kind of different experiences that we couldn't relate to, regardless of who we were." When Jacqui stayed in the sun too long, her sunburn surprised the white girls. " 'You get a tan?' 'Yes, I do. If I stay out there too long, I'm gonna turn red and I'm gonna burn,' " she informed them. Jacqui believes that "the cabins were as much a classroom as being in the workshop, because we actually got a chance to share. We'd sit on our bunks and we'd just talk, and we'd say, 'Gee, I do that too.' "[26] Bodies shifted their meanings. Young people could find commonalities among bodies that had been racialized as irrevocably unlike. If bodies did not cause the differences in racial groups, then all social arrangements based on race became open to discussion and alteration.

Young people from nonwhite neighborhoods might have some political ideas about racial inequality. But young white people came from a culture and neighborhoods that stressed the inevitability of white authority. The members of the dominant group had a lot to learn, the camp directors assumed, in order to give up their unexamined assurance. The camp programs depended on the presence of young leaders of color to disrupt white assurance so that white youngsters could begin to take in factual information about how social dominants helped perpetuate racial systems.

The official camp schedule included morning lectures, afternoon workshop discussions, a few hours of recreation, and then evening programs of entertainment, which often had informational elements. In 1959, under the overall theme "Education for Tomorrow," successive morning lecturers at the New York camps talked about America's Protestant, Catholic, and Jewish religions; Puerto Rico; and juvenile delinquency. Campers then discussed topics like segregation and discrimination, interracial and interreligious dating and intermarriage, separation of church and state, and a code of behavior for teenagers. The titles of the New Jersey Institute's five morning sessions in 1964 were "Equality for All Americans," "Human Relations in the Space Age," "Understanding People of Different Religions," "The American Political Scene," and "Re-entering your Home Community" (after camp).[27] In 1966, the Los Angeles camp's theme, change, included sessions titled "The Changing World of Racial Unrest and Vietnam"; "Changing Community," on police and free speech; "Changing Education," about unrest at schools like UC-Berkeley; "Changing Family," on interracial, interreligious dating; and "Responsible Action."[28]

Although adult resource persons delivered some of the morning talks to provide material for discussions, the camps minimized distinctions between authorities and learners and encouraged campers to analyze the connections between new information and their own experiences. On both East and West Coasts, former campers modeled collegial behavior, acted as cabin counselors, and led late-evening talk sessions after the boys returned to their cabins and the girls to theirs. The West Coast directors usually hired schoolteachers or counselors as staff, at minimal pay, though sometimes former campers, now in college, came back as counselors. In the New Jersey camp, Walt Chambers recruited college students as unpaid camp counselors to lead discussions and run sports, crafts, and entertainment. All the official camp leaders were taught to encourage camper participation, and the counselors—diverse in race, religion, and gender—

modeled leadership by groups not historically in charge. Walter Chambers alerted counselors that the "important thing to remember is that the [campers] select their own discussion leader, who conducts the session." Adult leaders might offer facts, but these should be "contributions, rather than final wisdom about which there can be no debate."[29] Camper Nina Asher remembers the feeling of responsibility of "staff people not necessarily expressing a whole lot of their opinions or feelings, at least initially, and really letting kids kind of get into their own experience more." The adults conveyed the idea that campers' thoughts and responses were valuable and that young people could be in charge of their responses.

Camp directors also helped adult resource people and student cabin counselors learn techniques to help campers move beyond the settled ideas they came with. To embolden campers to try out new ideas, to test them in discussions, and to revise them without penalty, the camps instilled norms of candor and questioning. New York camp director Margaret Gillmore remembers that the white gloves came off, and directness replaced evasive politeness. Campers learned "to frankly say, 'This is the way I feel.' Because, up to that time, [in] polite conversation you didn't mention religion, race, politics, etc." These potentially conflict-laden topics might cause hurt feelings or trigger animosity, but the camp environment implicitly promised students that adults would watch out for every camper and not prejudge a young person's ideas.

The camp promised safety for white campers, but the racially diverse leadership certainly intended to disrupt white assumptions that the United States was a fundamentally nonracist country. At one of the Newark camps in 1962, Jim Horton preempted a common position of white students: "I know everybody would say they're not prejudiced," he remembers opening one session, "because you're all nice people. That's why you're here [at a Brotherhood Camp]. However, this [racially prejudiced world] is the society we live in." Opening up consideration of the images and values created in the larger society helped campers contrast the reality at camp and that in their segregated neighborhoods. Horton remembers asking questions that highlighted the prevailing identifications of God and Jesus with white skin: "Is God black or white?" Or, forcing the young people to think about the unspoken assumptions that governed white churches and many white families: "Did God intend us to be separate from each other?" The safety of the setting allowed campers to try out the old rationales for segregation and to assess their inadequacies.

Discussions also disrupted white teens' assumption that their individuality was largely unaffected by their racial identification, in sharp contrast to the experiential knowledge of nonwhite teens, who had felt discrimination or seen its effects in their families. White students had never experienced the common black complaint that white people could not distinguish individual African Americans and thought all black people looked alike. White campers were shocked to realize that racial segregation also put all whites into an indistinguishable group. Gail Kern remembers a discussion when

> an older guy, somebody who had graduated, said that he had gone to a high school where most of the people—it must have been in Brooklyn, a big, big city high school—were black. And he (this was a white guy talking) found that when he came out of school and he went into white situations, he thought that all white people looked alike.

In a social context where he needed to recognize black classmates, a young white man had distinguished them. But the outsiders, the whites, now bled together. As Gail concludes, "Clearly this has stuck in my mind." She felt the truth that she, a talented and ambitious young woman, might look like any other white person when defined only by skin color.

Stereotypes had typically been hurled at groups considered outside, or marginal to, a white mainstream. Camp leaders used a technique to permit conscious recognition and analysis of the pervasive insults young people had learned. As a group people would shout out "names like spic, nigger, wop, whatever" and role-play responses to rebut these demeaning words. The group improvised responses, Jacqui remembers,

> based on, if someone called you a name, you'd try to educate them as to who you were and what you were all about. You'd tell them that you can understand that they might not like some black people, but they couldn't say they don't like all black people. Because they don't know [all black people], first of all.

At the camp, Puerto Ricans, black people, and Italians stood up to demonstrate that a fellow camper did not fit the images associated with those epithets. They upset dominant views of a racialized Puerto Rican, black, or Italian person and asserted their own individuality. Counselors and campers of color were able to present a worldview in which they did not seek simply to blend into white counselors' and campers' understanding of the United States.

The camps provided spaces for nonwhite groups seen as marginal to lay out their claims for being as central as white Americans in the national story. Nonwhite campers were not willing to give up their own family stories in favor of a white national narrative. A fairer society and better understanding came, as Walter Chambers said, in "an environment where a person can be accepted as an individual, *without forgetting the ethnic aspect of his identity,* [and] an environment where equal treatment is the principle and practice of *daily living.*"[30] Accounting for the "ethnic aspect" (a polite displacement of "race") of his own identity, for instance, required confronting what he saw as limited and unrealistic representations of the past and present of the nation. Using the locution of the early 1960s, Chambers told how he had loved education and especially learning about his country, "until we reached that unit on the Civil War. . . . Here, the Negro was a slave, a war was fought over him, Lincoln freed him—this is the three-act drama that is the Negro [in the American story]." When he asked himself what acts preceded or followed this antique play—What had the African brought to the New World and what had the African American done for himself and the nation since the Civil War?—little information circulated.

> Books? Magazines? Plays? Movies? Television? Radio? Most of what we read, see, and hear supports the image we learned so well. When I am not being depicted as the maid, chauffeur, criminal, musician or scarecrow, there are any number of documentaries and specials on the "Negro problem" to fill the void. Seldom, if ever, can we find a characterization of the plain, ordinary, law-abiding, Americanized, middle-class, worried-about-the-mortgage Negro family. . . . Where is my identity, when all they say is so different from what I know?[31]

Chambers concluded, "Every ounce of my pride is invested in being the Negro that I am." He did not want to be accepted as an individual who had escaped the past, but as a valuable person whose ancestors and family had earned recognition in the present.

Chambers's assertion of integrity resonated with some of the youth leaders. Jim Horton, for instance, had learned from his father about the record of segregation in North Carolina, a state his father had left to seek opportunities in New Jersey. Horton remembers his father's quiet assurance on the day the Supreme Court ruled against segregation in *Brown v. Board of Education*: "They [white segregationists] can run, but they can't hide," his father said firmly. Young African Americans often brought to camp family ideas at odds with those that circulated in white neighborhoods and provoked their white campmates to see beyond the limited depictions of the standard histories and popular media.[32]

In the midst of a civil rights movement in which media attention focused on the struggles of African Americans in the U.S. South, the camps' diversity revealed other stories of discrimination, shifting focus from a black "problem" to a white pattern of racial exclusion. On the East Coast, Puerto Rican students educated their peers about segregation and the U.S. control of Puerto Rico. On the West Coast, nonwhite students disrupted white ideas about other racialized groups, including Asians. Elizabeth Louie went to camp first in 1967 and found her family's Chinese American story unknown to most of the other campers. The white students in general had very limited experience with and knowledge of groups other than their own. "They said," Louie remembers, "and not in a mean way, 'Oh, but your English is very good.' Or someone spoke very haltingly, thinking that I wouldn't understand. And they [never imagined] that I was a fourth generation, that my family had been here longer than other people's families."[33]

Louie had learned pride in her family, which her father did not define in terms of assimilation to white racial views. When she attended camp, Louie lived in a middle-class Los Angeles neighborhood, Crenshaw, which white families were fleeing as black families began to buy homes there. Her father, a professional at the Internal Revenue Service,

> had very strong feelings that we grow up in an ethnic
> minority neighborhood that was not a predominantly Chinese
> neighborhood. . . . And I can remember very clearly a citizen
> organization that they belonged to, which was all Chinese, making
> statements, "If you really cared about your kids, you would move
> to the suburbs." And I am clear about my father's saying that we
> needed to survive and we needed to learn how to be with different
> people.

Sponsored by the Chinese American Citizens' Alliance, Louie brought to camp her father's disposition to uphold his Chinese heritage. Unlike many in the Alliance, though, she also applauded his refusal to align with white dominants and abandon racially mixed neighborhoods.

For campers like Nina Asher, her camp peers' varied lives raised anxieties about the unfamiliar. The other campers were bright and engaging, but they were not just like her. "This wasn't just a fun camp. Not that we weren't supposed to have fun, but there was a seriousness about it, that people were to be taken seriously about what they said or what they were thinking. And I think I remember feeling slightly intimidated by that. It sort of made you reevaluate things you were saying." Her campmates disrupted Asher's teenage assumption that her own life was the norm. "There was an intensity about [camp] where you really had to think about things, and you had to talk about things, and you had to try to define yourself, and you had to really listen." By teaching campers to speak out of the realities of their own lives, to confront each other, and to listen, counselors taught the conversational skills necessary to exchange emotion-laden, novel information. Then counselors gave emotional support to help campers incorporate new facts into their new self-images.

## Associating Interracially

The camps' success depended on the passionate, casual ease with which teenagers use their bodies. From the moment they met at the buses, campers were in a world that removed the everyday barriers of residence, custom, cultural norms, and, sometimes, law. During the course of the six-day sessions, they moved from cautious observation to embrace possibilities for physical, as well as intellectual and emotional, expression that the camp session permitted.

Campers were always nervous when their parents delivered them to the buses, Walt Chambers remembers, anxious about what would happen and where they'd find a comfortable group. The general teen angst about fitting in played against a backdrop of national uneasiness about racial integration. After the bus adventure, campers moved into their racially and religiously integrated cabins and negotiated with people they had learned, from a variety of sources, were not like them. They had meals together in settings where the white kids were not in charge and the kids with darker skins were not servants. They swam together and lay on towels in the sun next to each other to dry their wet suits. All of these acts—integrating buses, swimming pools, and dining-hall tables—had been flashpoints for the assaults on, and defense of, legal segregation in the South. In the North, social norms and housing patterns, not law, had made interracial living, swimming, and meal sharing unusual. (A 1963 national opinion survey found that fewer than half of white Americans would "have a Negro to dinner."[34]) So every day the campers lived together, they enacted nonconformist behavior that they found to be pleasant and unremarkable. Their actions often defied the norms of their neighbors and the white-exclusive representations in the popular media; their daily routines demonstrated peaceful possibilities at odds with the violent images broadcast from civil rights conflicts.

Simply enjoying the connections of young bodies of different colors disrupted national norms. Besides lectures and scheduled discussions, young campers gathered around campfires to sing in the evenings, practiced songs and dances and skits for the talent show night, danced to favorite records brought from home, and played and tentatively flirted and kissed. Every evening concluded with holding hands and joining voices in song to send people off to bed—or to late-night talk sessions in the cabins. Some evenings featured dances, for which the young people prepared with all the seriousness of presenting themselves well to the particular boys or specific girls who had attracted them during the day. Dancing let young people touch each other, express attraction, and pursue a romance that parents and friends at home might disapprove. At an interracial co-ed camp, the simple pleasures of singing, dancing, touching, and pursuing and exchanging a kiss overturned the social order instead of reinforcing it. (The sexual expressions were quite innocent, all the former campers assured me, and modest compared to the intercourse or genital intimacy more common among teens by the 1990s).

Camp leaders set a standard of general affection that inspired and authorized displays of affection. Clabe Hangan, music director for many of the Los Angeles camp sessions from the early 1960s through the early 1970s, expressed the optimistic purpose of the adult leaders and the adventurous delight that attracted young people. Hangan grew up in a black Baptist family in Redlands, near Los Angeles, and became a folk singer in college. In his teenage years, Clabe had tried out different religions. He had been attracted by the Quakers with whom his Redlands church held interracial services. When he had worked in a Jewish summer camp, he had been struck that Jewish people "seemed so African. They're Arabic, they're

Africans. . . . Somehow I had an emotional tie."[35] He had noticed the conversion to Judaism of the black entertainer Sammy Davis Jr. and had considered following that model. But then Clabe had married a woman he met
at the Friends meeting and continued his spiritual search as he finished
college, became a probation officer, and joined the NCCJ camp staff as a
song leader. Like Chambers, Hangan wanted the young people to respond
to other kids as interesting and attractive, not as "problems." They didn't
let campers talk about "interracial and interreligious," as if these represented a mixing of ineradicable differences, he remembers. "Those are just
terms, just words for people getting together."

Camp leaders created a set of living, playing, and debating structures that put campers on an equal level, and then encouraged them to
talk about the differences in their daily lives. "We didn't [deny] those differences. We said, 'Those are real, they're here. We've got this language
situation, we've got education, we've got income, we've got different levels
of cultural things.' " But in the camp setting these and other differences
were "talked about in the context of people talking to people" and learning, as Clabe Hangan explained, how to think about "what it's like to be
us." The camp leaders' acceptance of campers' affections for and attachments to each other was strikingly at odds with what most had experienced in their schools and families. Gail Kern, the white girl who kissed
a black boy when they said good-bye at camp's end, had learned even in
elementary school the tensions created around white girls being close to
black boys in social settings, specifically around the "one black boy in
my class at school" on Long Island. When the teachers organized dance
classes in gym, mostly square dancing, "there were the charged moments
when somebody [white] would dance with him. . . . [This] was a situation
in which his difference mattered, which other playground or classroom
situations didn't have."

Black teens had also learned to follow norms intended to avoid the discomfort of interracial boy and girl social contact. Jim Horton had grown
up in integrated Newark neighborhoods in the 1950s and, throughout his
elementary, junior high, and high school years in the late 1950s and early
1960s, had lots of friendships with white classmates who were boys. It was
all right for an interracial group of guys to play sports and hang out together after school. In high school, the taboo against relations with white
girls became evident, Jim reported. "Blacks didn't [usually] go to the high
school dances." On one occasion, he and some black friends decided to

attend a school dance and were surprised that the boys they had known only "in class and in sports and stuff" did not dance. The white guys stood along the walls, and the girls danced with each other. As young men who danced at family gatherings and in their families' social clubs, Jim and his friends seized the opportunity and asked the delighted girls to dance with them. But the black boys also didn't follow up after this one event; the dance didn't lead to the black boys being friendlier with the white girls at school.

Jim remembers that NCCJ, by contrast, "was the organization where you could really *associate* with white people." The distinguishing marks of association were heterosexual dancing, hand-holding, and kissing, which transmuted the old sexual fears surrounding interracial connections into adolescent curiosity and pleasure. Interracial sexual connections, especially between a white girl and a black boy, remained almost invisible and popularly inconceivable in the late 1950s and early 1960s.[36] The prohibition against white women's social and/or sexual involvement with nonwhite men had justified legal segregation and white violence against alleged offenders for well over a century. For many young black men and women, the brutal 1955 murder of the teenaged Emmett Till for speaking flirtatiously to a white Mississippi woman was a reminder of the still-potent danger of interracial encounters with even the mildest sexual undertones.[37] Even white adults who considered themselves nonracist continued to deflate the pretensions of white desegregationists by asking, "Would you want your [white] daughter to marry one [a black man]?" However much white Americans acquiesced in desegregation of public places, a majority still assumed the perpetuation of racial segregation or "social distance" in private life.[38]

The implicit message of cultural and legal opposition to interracial intimacy and marriage, one contemporary religious commentator argued, was that African Americans (and other racially marginalized people) did not belong in the same human family as white Americans.[39] Throughout the early camp era, directors and campers adopted a new humanity that the nation's legal system endorsed only in 1967 when the Supreme Court, in *Loving v. Virginia*, declared unconstitutional the laws still extant in almost twenty states against interracial marriage.[40]

The camps used a variety of techniques, from cabin conversations to role-playing, to allow young people to verbalize the rules against interracial intimacy so that they could directly examine the often unspoken norms. Gail Kern remembers how the counselors would assign us situations, and we would have to go act them out and then bring them back to the group. And so our group's problem was telling your parents you're dating a black kid. . . . And my job was to be the daughter, and I remember becoming—this was method acting—getting very, very, very upset and acting out my outrage that my parents would have objected to [my dating a black classmate].

Once the prohibition was voiced and the structure named, it could no longer be rationally defended. Perhaps this was what emboldened Gail to kiss "a black kid" on her return from camp when her parents could see her. She was no longer going to discipline her physical affection to conform to the prevailing codes of social segregation.

In the 1950s, changing ideas about public roles and responsibilities for women offered white girls the possibility to imagine more expansive roles. During the decade, white Christian and white Jewish girls participated in extrafamilial activities with what historian Joanne Meyerowitz calls a "bifocal vision of women both as feminine and domestic and as public achievers."[41] White girls were groomed to become housewives, and they also were expected to assume new civic roles. The opening into public life was not expected to challenge racial norms of social distance, however. White girls enjoying the companionship of black boys, no matter how young or innocent, made apparent the segregationist norms prevailing across public and private life.

By the early 1960s, a girl poised to make a significant social contribution found in the NCCJ camps a place where an interracial romance simultaneously expressed political commitment to equality *and* personal independence from older norms of female sexual passivity.[42] Cultural historian Susan J. Douglas sees in girls' new sexual assertiveness an increased sense of power, not to dominate but to move and to act freely in the world. In what she calls "the best part of 1960s adolescent femininity, [girls displayed] an eagerness to reach out to others, a faith in love, a belief in progress, and a determination to leave behind hoary conventions about staying in one's place."[43] In confronting a racial system built on regulating white women's contact with black men, private acts of affection were public challenges to segregation.

Cross-racial sexual contact in the United States had a different history and meaning when the men involved were white and the women were not. White men's cross-racial desires had posed a threat to communities of color, because white men had long been permitted to pursue American Indian, African American, and Asian American women as sexual mates, though not as marriage partners with whom to raise legitimate families.[44] The camp gave different meanings to these attractions—such relationships could be both safer, because nonwhite girls had more power over the nature of the encounter, and more potentially engaging, because prohibitions against interracial marriage were being struck down.

The young people overturned ideas that girls of color were less attractive than white girls and properly relegated to romance's supporting roles. At a 1964 camp, a shared love of singing brought together Jacqui, a talented singer, and a new boyfriend, Tom, a guitarist and the son of Jewish concentration camp survivors. They continued to date into the fall, and Tom invited Jacqui to visit for a weekend. Jacqui was quickly aware that Tom's "lily white community" had never accommodated anyone with dark skin "except during the week when the maids came in." Facing Tom's shocked neighbors, the young couple decided to enact one of the role-playing principles from camp: to "take something and just kind of turn it around." At the local shopping mall, Jacqui said,

> We decided to go over to the jewelry shop and look at rings. And he'd say, "Well, what do you think about that one, sweetheart?" And I'd say, "Oh, that's really very nice. Don't you think it's a little small?" We went through this whole thing, we tried things on. And, of course, they didn't want us trying on their rings, but what were they going to do?

Acting out the neighborhood's fear that an attractive black woman and white man might marry, the teens revealed the white community's pattern of expressing polite disapproval and its usual equation of "black woman" with "maid."

In the egalitarian and protective camp environment, girls of color had a social power not historically available to them, even as they perhaps continued to represent, for white boys, a fantasy of freer sexuality than white girls did. One young white boy, Crilly Butler, who attended the Los Angeles camp in the summer of 1967, remembers that he felt "unlovable and unattractive" around teenage girls. The son of a comfortably raised white Protestant father and a Jewish working-class mother, he had moved from Hollywood to the Burbank suburbs for his father's job and found himself an outcast: a boy wearing "slacks and black shoes when everybody else had blue jeans and tennis shoes." He hoped to reinvent himself at camp and to overcome his outsider position at school. When he got to camp, he said,

> everybody had this kind of sparkle in their eyes. . . . We arrived in early afternoon, and by that evening we were doing this circle dance. I remember there was this girl—she was Chicano—and she was really cute and effervescent, bubbly, and she sat next to me in the circle dance holding my hand. . . . And she would squeeze my hand every now and then, and when we stopped between songs, she kind of put her arm around me. And I was half terrified and half ecstatic. And then after the dance, she just turned and gave me this big hug and looked up at me with this incredibly beautiful look on her face, and I kissed her. And this would have been so out of character in any other venue of my life.[45]

The Mexican American girl who transformed young Butler's view of himself did not seek him out again or follow up on the kiss. Exerting her control, the girl had been the leader in their tentative kiss, without any hint of a white boy's prerogative.

The girls' presence in a setting designed to bring about change gave the signal that the camp was a new space in which old rules of racial distance did not apply. For many girls, NCCJ camps allowed expressions of unprecedented sexual, intellectual, and political power, but in a well-supervised environment. Especially for white girls, charged with protecting family and community by strict sexual behavior and racial aloofness, the camps allowed experimentation that would be risky outside. Jim Horton remembers being sixteen, kissing a white girl, and thinking "this was bizarre. I knew so many white girls in school. I found some attractive, obviously, but I never really thought about the prospect of dating them. I'll have to say that there was the sense of 'What would the kids at home think, or say?' And I thought the kinds of things that sixteen-year-old boys think, and that is, 'Boy, would people think I'm something because I'm kissing this really good-looking girl.'"

The teens' sense of expansive freedom of association contrasts with historians' accounts of the sometimes violence-tinged interracial sex between young civil rights workers, notably in the cauldron of Mississippi's 1964 Freedom Summer. The hundreds of young white women who came from outside the South to work on voter registration, teach in Freedom Schools, and staff movement offices sometimes felt affection for the young black men in the movement, who reciprocated because of shared attraction, mixed, undoubtedly, with the cultural imperative for a young man to seek sex. In the politicized South, however, these relationships attracted dangerous hostility from local white people, demoralizing envy from black women colleagues, and defensive assertiveness from white women, who defended their actions either as proofs of antiracism or, at the least, as merely personal expressions of physical attraction.[46] The sexual encounters of the young adult civil rights workers precipitated danger, fear, animosity, defensiveness, and hurt. In the protected camp setting, the rather innocent though sexually charged pleasures of young teenagers sparked curiosity, expressiveness, friendship, and hope.

## *Singing Empathetically*

Music was a force that simultaneously drew campers together and extended their worlds. Kids sang on buses on their way to camp to discover a shared culture and on their way home from camp to cement their new bonds. Music ritually marked each day's close and filled up spaces and hours during the day. Kids gathered during afternoon recreation hours to sing and to prepare for the talent show that marked the Thursday night finale for many camps. Before heading to cabins and late-night discussions, campers and leaders gathered almost every night for a circle sing. Music, even more than talk, opened up campers' physical selves and spirits to different musical heritages, treated as equally and delightfully valuable.

By the mid-1950s, two important musical innovations marked the generations coming of age after 1955 as different from their parents and the camp leaders: a revival of interest in folk music, and a synthesis of black-identified rhythm and blues and white-identified country and western music into the rock 'n' roll that hit the airwaves in the early 1950s. These two musical expressions, rock 'n' roll and folk, contrasted with the swing, big band, and pop music commercially dominant in their parents' youth and gave an interracial, social justice sound track to the camps.

The NCCJ camps relied on folksinging. Walt Chambers, who says that he hated folksinging "with a passion," was able to enlist nearly all of his counselors as volunteers, except the music director. "I had to pay that person, but I would have to recruit a very good folksinger. And every time they got together in general sessions or whatever, [they sang]. And I would disappear." Clabe Hangan, who directed music at many of the Los Angeles camps, saw music's pleasures as essential to attaching the kids emotionally to each other: "Music is the spiritual substance. . . . It's the gilding, it's the glue, and it's the glitter, it's the glamour."

Chambers experienced singing as entertainment, but Hangan envisioned the music as teaching psychological empathy across different life circumstances. The campers sang songs like *Let There Be Peace on Earth* and *No Man Is an Island*, which stressed the necessary cooperation of all people.[47] As Hangan says, even a civil rights anthem like *We Shall Overcome*, which was a standard at camp, could arouse a white, middle-class youth—not to feel pity for the less fortunate, but to identify with struggles to live better, because "there's not a child in the world that doesn't have something to overcome. . . . We were doing the real people thing. It was people [that we were teaching], it wasn't doctrine."

Folk songs came out of two somewhat contradictory movements. Many songs had been collected from rural people by 1930s New Deal arts programs inaugurated to save parts of the nation's vanishing rural culture. One category of rural song, the "Negro spiritual," as collectors labeled it, had been linked to the fortitude of a people, first in slavery and then in a white-dominant caste system. But other folk songs had been written in the 1920s through the 1940s as tools of union organizing and self-conscious social protest. By the early 1960s, camp song sheets included *If I Had a Hammer*, an old leftie protest song written by Lee Hays and Pete Seeger in the late 1940s and made popular by Bob Dylan on a 1963 recording. In the postwar era, collections of traditional songs of America's various peoples became standard texts for teaching the pluralistic meaning of national identity, evoking, one scholar says, a "broad typology of the American character and with it the principle of cultural democracy."[48] Many campers knew these songs from school music programs and the new commercial releases.

Dismissing the influence of musical pluralism, the major scholar of the folk song revival, Robert Cantwell, contends that the revival often erased the political messages of the old songs. "The mode of the 1960s seemed more like a collective adolescent quest than a political or even a cultural revolution; the folk revival had no political agenda beyond being vaguely against racism and war." Singing black spirituals might even, Cantwell argues, create an impression of black people as the "stereotype of Christian patience, humility, and other-worldliness."[49] As Jim Horton recalls, "White kids knew a lot about black music, but nothing about black people." At NCCJ camps, however, white kids learned the songs as they applied to actual people. When campers at an interracial camp sang a song like *This*

*Little Light of Mine*, they were more likely to envision emboldened Southern civil rights protestors than wistful petitioners.[50]

The camps also operated in a time of expanding, commercialized teen culture that, especially with the rock 'n' roll music popular after the mid-1950s, was implicitly interracial.[51] All teens knew the lyrics and tunes of the best-selling songs. Jim Horton remembers singing early Elvis Presley, but for him, the Coasters' *Poison Ivy* became the definitive camp song after one camper played it on a portable record player at the highest possible volume every morning at 7:00 A.M. as a wake-up call. The story of two young people who break out in bumps after they've accidentally cuddled in the dark in a patch of poison ivy, the infectious song celebrated teen romance even as it reminded kids that they were taking risks breaking out of the old, settled norms of affection. The mid-1960s brought the Beatles' English invasion, and campers cheerfully sang *The Yellow Submarine,* a testimony to youthful fun.[52] In the 1950s and early 1960s, popular culture's musical messages reinforced the camp theme that a variety of humans could come to empathize with and to understand each other.

Music "brought the songs into the heart, planted the words in there, motivated people, had them looking at themselves, looking at their society," Clabe Hangan believes. The ease of the songs led campers to ask, "Why couldn't the world be like Brotherhood? What is it that gets in the way of our loving each other?" When young people left the camps, they continued to ask these questions and to search for settings that reproduced the camp closeness. Although the NCCJ camps didn't turn students into an organized political force, the setting changed the singing experience from one of white appropriation of spirituals and protest songs to recognition of the circumstances and communities that had created such songs. The new understanding expressed a longing for, and held out hope of, connections that healed past injustices.

## Going down the Hill

At the end of a weeklong idyll, young campers went home, or "down the hill," in camp lingo, to segregated neighborhoods and schools where interracial association was not encouraged. For young people to put their good intentions into practice, the regional NCCJ offices sponsored events to keep them involved in the organization's work. NCCJ encouraged campers to start human relations clubs at their schools; these could respond to inflammatory rumors about various groups and speak at school assemblies to model and advocate interracial collaboration and friendship. Usually a fall reunion and a Christmas holiday meeting brought campers together to talk about their activities and plan either school or neighborhood work. Camp alumni met in spring to offer suggestions for the upcoming summer's camps. Campers typically stayed engaged with NCCJ activities for about one year; for those who returned as cabin leaders, the involvement lasted two years or more. But the campers were young, usually not yet out of high school, so the result of the camp experience was not political engagement, but a new vision of human acceptance and connection. They had become different in themselves, but these young people did not have social institutions to support changed behavior while they still lived with their parents.

For white teens, camp inspired a rethinking of basic assumptions about how they were different from their brother and sister campers of color, among these the belief that white Americans had higher claims to college education or to good neighborhoods. Margaret Gillmore remembers that when campers discussed their future plans, students of color realized "the whole idea of, 'You're going to go to college? Hey, in discussion groups, you don't seem much smarter than I am.' So the youngsters from schools where they hadn't thought in terms of college, for the first time they began to talk [about going]. And the youngsters who were headed for college also recognized in the youngsters they were dealing with, 'Hey, wait a second, I've heard certain things [that aren't true].'" Campers recognized that college attendance did not simply reward ability; white kids in predominantly white schools had a racial advantage, they now realized, which couldn't be justified, as they had believed before camp, by superior white intelligence.

For white students who had assumed their nonwhite peers had different life ambitions, the camp talk opened up new insights. Mary Hart, a young white Christian girl who was somewhat shy, recalls meeting two young black men, one from Newark and one from Harlem, in her early 1960s camp. She remembers "being good friends with them in the way you would be friends with anybody [white]. Just being able to sit and talk with each other about the things adolescents talk to each other about— your dreams and what you wanted to do with your life and things you might be afraid of."[53] For Mary, the distant worlds of Harlem and Newark now became embodied in young men with aspirations like her own. When she grew up and worked as an art therapist in Philadelphia, she thought it helped that she had learned that "neighborhoods are home, no matter what the problems. There are always *people* who live in neighborhoods—mothers who have children and care about them, and friendships." When she saw dark-skinned people now, she knew they had values not so different from her own, even if they lived in neighborhoods that were much less prosperous and comfortable than hers.

White kids' transformations came in response to meeting black, Asian, and Mexican American kids who didn't follow the cultural scripts that made white dominance appear the natural consequence of biological or cultural superiority. The confidence the egalitarian camps nurtured in nonwhite campers enabled them to challenge white ideas of preeminence and to offer a promise that ending racism would create a wider realm of freedom for everyone. Jim Horton spent four camp summers—from 1959 to 1963—as camper, cabin leader, and counselor, and long before his final years, he says, "I was at ease in white society. I realized that the white society was different from the [black community] I grew up in. But I could handle that difference." Elizabeth Louie started at camp in the summer of 1967 and stayed on for another year as recruiter and counselor. Nancy Trask invited her home and showed her she could function outside the isolated world of Crenshaw or the Chinese American Association, Louie recalls. "Brotherhood opened the door for me not to be afraid to look beyond someone's face, whether it be their color or their gender or their religion. It gave me that curiosity, and also that confidence that many people want to know me and will like me." For most of the white kids, their ability to act on the hopes raised at camp came only when they left home for the more open situations of college. Crilly Butler recalls that when he returned from camp to Burbank, not only were there no nonwhite classmates in his school, but "there weren't any in my whole town." So, although he talked with classmates about racism and "how we felt about being white," these conversations could not change the segregated environment their parents had constructed. It was not until he started college at the University of California at Santa Cruz in 1968 that he "moved immediately into friendships with a lot of different races, a lot of different religions, a lot of different cultures, very easily and naturally." What Brotherhood Camp did, Crilly decided later, was take the fear out of meeting people defined as racially different from him. "It made us intrigued and interested and curious and excited about learning about other cultures and other races and other experiences."

The understanding of the white campers of this early era evolved through a series of responses to the civil rights movement and its expressions among their campmates. From initial denial that they had participated in any way in racist actions or had held any racial prejudices, white teens learned about silent assumptions and became aware of cultural practices that defined a different humanity for white and nonwhite peoples. For many, the new insights led to guilt about their historical advantage. For many others, defensiveness metamorphosed into curiosity about, and then affirmation of, the new people they had come to know at camp.

By 1967, however, despite passage of two major civil rights bills, the shapes of new systems for sustaining white advantage were emerging: the residential segregation of white suburbs, the foreclosed education and job opportunities that followed, and whites' persistent obliviousness to the racial consequences of their self-protective isolation. Urban uprisings that began in the Watts section of Los Angeles in 1965 expressed inner-city anger at white unwillingness to open up suburban housing to other races. The earliest draft and casualty figures from the Vietnam War showed that these same inner-city neighborhoods carried a disproportionate burden in military service. And, as the Kerner Commission reported in its spring 1968 analysis of the civil disorders: "By and large news organizations have failed to communicate to both their white and black audiences a sense of the problems America faces. . . . The media report and write from the standpoint of a white man's world."[54]

In this context of heightened anger and fearfulness, the white orientation of the NCCJ camps became more evident. The majority of campers had been white. The camp leaders had emphasized contact among young people and focused on individual transformation and not on institutional change to reduce systemic white advantage. In these ways, the camps reflected the limitations of white America generally.

But the camps had two virtues that contrasted with most white-directed institutions. First, they created settings in which white U.S. teens learned that homogeneity was not only an untrue picture of the nation, but also a worldview that narrowed their own lives. The young people had been able to recognize that the price of white dominance was constant emotional, mental, and physical self-policing. Second, the camps provided a safe place for white kids to take in the worldviews of nonwhite youngsters. Both experiences were rare for young white suburban Americans.

# 2

# Respecting All
# the Brothers and Sisters

*Brotherhood Camps, 1968–1974*

When you're talking about brotherhood, then you want all
the brothers. Want to bring all the sisters. We'd bring it all
together, all the other brothers and sisters, religions, cultures.
—*Clabe Hangan*

In the hard summer of 1968, just after Martin Luther King Jr.'s assassination in early April and Robert Kennedy's in early June, thirteen-year-old Julie Cohen arrived at NCCJ's Brotherhood Camp from a liberal, North Hollywood, white Jewish household. She anticipated a week of interesting conversations, but when she located her cabin, she remembers, "I felt some anger [there]. There were a few black girls. I think there were Chicano girls, and it was like, finally, we were all on equal turf. I didn't have 'my people,' my background, my support system. *I didn't have any more say in the matter than these people did.* [So for the first day or so it's a question of] are we going to be friends, or are we going to fight out the differences?"[1] By 1968, the combination of white suburban segregation and African American, Mexican American, and American Indian separatist positions revived a public discourse of racial animosity. Contemporary liberal support for unified universal ideals of equal opportunity, the racial power groups argued, could too easily enforce homogeneity under white leadership. At the Brotherhood Camp, however, Julie found a third possibility: self-respecting negotiation of presumed equals. "What happened was, through time, interacting, and sparks, some friction, I started to learn how to take some of the shots, and I started noticing that we were all sort of having to. And I started finding a way to be myself, not hav[ing] to interact in the way these other people did, but be able to be receptive to it. I started to learn that I could be different and yet equal."

A nice, unprejudiced person like Julie couldn't succeed at camp with only good intentions; the white campers would be pressed to take some responsibility for the reality that white Americans lived in increasing isolation from nonwhites.[2] Like young people of color, white kids had to figure out how to act from their racialized identities and social situations. Julie found herself able to listen to her cabinmates' anger and to begin crafting a new kind of white identity that did not entail dominance, but did carry some obligation to affirm the feelings and views of the girls in her cabin. The camp challenge of the post-1968 era was to sustain interracial dialogue and connection amidst nonwhites' cultural nationalism and whites' detachment from race as an issue.

## Racial Power

After 1966, as historian Bruce J. Schulman sums up in his classic study of the 1970s, African Americans shifted their goal from integration to "black identity and cultural separateness, [and] the Chicano movements and those of American Indians and Asian Americans almost immediately advanced an anti-assimilationist, cultural nationalist agenda."[3] Groups the white, dominant culture had viewed as minorities or as aliens in the historical development of the nation now argued that their histories and cultures were central to the national story. These marginalized groups could gain recognition and power only as separate, race-specific entities, not from integration into white-run institutions.[4] The upshot for the Brotherhood Camps was that in the minds of African American, Asian American, and Mexican American campers, white people had a lot to learn.

In response, Brotherhood Camp leaders sought ways to support some students' racial power assertions, give white students enough security to hear new ideas, and enable young people from various groups to feel some responsibility toward each other. Acting on their belief in democratic principles of inclusion and dialogue, leaders welcomed each camper—and the history, culture, circumstances, and political ideas that each brought. Their even-handed willingness to allow campers to express a diversity of views accorded legitimacy to ideas generally treated as dangerous to the dominant white culture. In this special space, young white people found that authorities, quite radically, backed all the campers equally, instead of assuming the innate higher intelligence or better sense of a white child versus that of any child of color.[5] As Clabe Hangan promised, all the young people would be equally valued, but peers would push white teens to consider how they might undo some of the behaviors and institutions that racialized differences and rationalized inequality.

The NCCJ camp leaders' willingness to give a respectful hearing to racial power arguments ran against the current of dominant white opinion that the civil rights era had successfully concluded about 1965. Whites who saw little need for more civil rights activism could cite Supreme Court rulings against segregation, congressional passage of significant legislation, and white popular acceptance of African Americans' innate equality. Attitude surveys showed that over the course of the 1960s, white Americans had given up old biologically based views of racial hierarchy. White Americans claimed that they no longer supported racism; they had become color-blind and able to ignore racialized identities, which only the racial power movements, paradoxically, kept alive. Some skeptics argued that the "unfashionableness of blatantly avowed racism" had shamed white Americans into saying they believed in racial equality. Many white Americans now explained away ongoing inequality as the result of laziness or lack of interest in education on the part of nonwhites; white respondents to social science surveys had learned to offer a socially acceptable "motivational" explanation and not a discredited "genetic" one.[6] In this context of a majority white opinion ready to be done with discussions about racial inequality, the camp leaders opened up space to talk.

## Unsettling Encounters

New practices of confrontation required new leadership. While some of the 1968 campers found the new environment unsettling in positive ways, longtime director Nancy Trask found it disturbing. Bernice Van Steenbergen, who would take over camp leadership in 1969, remembers that Trask "felt very concerned when she saw blacks starting to group together." The camps had been "we shall overcome [racial segregation], and it was getting very separate. . . . People were starting to get into their own ethnic groups and [to ask], 'Who are we?' "[7] The 1968 camp theme was "Building a New America," and Trask and the staff defined six daily discussion topics for the week—"race relations, education, housing, religion and morality, employment, and foreign relations"—for campers to formulate shared political positions.[8] Trask was still emphasizing that campers could debate and settle on singular solutions to political "problems," and campers obligingly agreed on a series of recommendations: "Move more jobs and businesses into the ghettos" and "balance already integrated neighborhoods so the balance doesn't shift in either direction." But campers also advocated "exchange programs so that black and white students could live in each other's homes while attending each other's schools" to reduce residential and school segregation. Campers articulated plans to learn about worlds that had not been in the official curriculum of their predominantly white schools, calling for "mandatory study of minority group history, for instance the history of Mexican Americans in Southern California,"[9] backing up demands Chicano activists were making.

In 1969, Bernice Van Steenbergen became camp director and tentatively but conclusively turned the camp away from a focus on learning about political issues and toward an emphasis on learning empathy for various religious and racial situations in the United States. She had come to the camp first in 1968 along with her husband, a high school social studies teacher recruited as a counselor. Having interrupted her own college degree, first to work and then to support the family while her husband finished his degree, Van Steenbergen was completing a bachelor's degree in English, raising children, and volunteering. She had no human relations training and no relevant background for the camp directorship, "except that I was interested in people." Having grown up in Montana, where "the only people that weren't white, Anglo-Saxon Protestants were some Native Americans that we would see coming into our small, little town," she had not known much about interracial work. But, in her first few camp sessions, she had seen "the growth that it gave others and myself. . . . a tremendous closeness that developed at camp."

Candor, confrontation, and respect did not come about through avoiding conflict, Van Steenbergen concluded, and she quickly began to learn human relations techniques. She maintained earlier camps' emphasis on honesty and reflection about feelings, but campers' work now extended to the emotions aroused by examining history, past injustices, and current politics—feelings of fear, anger, and shame, as well as of attraction and empathy. She initiated more training for the staff, who were usually recruited from schoolteachers and counselors free during the summer months, and included the campers who came back for a second summer as cabin leaders.

Counselors and cabin leaders learned basic human relations techniques for enabling constructive disagreement: articulating one's feelings, stating one's own experience, and giving feedback about the effects of someone else's actions. Van Steenbergen remembers that "we really focused on speak for yourself. You can't speak for anyone else but yourself. You can't speak for your race." Campers were taught not to say, "Whites do this, and Mexicans do that," as if there was a universal truth about a group's nature or behavior. Instead, campers had to speak only for the "I," for what they knew about themselves. "It's a hard thing to confront somebody if you don't like what's happening," Van Steenbergen says, and people had to master how to do that without name-calling. "It's a real learning experience not to say, 'You make me such and such,' but to say 'I *feel* such and such [in response to what you said or did].'" With these simple techniques, counselors and cabin leaders taught skills that allowed campers to talk about the communities, neighborhoods, and schools they came from without one taking precedence over another.

The camp sessions typically opened on Sunday evenings with ice-breaker games to let young people meet, find similarities besides race and neighborhood, have fun, and act silly. Just-arrived campers were instructed to find somebody with the "same color socks and hook arms," and later to find "somebody with the same color eyes [or] the same color jeans" and link arms. Young people paid attention to qualities besides race and gender as they scrambled to locate a partner. Bernice Van Steenbergen remembers that the physical games forced undignified intimacy for the teens, who were protective of their images of self-assurance. In the circle sit, for instance, the order would come to sit, and "all of a sudden here's this group all sitting on each other's knees all around the room." Adults joined in, too, which may have relieved the pressure for teens to maintain poses of detachment.

As campers quickly learned, each day ended with a circle sing, where campers and staff sat on the ground in the evening's dark, sang together, and felt the physical presence of an inclusive group joined to make music. Although the music had always been diverse, with a new consciousness of cultural inclusion, the song sheets now included, Clabe Hangan remembers,

> songs in Spanish, Hebrew, Japanese, Russian. [Because] when you're talking about brotherhood, then you want all the brothers. Want to bring all the sisters. We'd bring it all together, all the other brothers

and sisters, religions, cultures. So we could all know that each and all is equally real.

Then the campers walked home to their racially mixed cabins for a final hour of getting ready for bed. "They'd have cabin meetings every night before they went to bed," Bernice explains. The cabin leaders "were trained to talk about what the day was and what the kids felt. Sometimes it was difficult for the cabin leaders because they were pretty much the same age; it was tough when you're trying to keep order, be a leader, with your peers."

The counselors set norms that encouraged teen responsibility and fun. Bernice recalls that she persuaded the Los Angeles School District to certify the camp experience for school credit. When she recruited in high schools, she promised students not just the tangible benefits of credits, but also the chance to get away from home for a week, and, for the boys, a place to meet girls. The camp director and her staff monitored young people to make certain that late Sixties' mores did not bring drugs and sexual intercourse into the camp. But the staff did not interfere with campers' flirting and kissing and allowed students to meet at a smoking tree for hard conversations and cigarettes.

In the 1969 transition year, Van Steenbergen's program meshed the sorts of political discussions usual in earlier years with the personal examinations provoked by human relations techniques. Held at a moment of intensifying opposition to the Vietnam War, campus protests about the military draft, and student demonstrations to adopt black studies and Chicano studies history and literature courses, the theme for the 1969 summer camp was peace. Instead of hearing lectures, each day the campers contemplated a set of questions: "How do I find peace within myself? How can peace come in black/brown/white/yellow relations? Is peace desirable or possible in the world? What can I do to bring peace?"[10]

Evidently, the campers were inhibited by the imperative of agreeableness and agreement implied by the goal of peace. After four days of the usual discussions and workshops, the director and cabin leaders enacted a secret plan. The student cabin leaders provoked campers to imprison the adult counselors, take over the camp, and formulate plans on their own. Arguing over how to run the camp, campers finally sought help from the counselors. The day ended with the staff back in charge, but with a very different dynamic. The incident had demonstrated benefits of some order and shifted the power dynamic from a contest over whether adults or youth were in charge to discussions about how to use authority.

Freed from the need to challenge adult leadership, the campers refused to smooth over their unsettled feelings that peace could not be gained by dissolving racial differences. On the last night, the campers created a skit, "Look for America," in which each of the camp's racial groups conveyed its significance within the nation. The enthusiasm students showed for this prickly, confrontational production contrasted with their apathy to a "traditional play on the theme of brotherhood," noted one adult observer.[11] An old ideal of "all getting along" without disagreement seemed naive. Peace, the campers implicitly argued, could emerge from empathetic and ordered recognition of different racial positions.

For the summer of 1970, Van Steenbergen recommended a smaller camp where campers could confront the new racial reality—that young people "are dealing more with separation than brotherhood, more oriented to action and hostility than to love and the brotherhood principle." She argued with her boss to reduce the camp size and to hold three small camps of about 100 instead of two big ones of about 300, so that young people could have more interaction and individual counselor attention. From the 1970 camp on, the morning sessions focused on "Racism" and "Sexism," followed in the afternoon by less emotionally stressful interest group meetings in activities like dance, music, film, arts and crafts, and sports. Staff worked in the morning sessions on communication skills, so that students could learn how to convey their understanding and experiences to each other. Even more explicitly than Walt Chambers's New Jersey institutes, Van Steenbergen's camps gave students structures to teach each other "what it feels like to be *me*" and to recognize that *me* exists not only as an individual but also within an historically racialized social realm.

In moving to hold meetings in racialized and gendered groups, Van Steenbergen adjusted the camp direction to the temper of the cultural nationalist times. By contrast with those who saw cultural nationalism as divisive, Brotherhood Camp sought to incorporate group identities into a revised history of the nation and a contemporary politics of interracial collaboration. Unlike others who simply celebrated the end of longtime pressures for all Americans to conform to the values of the dominant WASP culture, NCCJ tried out processes to transform cultural diversity into a conscious, respectful exchange of viewpoints.[12]

The emphasis on emotion was essential, Van Steenbergen believed, to disrupt the intellectual rationalizations that young people had absorbed. As she had figured out, "Some of the people tried to stay in their heads and to keep from getting emotional. If you don't want to look at the issue squarely, you'll try to stay in your head" and ignore the sadness, anger, and self-defensiveness aroused by a campmate's words. To imagine the possibility of new kinds of relationships that accepted racial differences without sustaining white dominance, the young people engaged in talk and argument that encouraged them to try something new. The camp events were designed to "hit the heart," Bernice said, and to move the young people beyond "tolerance" to a desire to "really know people, somebody from another race that they never would have met and known as a friend, a human being." In her camp memories years later, Julie Cohen described the difference between an idea of brotherhood and its feeling as that between the "intellectual heart" and "your *true* heart."

The racial composition of the camps changed as a reflection of, and reaction to, the new willingness to accept conflict as part of a process of change. Van Steenbergen more carefully recruited a diverse racial array of students, and her camper lists use marginal notations to identify campers as "w, b, br, As, I" to keep track of the percentages of white, black, brown (for Mexican), Asian, and American Indian young people. As the percentages of nonwhite students rose, fewer white students signed up to attend sessions. Some white decline was institutional; white parents, especially in the San Fernando Valley, were pulling their children out of the public schools that had typically been recruiting centers for the camps. Some was the result of white fearfulness; with young people of color in the majority, white youngsters were in a minority position and, as the available representatives of the nation's historically dominant group, easy targets of blame. In 1969, white campers were just above 50 percent of the total; in succeeding summers, the white percentage dropped below 40, with black and brown campers each making up between one-fifth and one-third of campers, Asian campers posting close to 10 percent, and a few American Indian campers in some summers. Through the first years of the 1970s, the appearance of the camps changed from a white-dominant space with some racial minorities to a racially diverse space.

The gender dynamics of the camps also shifted, as the women's movement added questions about gender inequality to the public debates about racial inequality. The attractions of adolescent flirting continued to entice young people to a space where boys and girls could cross their everyday boundaries, safely supervised by friendly adults. The boys' and girls' cabins now became centers for more serious racial discussions, as Julie Cohen found. At the same time, the political inspiration of the women's movement enlarged the camp focus to include a more general examination of social inequalities.

As the campers of color took a high ground of historical hardship, loss, and political activism, white campers were challenged to conceptualize a white identity that did not rest on racial dominance and exclusion. They listened to nonwhite campers with varied reactions. Campers' responses articulated in their camp memories reveal a developmental pattern: movement from denial of white advantage or deflection of the advantages of their white identities to curiosity about their campmates and, sometimes, to affirmation of a nation built on the respectful negotiation of racialized differences. Not every camper worked completely through these stages, and any single young person might express a number of them during the session, but the camp procedures offered a rare space for white young people to examine the effects of being white in the United States and held out inducements, especially of friendship, to join in changing the structures of white advantage.

### Imagining a Racially Egalitarian America

During the 1968 and 1969 summers, campers still met in racially mixed discussion groups after the morning lectures. Infused with the ideas of power politics sparked by Black Panther prominence in California and angered by the inattention to inner-city poverty and the rising costs of the Vietnam War, African American and Mexican American young men arrived at camp ready to speak out. Van Steenbergen remembers the "big heavy, macho guys with the bandana around their head, and the Afros, . . . and some of them used [the style] to intimidate, because it's kind of fun to get your jollies back." As the African American and Mexican American young men enjoyed an unusual freedom to criticize whiteness, they baited the white teens. White kids had the choice to avoid these threatening campmates or to hear what they had to say.

Having found her voice among her cabinmates, Julie Cohen participated in an afternoon workshop dominated, she recalls, by two "black militants" from poor Los Angeles neighborhoods who had come to camp ready to berate privileged campers. Julie remembers that they were "educating us about what was going on in the ghetto" and "how different their experience was from most all of ours." The young men spoke about "the history that had brought us to this point" and refused to accept the easy white sidestepping—"Oh, let's be friends and let bygones be bygones." They would not accept a compromise that required them to give up "venting this anger and informing us," Julie says. Taking advantage of the orderly camp schedule and the requirement that they show up for their daily discussion sessions, most of the white teens kept coming back to listen and argue, and so did the black guys. The white kids argued against the ghetto pessimism, but "there was something about their passion and truth" that pushed the white kids to believe in the realities described by the black guys. Even when faced with anger, Cohen didn't succumb to fear and walk away. As Cohen concluded about her particular exchange, "There was something about our persistence that actually got to them [the black nationalists]." And the young black men, Van Steenbergen believes, realized "they didn't have to be the tough kids all the time."

Disarming the anger sometimes required to fight white dominance occurred within groups as much as across them. African American camper Teresa Miles remembers that in a 1971 session, there was a group speaking up for "the Black Panthers. They were strictly militant, and they were basically saying that the blacks should take over everything. These guys were just ready to overthrow [the existing order]. After we had a campwide discussion, they kind of isolated themselves for a couple of days, and then they kind of mixed back into the [black] group—four or five of them, out of forty or fifty of us."[13] Black campers like Miles supported black power positions of pride and assertiveness, but they did not get caught in the trap of replacing white dominance with black.

Starting in 1970, camp sessions included activities that pushed students to give voice to existing social patterns of power and authority; without a conscious recognition of unequal power, there was no urgency to undo it. At an evening session early in the week, students would be asked to place themselves along a "power line." Bernice remembers that, "if they felt they were in the wrong place, then they'd try to fight to get themselves up to the front." After struggling in the power line, the teens would draw a grid that placed groups in their social rankings. Some, Bernice said, "felt the white were on top, the black were next. Or the Asians were next, then the blacks, and the Latins were on the bottom. And then people had to look at how they felt about that. It's stuff that is painful." As the young people acted out their shared and demonstrably broad knowledge about who exercised control in the United States, white kids had to face the reality that they enjoyed advantages over other kids just because of their race. They had not asked for privileges, but they also could not evade responsibility. The kids of color had the discomfort of articulating a social system that devalued them and put them in competition with each other. But they had the assurance that their ancestors were not to blame for the nation's historic racial hierarchy.

The camp design provided space for presenting the developing views of racial power groups. Racial power analyses were rewriting U.S. history to stress a white history of conquest, violence, expropriation, and obliviousness to the endurance of oppressed minorities. White campers had to bear the burden of a narrative that stressed white villainy. The camp norms allowed the young people who had been silenced in school to speak out, which often left the white campers speechless. An emerging politically minded young man like Fernando Huerta, whose father worked at a warehouse management job after emigrating from Mexico, had been inspired by Chicano politics, especially Cesar Chavez's farmworker organizing in the large agribusinesses of central California. But Fernando's enthusiasm led him to fight with a high school teacher. When the school started to call the police, another teacher intervened and proposed that she take Fernando in her classes. She then recruited him for Brotherhood Camp, where Fernando found his version of U.S. history affirmed:

> I was angry at that time about how Chicanos were being treated. . . .
> I was angry at the history that was portrayed in the books and
> how I perceived myself to be, from what [the books] told me. The
> way history is outlined, it looks like the Mexicans were a bunch of
> lazy people, caught up in superstition and stuff rather than convey
> how much science, how much of the food that's saving the world
> today came from [the] America[s]. We just hear that [Mexicans]
> were conquered very easily by a handful of Spaniards. [And
> then we're called] Spanish Americans, as if we weren't Mexican
> Americans and native to America.

Although the camp staff didn't advocate a particular historical narrative, at Brotherhood Camp Huerta didn't have to fight for his Chicano version of the past or his claim to a status as valuable as that of European immigrants racialized as white.

Like Fernando, Teresa Miles had felt her worldviews criticized and constrained in her high school. Teresa, who arrived at Brotherhood Camp in the summer of 1971 and returned in 1972 as a cabin leader, found the camp "a release. At last I could talk to people and see things and be myself." Teresa's mother, a schoolteacher before working in administration at the University of Southern California, and her father, a postman, had bought a home in Compton when it was one of the two middle-class Los Angeles neighborhoods (along with Baldwin Hills) open to black families. But her parents had separated, and her mother was raising six children. Along with other middle-class black parents, Teresa's mother sent her children to private Catholic schools, and Teresa's childhood occurred safely within the bounds of school, Catholic Youth Organization, and home. After meeting Bernice Van Steenbergen, Teresa's mother decided that Brotherhood Camp was also a worthwhile activity.

Teresa had confronted the Catholic school leadership, starting with a personal symbol of black power aesthetics: the dense halo that grew if she did not perm or straighten her hair. They "wouldn't let us wear the 'naturals,' the Afro, and so I led a protest march. They let us do it, but we only could wear them real short." Especially after scholar-activist Angela Davis was publicized across the nation as a dangerous communist and black power revolutionary, the image of a smart and beautiful woman with an enormous halo of hair became a model for young black women.[14] At camp, Teresa Miles let her hair grow and "after that people used to call me 'Angela Davis,' because I tried to get [my Afro] as big as possible."

For Teresa, the freedom to emulate a politically controversial black woman affirmed her own value; it distinguished her from other campers, but it didn't separate her. In a setting where "everybody came from a lot of different backgrounds," she found shared interests and intellectual nurture.

> We talked about everything, about all kinds of social issues, music—we talked about the Beatles, religion, the different kinds of religions, especially my being Catholic. . . . The adult leaders talked to you. They didn't think you were bizarre, that you're going to turn out to be a bad person. They didn't make value judgments about things that you said. . . . I got a ratification of my feelings and my opinions when I went to the Brotherhood Camp.

Although she hastens to add that her mother always supported her children's ideas and aspirations, it was different when adults in a "public," impartial place validated Teresa's questing thoughts. She felt able to express her views, act like a proud, black woman, be a Catholic, and find her place among the other campers, from black activists to white do-gooder kids.

Asian American consciousness had emerged in the late 1960s, particularly in the context of the war in Vietnam. Even as the U.S. government pulled troops out at the end of 1972, many young Asian Americans felt the U.S. assault on Vietnam as one more instance of a white U.S. history that demeaned Asians. A recent immigrant, Jai Hwa Lee, attended camp in 1972, and she and the other students in the Asian group volunteered to cook something Asian as a cultural gift to the other campers. Whether second-, third-, or fourth-generation, or a newcomer like Jai Hwa, the Asian teens used the moment to teach the non-Asian young Americans about the realities of life in countries like postwar Korea and wartime Vietnam.

> We wanted to share with people what it was like to suffer during the war, so [when we cooked for the camp,] we served boiled rice and water. And everybody had to sit on the floor. So people were really angry, because some were hungry, and there's this boiled rice and no utensils given. I didn't really understand what was going on, but there was part of me that felt kind of satisfied that there was this group of really privileged Americans that kind of had a sense of what it was like to be hungry and uncomfortable. Because to me, all Americans at that time, regardless of their race, were a privileged group of people.[15]

The Vietnam War had appealed to the knee-jerk anti-Asian sentiments developed historically in the United States through Chinese exclusion, Japanese internment, and the creation of Asian enemies in Japan, Communist China, and North Korea; the Asian American students identified their bodies with those being damaged in Vietnam and with a history of U.S. comfort oblivious to Asian hurt.

The NCCJ camps enabled students of color—black, Mexican, and Asian—to assert historical, political, cultural, and aesthetic positions unfamiliar to, and often unpopular among, most white Americans. Bob Jones, the Los Angeles NCCJ executive director in these years, was funding workshops for police officers to meet with residents of inner-city, predominantly black areas, as well as the Brotherhood summer camps. He concluded that the black participants felt that "their role was to be confrontive. They were to confront the terrible results of segregation and discrimination, and they could not play that role if they withdrew from the dialogue."[16] If the NCCJ had clear roles in mind for spokespeople from inner-city communities, the roles for white police and students were less clear. Jones reported that police often walked out of the workshops with the attitude, "Why should we stick around and have our noses bloodied?" But, he marveled, the young people at Brotherhood Camps would stick it out as "something you had to live with and work with as best you could." Not yet in positions of social authority and living with each other for the seven days of camp, teens battled through to new views of each other.

Paradoxically, acknowledging social differences freed campers to reject the social hierarchies of worth that had inhibited individual expression. Clabe Hangan concludes:

> This became our most constructive and creative era, where we started off separated and came together as ourselves. Black kids weren't trying to be white. White [Jewish] kids weren't trying to be Protestant [white kids]. Protestants weren't trying to be Catholic. Asian kids were trying to be Asian. They were trying to be themselves and appreciating each other. Letting [each other] be themselves and still caring. That was the pinnacle.

The appreciation of Americans other than those who were white made the camps a haven for those down the power line and a challenge for white kids, especially the Protestants, up the line. But all campers saw an environment where differences could be celebrated and negotiated, encouraging each camper to find her or his unique self without denying family and neighborhood.

## Searching for Freedom from White Dominance

For all the white kids, the challenge of camp was hearing things they hadn't known about before, growing into an understanding that people could be different from each other and still be in respectful relationships, and, if possible, taking away ideas for political change to reduce unfair white authority. Hearing from peers about circumstances of discrimination, isolation, poverty, and invisibility, white students often felt guilt and shame as the bearers of white history. To escape the heavy responsibility, young people often sought to substitute personal relationships for political involvement. Other white campers listened to expressions of racial anger and responded with curiosity, respect, and even appreciation. These young people often had parents who themselves had made interracial connections and worked against discrimination.

The camps had ceased to be a citizenship activity where a young person could prove his or her antiracism and instead had become a risky encounter. As a result, white campers now represented a narrower geographical and political range than had earlier campers. A large percentage came from the liberal West Side of Los Angeles, with a high proportion of Jews. Other white campers were recruited through church and family networks of liberal mainline Protestant congregations and from among socially conscious Roman Catholics. Growing social conflict and a fear of racial confrontation meant that white campers typically came from church, synagogue, or family backgrounds that taught the need to cross racial lines and to seek racial fairness. Such campers showed up with some assurance that they were on the right side of the historic movement to end racial inequality. Naïve hopefulness made it difficult for some to examine their own privileged assurance, gained from belonging to the white middle class; for others, church or family activist politics inspired attempts at positive collaboration.

To sustain campers as they worked in various configurations, and especially to balance the tensions of racial- and gender-separate groups, the camp directors encouraged imaging and practicing circles. Terry Odendahl, a white, suburban San Diego camper, remembers:

> We had trust circles. You stand in a group and one person stands
> in the middle of the group (I don't think there were more than ten
> people), and that person is supposed to totally relax and then fall
> backwards. And you have to trust. And then the circle pushes you
> very gently all around, back and forth. And you just have to trust
> the people in your circle to take care of you so that you won't fall.[17]

Each evening, the camp day ended with all the campers and counselors holding hands in a circle sing. "And rap [discussion] groups were always in circles, so I have this image of circles," Odendahl recalls. The circles physically embodied both shared work and secure inclusion.

When the camps began to organize the morning discussions in racial groupings to talk about what it meant to be black, white, Asian American, or Mexican American, white students had a hard time. In a 1971 camp, Fernando Huerta remembers, "the Mexican group took off and went over to the library, and the blacks took over the church, Asians took another section. And the whites were very reluctant to play the game and they wanted to infiltrate all our groups, and one or two Mexicans or blacks did, too. They didn't want to play the game, so they were kind of nomads."[18] The white kids did not want to work in a white racial group, Bernice Van Steenbergen decided, because "they have this taken-for-granted thing that, because you're white, you wake up in the morning and you have certain things you don't have to think about." Conceiving themselves as a racialized group instead of as unraced, normative Americans was not something the white teens came prepared for.

As children of the nation, white youth had no base in a racially identified culture. What performances, foods, music, and rituals defined whiteness? These campers felt they could claim only consumer culture, Van Steenbergen recalls:

> The kids would say, well, we've got Coca-Cola, we've got McDonalds. They really felt they had no culture, and they felt that the other people had it all together. They felt lesser in that sense. Especially when they're outnumbered, it was a struggle not to give in and think everybody else is better. [For the other teens], the color and the discrimination [bound] people together, and there wasn't much of anything in the white group to band them together.

Representations of whiteness in the racial power era were negative ones of unfair dominance and racist exclusion—an increasingly unpopular war in Asia and persistent racial segregation. Positive images that could be construed as white were limited to the brands sold by U.S. companies.

An important aspect of the lack of images of whiteness other than dominance was whites' near-universal experience of living in racially segregated neighborhoods and now being called on to see these not as simply good places to live, but as exclusively white. A Filipino American boy from San Diego, Myke Santos, had immigrant, professional parents who were becoming comfortably middle class in the 1960s but who bought a house in an inner-city residential area about one-third white, one-third African American, and one-third Latino/Filipino. At his camp session, Myke joined the African American campers for the racial breakout meetings, because there were too few Asians for an Asian group. The African and Asian American pairing didn't feel unusual, he said, "because I'd grown up in a diverse neighborhood and had close friends who were African American or Latino."[19] Myke had taken for granted the daily cross-racial encounters of a multihued neighborhood, so "it was an eye-opener for me to see a lot of Caucasians who didn't have this kind of experience. . . . I felt that I was pretty well adjusted and comfortable with people from other backgrounds. And I could see that some were not." Learning about racially mixed neighborhoods as a norm challenged the majority white concept of segregation as natural and not the result of racialized real estate practices and white families' home purchase decisions.

White youngsters who were aware of their family's racial animosity understood barriers better but also feared they would face merited anger from nonwhite campers. A white Protestant girl who focused on music, petite, blond, blue-eyed Dorothy Smith, "was a kid raised in white [San Diego] neighborhoods, raised in white schools for the most part, . . . in the natural boundaries of where you live. . . . It was sort of understood that there were different areas of town—blacks in southeast San Diego, and a big Mexican community in San Ysidro."[20] Dorothy's father had grown up in rural California, worked in farm fields, and developed hostility to poor Mexican farmworkers, whom he denounced to his children. Dorothy's adult mentor was a local Methodist minister concerned with people outside their white neighborhood, and she went to Brotherhood Camp in 1971 because she "cared about being exposed" to people she didn't see in her school. But she was also nervous, "because these were kids I did not come in contact with every day. And I didn't want to say the wrong thing, or do the wrong thing, or just seem racially stupid."

Dorothy's church had already been offering its young people experiences she imagined as alien to most whites. In one inner-city "plunge," where youth leaders created a situation to "make other people's experiences real for you," church young people spent a weekend living in an inner-city neighborhood with some of the limitations poor people faced. At one weekend's "have and have-not plunge," young people threw dice to determine who was a "have" and who a "have not." The lucky "haves" got tokens to buy food and to pay for a room. The "have-nots" had to sweep floors to earn more tokens and eat "spaghetti with no sauce," while their peers had "salad, bread, spaghetti with sauce, and ice cream," Dorothy remembers. The kids were encouraged to treat each other deferentially or disrespectfully, depending on their status, and Dorothy finally became so angry that she robbed the token box and distributed the tokens to all the "have-nots." Dorothy's "plunge" had let her identify with the anger of the outsider, which she feared racial outsiders might direct at her.

Other young white people attending these more confrontive camps came from families doing political work to reduce white advantage. Terry

Odendahl's mother attended a suburban Methodist church in La Mesa whose liberal minister and youth director had formed a partnership with a downtown church, Chollas View Methodist. The inner-city church had lost many of its middle-class congregation to white flight and now had a small but very active interracial membership. Young people from the two congregations came and went between the suburban and inner-city communities, learning about each other and their neighborhoods. In the church encounters, Terry learned to use the self-naming terms the black kids explained to her, "first of all talking about 'Negroes,' and then starting to talk about 'blacks.' 'Negro' was preferable to 'colored,' which a lot of people used then, but not that great. And when black power came in, all the youths from the black church were into black and black power."

In this parent-sponsored setting, when Terry's cohort asserted black power, she took it as their claim to political presence, which didn't necessarily entail separation from white people. The black teens were feeling their way out of the old relationships of white authority and black acquiescence into the more mutual connection their church elders were encouraging. Disrupting the old power *line*, the kids of color modeled a power *circle*.

Confrontations in an egalitarian circle had a different effect, as well as a different affect, from those between firmly positioned, oppositional groups of unequal social status. The camps continued to recruit outspoken kids, and the universal acceptance by camp authorities supported young peoples' talking to each other from positions of rough equality, regardless of differences in social status outside the camps. Eric Macy, a white Catholic boy from Point Loma, near San Diego, was recruited to camp through his mother's involvement with the NCCJ project, Rearing Children of Good Will. By 1971, when Eric went to camp, he recollects that his cabinmates and workshop peers were "a very articulate, go-get-'em bunch of kids. They'd really skin the top off an opponent" in an argument.[21] Eric discovered "how many smart people there are, no matter where they're coming from." The camp discussions, he concludes, "were billed as leadership-training groups, as opposed to promote racial harmony, and getting people to interact on a more consensual, as opposed to dictatorial, basis."

Eric had grown up in a household with an architect father and volunteering mother active in the YMCA and other social work groups. Eric had observed them consistently act on "the sort of Golden Rule type thing— for people to treat you the way you treated people." The family had moved from downtown San Diego to an all-white suburb in the 1960s, but his parents tried to make sure their children got "a realistic view of things," that is, most of the world did not look like white U.S. suburbs. The Macys served as a host family for African and Asian students attending local universities, informed their children about politics, and took them on peace marches against the Vietnam War. But Eric found that hearing the realities of someone else's life in person was more mind opening than having his parents transmit their political views. He remembers being struck by a camp conversation when

> people were sitting around and talking about what they would least like other people to take from them or know about them without their knowledge. I was more worried about personal things, and some of the black kids in the group were more worried about *things*. Like their cars. And that struck me as something you wouldn't really worry about because you could always get another one. But I guess you couldn't always get another one if you didn't have access to the tools to get another one.

The campmates' talk conveyed the reality of being poor, a class difference layered onto race that this liberal white American understood only when he reflected on his campmates' unexpected responses. Eric's kind and well-educated parents could only prepare him to hear what the other kids said; arguing with teenage peers helped him reflect about his own comfort and the struggles of other boys.

For many white teens, the desire to accord recognition to people of another race or religion pulled against the dominant impulse to ignore differences. Even as Terry Odendahl accepted that other kids distinguished themselves from her and wanted recognition of their identities, she recalls her feeling that "at a personal level, differences [of color and religion] were more skin-deep; they were superficial differences." Even though her camp held racial group meetings, for Terry the most important symbol was the camp T-shirt with its revered civil rights image of "clasped hands, a black hand and a white hand clasped," which she treasured until she wore it out.

Terry's camp memories revolve not around racial group sessions but around the music workshop, where she connected with other campers without having to focus on how racializing divided their experiences: "I couldn't wait to get back together with the music group." That group had black boys who sang, and Chicano boys who played guitars, and white kids who did one or the other or both. In the eclectic folk song and popular song mix of the early 1970s, Odendahl sang spirituals associated with the civil rights movement, union songs, ballads by singer-songwriters (such as Neil Young, Leonard Cohen, and Bob Dylan), and almost anything from Joan Baez's repertoire.

Dorothy Smith, like Terry, managed the potential emotional conflicts of racial groupings and confrontations by focusing on music. Jim Strathdee, a musician composing new hymns (usually with guitar accompaniment) for Methodist church services, had become one of the camp's regular musical directors in the early 1970s, and he inspired Dorothy to see music as a means of instructing and uniting. Singing songs like *We Shall Overcome* and *Oh, What a Beautiful City* identified with Southern civil rights battles, Dorothy found the camp a place she could join an interracial world. Looking at a 1972 camp photo with a "guy with an Afro on one side of me, and an Asian on the other side," she says, "I was a happening babe," a white girl who could align herself with civil rights history and commitments.

## Girl Power

Girls were in the majority in every racial group at camp, and their willingness to talk with each other and to push the boys to open up emotionally provided essential cement for the camps' often-fractured discussions. As the majority group, white girls, Jewish and Christian, set the camps' dominant tone. Marjorie Baer, a young Jewish camper from North Hollywood, remembers that in the summer of 1968, her cabin was like "any other group of women [I've met] since then. We put them together and they get down to it immediately, talking about who they are and where they're from. I remember there just being a lot of energy."[22] Reflecting on her youthful naiveté: "We just were hopeful that by being friendly and open and showing the world that there's no need to be prejudiced, we could make changes." The older Baer knows such openness was not sufficient for changing the racial order, but she also experienced how girls of all racial groups took on the tasks of social communication.

With an immigrant ambition to learn English and to meet non-Koreans, Jai Hwa Lee answered an ad her mother saw in the Korean church newspaper for Brotherhood U.S.A. When she arrived at Exposition

Park to get the bus to camp, she thought "everyone looked like [strange] hippies. I was very intimidated." But almost immediately, a couple of girls on the bus whom she later figured out were a black girl from South Central, Los Angeles, and a "very upper, middle-class white girl" from Long Beach were friendly to her. "It was clear that it was okay I didn't speak much English, and they would try to slow down and talk to me more slowly."

Girls' curiosity about others—their willingness to go up to people and ask questions—was essential to the exchange of stories that broke through the preconceived ideas young people brought to camp. Julie Cohen remembers that it "just sort of happened naturally" to compare her life experiences with others. "It was shocking or at least a little bit bewildering that someone had been living such a different life for so long while I was living my life and was unaware of [theirs]." The campers sang the Pete Seeger lyrics about the "little boxes" made of "ticky-tacky"—postwar suburban homes—but turned the reference into a view that their families and neighborhoods boxed them into discrete, small-minded, racially isolated existences.[23] For Julie, a new insight was that in her family going to college was assumed, while some of her campmates "were going a different route, whether it was manual labor or going into [military] service." For the first time, she became aware of the luxury of her own choices and of their limits: "Sameness was really terribly boring."

The proximity the camps made possible and the disagreements the counselors facilitated made evident a disjunction between the conscious white ideal of informed tolerance and the fearful ignorance that was not apparent in the day-to-day lives of self-segregated white America. Even as she felt buoyed by curiosity and new realities, Julie realized her own ignorance and fear.

> I thought I knew a lot more than I did about these people from other backgrounds, and I learned that I had to start at ground zero. I [knew] nothing. And when I finally got to that [admission of ignorance], which was not as easy as it is to say, then [it was hard] seeing the prejudice in myself. . . . You have this ideology [of open-mindedness] and then you have your gut feeling. . . . You see someone who fits a certain description and they're not looking particularly friendly and they have this kind of skin, and then suddenly you think, "I have to be careful."

Julie was probably applying her adult reflections to the camp experiences, but her discovery that she had believed herself to be tolerant and had all along harbored firm though unconscious prejudices was common in the camps.

The presence of girls was essential, Fernando Huerta remembers, because they "forced us to get a little more serious than we [boys] wanted to." Girls rewarded boys with flirting, dancing, kissing, and friendship. The camp relied on and encouraged the culturally approved norm of boy-girl teen attraction. One of Myke Santos's vivid memories is the excitement of the evening "square dancing, and conga line." At the last night's big dance, all the boys in his cabin "were doing their best to take showers and get foo-fooed up, and we ran out of underarm spray" as the boys all made sure they smelled and looked good. Myke was a bit too young to imagine a full-blown "romance," but he did meet a girl, who was "a good friend I could share with." Instead of seeing girls as awesome creatures to woo, Myke found they "were human. They were somebody you didn't have to be intimidated by. They weren't scary. They were nice. They were people also, and if you treat them well, they listen to you." Girls' social skills and the premium they placed on interaction helped boys talk, and the breakdown of girls' sexual regulation helped them to bridge the racial divides that their sexual protection had helped to enforce.

## Accommodating and Unraveling Whiteness

Challenged to find ways to reinterpret the nation's past and their present role—to diminish white dominance and historic privilege—white young people responded in three notable ways: opting out of whiteness as Jews; bridging separation with sex; and evading political demands with personal cordiality. Each of these gambits offered a means to deny or to deflect responsibility for white advantage. Each also provided a potential path to empathy and affirmation.

### Balancing Whiteness and Jewishness

Unlike the white campers from Christian backgrounds, by the late 1960s and early 1970s many Jewish campers simply denied that they were "white," as this term operated in the United States. Their unwillingness to be clumped with the Christian white group that had dominated the nation may partly explain the dearth of white campers willing to attend the racially designated morning discussion groups. (Once the Jewish campers took themselves out of the category, the white campers remaining would have been a tiny band.) The Jewish students' reluctance implied that the benefits and histories typically associated with U.S. whiteness had been grounded in Christian religious identity, too.

American Jews had found confirmation of a distinctive identity after the Six-Day War in 1967, when Israel defeated the combined forces of Egypt, Jordan, and Syria. Anxious and elated over the fate of Israel, in the war's aftermath American Jewish congregations bonded as something more than one of the three semi-authorized U.S. faiths. Coupled with renewed attention to the heritage of the European Holocaust that destroyed Jewish communities and killed millions, the Six-Day War solidified American Jews as a people with burdens and responsibilities different from those of other white Americans. The new closeness to Israel provided a nonwhite cultural identity that the counselors seemed to accept when they planned evening entertainments of "a Soul night, La Raza night, Jewish night" [of Israeli folk dances], and worried about how "the other whites [might] deal with a night of their own."[24]

African Americans, especially, rejected the Jewish claim of detachment from racialized white dominance in the United States.[25] By the late 1960s, in Los Angeles as in other large cities, Jewish families enjoyed the same home-buying opportunities as any white American and participated in the suburban migration away from racially mixed or racially isolated inner-city neighborhoods. Jewish access to housing and schools had become indistinguishable from that of any other group of white Americans. Moreover, in the 1950s, African Americans had conceived an affiliation with Arab peoples as another racially abused people; members of the Black Nationalist Nation of Islam, especially, celebrated a faith not implicated in the white racial colonialism practiced by Christians and Jews.[26] Many African Americans interpreted the Israeli victory that heartened America's Jews as just another exercise of white dominance. In this context, when campers tried to "back out of being white" on the basis of being Jewish, Van Steenbergen said, everyone else looked at them and said, "Yes, you are white."

Jewish campers called on three themes to explain themselves as different from white Christians in terms of racial discrimination.[27] First, they claimed a heritage of racial discrimination against Jews as the basis for their identification with suffering and their commitment to confronting oppressors. Some campers specifically inherited family stories that emphasized Jewish people's affiliation with African Americans in historical struggles for equality. Julie Cohen's family did not attend synagogue regularly or join political demonstrations, but family stories conveyed a legacy of empathy and fairness. Her Lithuanian Jewish grandparents passed on stories of pogroms in Europe and a family morality that "rose to how you treat another person." One of her mother's stories was about her own childhood, when the family drove from the East Coast to settle in California. They stopped in a restaurant someplace in the South and were about to sit down, when a black family came in and was told to leave. "So my grandfather said, 'If they can't stay, we're not staying.' And they left. That impressed me, . . . how my grandfather felt very strongly that everyone should be treated with the same respect and as if they had the same quality," and that he acted on that feeling.

The second theme was the immensity of the European Holocaust, invoked to convey the great depth of Jewish social responsibility. In her "white, Jewish, middle-class" home, remembers Marjorie Baer, a budding ninth-grade intellectual when she attended camp in the late 1960s, the family "didn't go to synagogue or observe high holidays" but were "what I think of as typical, assimilated L.A. Jews. Dime a dozen." Her father, however, had emigrated from Germany in the 1930s, just avoiding detention and likely death. Even though her parents didn't "inculcate us with values concerning racial equality in any kind of direct and concrete way," she knew that they had opposed California Proposition 14 to repeal the state's fair-housing legislation, probably as a result of her mother's participation in the League of Women Voters. She also knew, from reporting about Watts, that slums existed in Los Angeles and that she lived in a comfortable, middle-class suburb, cut off "from poor people or very many people of other races or cultures." Perhaps because of her father's fortunate escape, young Baer had felt that her life was "lucky, that I'm white and well-educated and middle class and healthy." Her good fortune, she believed, had been gained in tandem with others' less good luck. After camp, she remembers, she felt some "guilt," which came from "feeling concern for people who have less and who have it worse than I do, sort of survivor's guilt," perhaps similar to that her father felt about his escape from the Nazi regime.

By the early 1970s, the camp opened up discussions about the European

Holocaust, viewing the film *Night and Fog* at one of the evening programs. All the "kids were walking around kind of like zombies after that," Van Steenbergen remembers, absorbing information that was distressing and, especially for the non-Jewish kids, a new set of facts that didn't fit the notion of whites as uniformly powerful oppressors. For Jewish young people, choosing to ignore the differences of poverty and social isolation in favor of a connection made through historic suffering was tempting amidst the heightened demands on white campers to take on some responsibility for the white nation's oppressive past. Jewish emphasis on past suffering could offer evasion or it could inspire deeper association, and campers might move between these with little self-consciousness.

Finally, the third theme recognized that Jewish religious identity had become more assertive in the post-1967 era, both as a commitment to distinctive religious practice and also at a moment when other white ethnics were distinguishing themselves from the heritage of WASP America.[28] Terry Odendahl had learned the lesson at school, where she was in an honors track with many Jewish teens who

> were making it really clear that they were Jewish. It was very important to them for us to know that they were Jewish. . . . I wasn't very aware of differences with regard to religion. And I thought it was really kind of peculiar [that the kids asserted their religious identity], because here were these kids who *looked* just like me, and yet it was really important to them [not to be considered Christian].

Especially since the Jewish students made up such a large part of the camp's white cohort, Terry found that the people who looked like her did not necessarily start from the same assumptions or traditions. With race as the prevalent default of difference in the United States, especially white-black, came an assumption of sameness among whites that disallowed significant religious differences. White Jewish young people had to assert themselves in order for white Christian kids to allow them a distinctive culture and history.

For a young Catholic boy like Myke Santos, whose racially mixed neighborhood was entirely Christian, the Jewish presence was also surprising. What struck him years later was that one camper, particularly, "was very outspoken about being Jewish" and not willing to be quiet about it. "I never had the opportunity to meet anybody who didn't believe in Jesus," he recalls, "who had an entire culture and background that was so divergent from mine." Perhaps for a Filipino like Myke, it was easy to understand that those who practiced Judaism were "another culture, just as mine and everybody else's." Whether campers' reaction was sympathetic, surprised, or angry, they found that Jewish campmates refused to blend into homogeneous whiteness.

In the new global context of the exhibition of power by a Jewish-identified state and the Los Angeles context of well-to-do Jewish families living in white, predominantly Jewish suburbs, some Jewish campers evaded responsibility for whiteness by appealing to their historic status as a threatened people and now a menaced nation. But other Jewish campers asserted a historic Jewish ethic of social responsibility and fairness.[29]

## Sexualizing Whiteness

In the integration-era camps, when white girls had tentatively enlarged the range of acceptable romantic partners and friends to include the dark-skinned boys who had been off-limits, their acts of association had challenged the old segregationist norms of white social distance. Now the message sent by a white girl attracted to a black, Asian, or Mexican American boy was more complicated. White girls' social pairings with boys of color could express a range of motives—from denying racist feelings and deflecting responsibility for white authority to expressing curiosity and affirming another's worth. All four responses might be intertwined in any particular relationship.

Although white girls' bodies had lost some of their historical salience as precious and protected symbols of white virtue, they remained talismans of desirable beauty. But for girls influenced by the women's movement's demands for greater independence, bodies were also tools for asserting personal freedom, often expressed as freer sexual behavior.[30] It was tempting for white girls to use personal, sensual attraction and affection, something over which they had control, to bridge their separation from and defuse the political anger of nonwhite boys.

White girls at camp could exhibit their nonracism through relationships of sexual affection. In the music group Terry Odendahl hung out with, there was a boy, she remembers,

> who was Latino who played guitar. And he and I were playing
> guitar together all the time and singing and playing guitar. And I
> was attracted to him. He was attracted to me. . . . There was a lot of

> sexuality in the air, all around. And especially at night, and around
> the campfire, and with the music. Things were charged in that way.
> We danced.
>
> And we kissed. . . . And that seemed to be just fine. I don't
> remember adults coming around and harassing us. That just
> seemed to be part [of camp].

The music group was electric with the boys' and girls' pleasure. "I don't re-member racial difference or politics," Terry laughs. "I remember . . . wide-spread affection and [sexual] interest and raging hormones." The camp setting didn't discourage the mix of personal connection with political ac-tivism; personal caring might not affect the relative power of the campers' families and neighborhoods in Los Angeles and San Diego, but it might lead white campers to take on greater responsibilities.

Young black and Mexican American men were not averse to taking advantage of the white girls' belief that their displays of affection asserted their power and demonstrated antiracism. Jai Hwa Lee remembers a scene that stayed with her from the 1973 session.

> Some of the African American guys got up in a town hall meeting,
> and they started yelling and screaming, and then one of them got so
> angry that he started breaking down chairs. And white girls from
> Palisades [a well-to-do neighborhood in west L.A.] started crying
> and saying, "I'm not responsible for what happened to you guys."
> And the anger and the violence was really shocking [to me.] Then
> the next day, all these black guys are walking around with the same
> white girls who cried in their arms. I just couldn't understand. One
> minute they are angry at these women, and the next minute they
> are kissing and making out. I said, "What's going on here?"

Young men ready to enjoy the favors of young women wanting to prove their racial open-mindedness offered these young women an easy substi-tute for political responsibility.

For the African American and Mexican American boys at camp, sex-ual relationships with white girls, while appealing, also alerted their self-protective instincts, the result of the fear of dark men that the culture still taught white girls. When black power and Chicano movements had ex-ploited this historical reputation through displays of aggressive masculinity, the bravado exhilarated young men but also perpetuated, and provided rationales for, the culture's encouragement of white fear.

Occasionally, the campers could spotlight the unspoken messages that made interracial romance both a test and a hazard and turn affection into positive understanding. Fernando Huerta remembers a particularly powerful moment in a 1971 session:

> One night they put some people in a chair in the center of the auditorium to talk about their fears, and a white girl [said] she was afraid of blacks and Mexicans. She said that she was very frightened of the black people there, and she thought they might kill her or something. And the Mexicans, she felt, were going to rape her. And she let this out, and it got dead silent in there. It was—it was powerful. I remember the black and brown hand came out to her. Pulled her up vertical. And once she said all this, she bowed her head and was just crying, and she was too embarrassed to move, she was frozen. And so this black guy and this Mexican guy went up there and extended their hands to her and pulled her up. That was very touching. There was a lot of intimacy, but not the regular kind. It was collective.

Expressing the fears her family and culture taught, a young white woman had opened a space for a young black and a young Mexican man to feel hurt and anger and to move from these to kindness. The public setting clarified the fears as collective and general. The confrontation revealed the reactions that young men of color faced when they walked down city streets and allowed these young men to express gentleness as an aspect of their Mexican American and African American manhood. The conscious recognition of the social patterns of fear and anger opened a moment, Fernando felt, when campers might forgive past hurts, abandon old fears, and shape their futures with more mutual trust.

The undoing of sexualized racial fears enabled white girls to imagine nonwhite men as friends and family. Julie Cohen begins a story about a "midnight lover," a young black man she "bumped into on the way to" her cabin on one of the first nights at camp. After the first accidental touch, the two met at the same spot night after night to "give each other a little kiss and this lovely hug and say goodnight. It was very romantic, but it was sweet romantic." After a day of hard angry debate, the brief affirmation of underlying affection was "comforting," she recalls. She concludes the story with a memory transformed from sex to fellowship: "It was almost like a brother, or something: being comforting with each other and saying, 'Goodnight. Have a nice sleep.'" The camps' closeness made possible an evolution of feeling from sexual curiosity to familial love, though such progressions were rarely articulated in any formal, daylight session.

## Personalizing Race

By the mid-1970s, the rich context of political action fostered by the racial power movements diminished, and the camps' message of "encounter, confront, understand, and reconcile" was detached from a widespread social message. The Black Panthers had shrunk to a small band in Oakland; the Chicano movement's push for an independent political party, La Raza Unida, had failed; and the American Indian movement had suffered a defeat in a confrontation with federal authorities at the Pine Ridge, South Dakota, reservation. Simultaneously, prospects for more-integrated schools collapsed with the Supreme Court's 1973 and 1974 decisions to absolve white suburbs from any responsibility for the de facto segregation of majority African American and Mexican American urban school systems. After the Court's decisions, white families could live in segregated suburbs and send children to segregated schools, so long as these had come into being by what was construed as a market process of home buying and not through government enforcement of segregation.[31] Finally, a language of color blindness was displacing the racial power and antiracism messages of white responsibility for undoing the effects of the nation's rigorously enforced, historic racial inequality.[32] The principle of ignoring a person's color, which in the 1960s had inspired actions for integration, was reinterpreted in the 1970s into permission to overlook persistent consequences of the nation's racialized past.

Despite the changed context, in the mid-1970s campers continued to arrive at Brotherhood Camp from their racially segregated neighborhoods and schools to meet each other on safe ground, to express their thoughts about race, and to replace their stereotypical images of another group by coming to know some of its members. Fewer white campers risked the encounter—just under 40 percent of campers in 1973—and a greater diversity of Asian, African American, and Mexican American attended. Increasingly, campers reflected the larger culture's movement toward a personalized, individualistic view of race relations. Counselors continued to push social analysis of how historical constraints and broad cultural messages affected individual lives, but campers increasingly attributed interracial conflicts to personal misunderstandings and not to social systems.

The mid-Seventies camps used the longtime tactic of calling on campers to name the stereotypes that everyone had learned from popular culture and families (even though proper people didn't use such words). The first general session included "each culture saying something against the white race, something negative about that particular culture, Jewish or white, for one minute," Darryl Smith remembers.[33] The sessions moved on to other racial groups during the week, "like a group therapy thing, these are things [people] are actually thinking but are afraid to say." The named group had time to respond to the stereotypes and, of course, pointed to themselves as evidence that the stereotypes were at best only partly accurate. But "white kids," Van Steenbergen says, were left "thinking they didn't have anything to be proud of, and feeling the pain of past racism, and saying they didn't have anything to do with it." They didn't want to accept the label, 'You're a racist,' " she said. Most of the white kids, Darryl remembers, "would respond, 'What did *I* do wrong? I'll be your friend. I don't mind being your friend.' "

The white response—to personalize race relations and remove them from issues of power and politics—coincided with a black and Chicano impulse to draw racial lines more clearly in the face of what they saw as another instance of white withdrawal from responsibility. Darryl Smith, an African American and a successful student from downtown Los Angeles, came to camp as a high school junior in 1974 and returned as a cabin leader in 1975. After elementary school in the center city, his parents had got him into the city's school choice program, and he had bused from downtown L.A. (and then moved in with an aunt) to attend an academically demanding, predominantly Jewish high school in the San Fernando Valley. At camp, Darryl's comfort with middle-class white youngsters, especially his affinity with the Jewish kids, made him suspect among inner-city black and Latino young people. Responding to the political abandonment of cities, they lashed out, especially at the black and Latino kids who had escaped urban life. "They would call me an Oreo or Uncle Tom," Darryl said. In other racial group meetings, he recalls, "the Hispanics were called coconuts, brown on the outside and white on the inside. And the Asians were called bananas" if they were friendly with white campers. Interracial couples still danced and kissed, but Darryl remembers some black girls giving a black guy "a hard time" for dating a white girl and some Hispanics "giving an Hispanic girl a hard time for hanging out with a white guy." The kids who opposed mixed dating thought "it would separate the race and make the race weaker" if someone dated outside the race, that it took emotional and material resources away from the group. At the same time, the campers persisted in talking across racial lines, finding innocent intimacy, and arguing about allegiances in one of the very few places such contact was favored, or even likely, by the mid-1970s.

## Back to the Real World

No matter how white campers responded to their campmates' views, they left the camps aware of the possibility of living in a world different from the homogeneous one most of them were used to. Usually they were unable to find another environment like that at the camps or to replicate the experience. Camp counselors worked to help students with reentry, as they called going back to their noncamp lives. The campers went home elated and ready to live as they had at camp, and "everybody didn't want to hear what they had to say," Bernice Van Steenbergen understates for effect. Their schools, if desegregated, continued to have racially divided groups. "They would go back and try to go into different ethnic groups," Van Steenbergen said. "A white wanted to go over to the black group, and they might not be accepted, where at camp they could go up and talk. So that part's hard." Young people kept an image of a magical place where they connected with each other, even as they argued, debated, challenged, confessed, and felt afraid.

During the racial power era, many nonwhite campers found the Brotherhood experience liberating; they saw themselves as central to an America that, as Jai Hwa Lee said, "was not white." Young people of color expressed pride in their bodies and minds, which had been invisible, fearful, or part of white culture; they constructed themselves as central actors in the camp's dramas and the nation's history. Ex-campers of color often joined racial pride organizations and introduced the possibility of alliances across racial lines that had often hardened in the competition to gain access to the benefits held by white U.S. institutions. Many white ex-campers, by contrast, returned from camp to few sustained efforts by white adults to examine and to alter the real-world "power line." White campers had a difficult time finding places away from Brotherhood Camp to enact their new hopes for affiliation and fairness.

One white response was to learn more about the worlds opened to them at camp. Marjorie Baer remembers a new interest in "reading books by black authors and listening to black music, which I always did." She was aware that

> the Chicano power movement was just firing up, and the progress in the Farmworker movement [of Cesar Chavez] was another thing going on in California culture that was of interest and concern. It's not something that we participated in, beyond boycotting grapes [to pressure owners to bargain with the union]. But you were aware of it and admired it, having some kind of vicarious pride that this was going on.

Baer joined the middle-class consumer boycott to aid Mexican American farmworkers, one of the few interracial political alliances of the late 1960s and early 1970s, but her sympathies remained distant, absent a political movement or adult status. Ongoing contacts to follow up on camp encounters were limited, Baer concludes, because Los Angeles sprawled, young people didn't have cars, and "to go from North Hollywood to Compton [in South Los Angeles] took tremendous effort and someone's goodwill and automobile."

White campers could refuse to sanction commonplace racializing comments and speak up when people around them made casually racist or unfriendly remarks. Though these young people still lived largely segregated lives, they had gained affinity and caring for the inner-city kids they met and were unwilling to identify themselves with the typical white dismissal of urban neighborhoods and residents. When Julie Cohen went home to her white neighborhood,

> I wasn't just who I was when I went there. I actually now encompassed also the experiences that [the black power advocates] shared with me and who I became when I was with them. . . . [When someone said something racist], I was able to represent [the people attacked] because they were kind of a part of me, [and] I was talking about my family.

Julie continued to feel this connection through college and chose a career as a teacher to be able to work with inner-city children, who had become like "family." Similarly, Marjorie Baer found herself encouraged by camp to be alert to the feeling that "white people shouldn't be like this, and to be on guard and ready to combat [white self-justifications]." These essentially personal solutions nevertheless allowed campers to find sympathetic white classmates at college and to welcome black, Asian, and Latino classmates there.

White young people had entered a different world at camp, and they carried its norms into any setting that accepted them. Eric Macy credited camp with his feeling comfortable among his diverse colleagues in pre-med labs at UCLA, where the "racial mix looked like a typical NCCJ camp: guys from Guyana, guys from Nigeria, people from Asia, a whole lot of women. It made a difference what was between their ears, more than what was on the outside, as to how you got along with them."

White Protestant campers from liberal church communities did find work to do when they returned home. Terry Odendahl's parents helped found a group to reduce housing segregation in their suburb and surrounding ones: the Heartland Human Relations Association (HHRA, pronounced "hurrah"), which had its first office in their Methodist church building. By the late 1960s, however, the church's minister, who preached Christian responsibility to "the least of these," was alienating members. More than half the members left in opposition to their minister's consistent call to do something about the powerless and poor.[34]

At the same time that white advocates of racial responsibility felt embattled (and HHRA did suffer a bomb thrown into its church office), the racial power movements, caught up in creating white antiracist politics, left them on their own. The white kids who had enjoyed the fellowship of camp felt abandoned. Longing for connections, the teenage Terry Odendahl could not see a means to work with a black movement that "was being transformed to a more Malcolm X, Black Panther" position that "was more separatist." She "felt very hurt. . . . And that's when I got more into SDS [the New Left Students for a Democratic Society], and more into anti–Vietnam War [work]."

Acceptance, caring, and the camp's gentle moments showed campers another possible world, where they could argue, pay attention to each other, show affection, disagree, and still remain together. One camper remembers as "the most exhilarating day of my life," when "Clabe [Hangan] was singing *Aquarius*. We got up and everybody started forming these circles and started singing [and moving] closer and closer together. I don't know how it happened, but I thought, 'God, this must be heaven!' " The weeklong practices of speaking up, disagreeing, reflecting on one's feelings, and sometimes merging into a moment of peaceful community gave young people a rare vision of how multiracial democracy might look in their country.

Despite becoming less politically oriented during the 1970s, the Brotherhood Camp still offered one of the few places that broke up residential and school segregation and let young people meet and listen to each other. When in 1981 a filmmaker documented a week's camp (with even fewer white campers than in the early 1970s), the program had added to its sessions on religion, race, and gender one about homosexuality as a source of social inequality. Kids confronted their fears about homosexuals and the way the term "faggot" was used to discipline young men not to show caring and other unmanly emotions. In a session whose topic was "What do people see the first time they see you?" girls expressed frustration that the first thing others saw in them was whether they met standard beauty norms. And a black teenage boy reported, "I have trouble with this, because I'm six foot four inches. So when people see me, they shy away. Because I'm big and I'm black." The nervous laughter that followed his analysis confirmed the accuracy of his complaint, and at least one of the white girl campers confessed that she had just figured out that, despite her best intentions, she did carry fears of black men as a legacy from her parents' warnings.[35]

The camp experience continued to help young people see the emotional fears, anxieties, and hopes they channeled through racial, gender, and sexual anxieties. By the end of the week, their reciprocal affection was evident as they sang *Lean on Me*, with its promise that "I'll be your friend/ I'll help you carry on."

If the first era of Brotherhood Camps, from the early 1950s to the mid-1960s, broke down centuries-old social and cultural prohibitions against interracial association, the second era taught young people to negotiate differences of history, circumstance, and power. They learned of varied accounts of the nation's history, of the myriad realities that existed in Los Angeles's and San Diego's varied neighborhoods, of the diverse individuality within racially defined groups, and of the unifying circumstances that sustained racial distinctions. Because racial power movements inspired teens of color to offer a worldview (or many distinct histories) at odds with the prevailing white conceptions of the nation, young white teens learned to see the nation as something other than a unity. Some white teens resisted, and some opened their hearts to new relationships and then their minds to accommodate these new ideas. In the terms of political theorist Danielle S. Allen, young people had been able to imagine themselves as a "whole" and not "one."[36] The campers enjoyed a utopian moment when they could imagine living together in a whole working, caring group that survived through negotiating differences and not through expecting the campers to meld into a harmonious one.

The NCCJ Brotherhood Camps never had the visibility and historical prominence of civil rights demonstrations and lawsuits. Their quiet, hopeful efforts to value each teen and to teach teenagers techniques for valuing each other resulted in no political organization. The teens returned to their homes with mental pictures and somatic impressions of newly possible relationships but, for the white teens especially, with few organizations to which they could devote their efforts. Instead, as white campers matured, many of them welcomed an array of college classmates and coworkers, contemplated and approved interracial marriages, moved into nonsegregated neighborhoods, and quietly backed political views advanced by peoples of color. In interviews, many expressed sadness that the nation had not moved closer to Brotherhood principles during the 1980s and 1990s, but all continued to carry a mental image of the camps as a bright, if wistful, hope.

Although the Brotherhood Camps affected only a small number of white teens (no more than twenty-five thousand in the New York City, Newark, and Los Angeles camps between 1951 and 1974), their historical record offers a counter-memory to the dominant picture of white American failure to act on the new possibilities of desegregation. As the nation invented a new racial order of residential segregation to replace legal segregation, most white teens continued to have few friendly contacts outside their racialized circle and to study in monochrome classrooms. White teens at Brotherhood Camps experienced, even as a momentary contrast, respectful and caring relationships across races. They learned it might be possible to embody a whiteness that incorporated discussions of color, a checkered national history, and respectful negotiation with Americans of other races.

# 3

# Making a Neighborhood

## Neighbors Inc., 1958–1965

It is becoming increasingly clear that the persistence and
growth of housing segregation threatens the gains made against
discrimination in other fields—and adds a few distinct problems of
its own. Its consequences are so serious that the struggle to end it
should be a concern for all Americans.

—*George and Eunice Grier,*
Discrimination in Housing, *1960*

"The shadows are coming; the shadows are coming," a man intoned ominously on the other end of Janet Brown's telephone line. Inside her large well-built home, the white housewife listened to the persistent real estate agent who had waited until the man of the house left for work to warn her that she and her young children might soon find their leafy, quiet neighborhood deteriorating. The caller hoped that she would panic and sell out, at a good commission for the agent, in anticipation of the effects of the "shadows"—black families who might move onto her block in Washington, D.C., in 1961. Brown felt more anger than fright, fended off many such urgent calls, and stayed to raise three children with her husband, Norman, in that comfortable urban home.[1]

The Browns' story offers a partial answer to an urgent postwar question: How could anyone hope to advance residential desegregation when the major suburban housing developments of the postwar period were constructed for de facto white occupancy? In the historical moment when a family home in the racially segregated suburbs fulfilled the American Dream of prosperity and comfort available to most hard-working families, where was an alternative? Some white Americans seized the new mix of spaces in cities left behind in the turmoil of postwar urban housing shifts to create housing that competed with the white suburbs. In contrast to ideals of postwar whiteness as suburban, racially exclusive, and focused on consumption, these groups constructed a white identity as urban, neighborly, socially conscious, and civic.

The stories of these urban efforts all but disappeared in the historical emphasis on the postwar population shift to largely segregated suburbs; the predominant narrative either ignores interracial city neighborhoods or dismisses them as paternalistic attempts that inevitably failed because white families expected to be in charge and to welcome grateful, assimilating black families.[2] But one Washington, D.C., neighborhood organization offers an essential memory that clarifies the complex motives of white Americans who loved cities, favored racial desegregation, and learned that both required a hard fight.

The Browns bought a home in the city at the pivotal moment when it seemed as if Washington might leave behind its segregated past and emerge as a model for racial integration. As the capital, Washington could symbolize the way the United States would protect democracy at home as it claimed Cold War leadership to protect freedom abroad.[3] Efforts to transform the city had begun in 1947 when President Harry Truman charged a President's Committee on Civil Rights to study and give guidance for necessary reforms. Embarrassed by conditions in the capital city, the committee concluded in its 1947 report that Washington's *"situation [was] intolerable."*

> For Negro Americans, Washington is not just the nation's capital. It is the point at which all public transportation into the South becomes "Jim Crow." . . . The Negro who decides to settle in the District must often find a home in an overcrowded, substandard area. He must send his children to inferior public schools set aside for Negroes.

The committee recommended that the U.S. Congress, which governed the District, move swiftly to end segregation in publicly funded institutions— schools, hospitals, parks, public housing—and to outlaw restrictive covenants that prohibited an owner in a white-segregated area from selling a house to a "Negro."[4] The committee's suggestions were bolstered in short order by the Supreme Court's 1948 ruling in *Shelley v. Kraemer* that housing covenants were unenforceable, and, in the companion case of *Hurd v. Hodge*, that the D.C. government could not enforce restrictive covenants in violation of the guarantees of the Civil Rights Act of 1866. In 1954, the Court decision in *Bolling v. Sharpe*, a partner case to *Brown v. Board*, decreed an end to the District's dual, segregated school system.[5]

Few white families were choosing integrated areas, however. By 1961, tens of thousands had moved out of the city. Better-off white families who did not want to  commute or to leave the city's cultural center had created a racially exclusive enclave to the west of Rock Creek Park, using the natural physical barrier of streams, hills, and woods that cut through D.C.'s northwest quadrant from the Maryland border to the Potomac River. "West of the park" had become a synonym for white Washington residences isolated from black sections of the city. Real estate agents assumed that families like the Browns would move out, and quickly.

# The Nation's Capital Desegregated and Resegregated

By the 1950 Census, Washington had become a majority-black city run by a white Congress and white elite. In contrast to the recommendations of President Truman's Committee on Civil Rights, which envisioned a less segregated city, congressionally controlled local authorities adopted policies that seemed designed to hasten white movement out of the city and to intensify black demand on the city's available real estate. To aid the growth of suburbs, the regional planning commission had proposed new freeways to connect the suburbs with the city center, still vital for work, shopping, and leisure entertainment. Building the freeways also had enabled the planners to solve what they saw as another problem—clearing out an unsightly working-class, racially mixed area that marred the vista of the Capitol. In the mid-1950s, Congress authorized demolition of the densely settled neighborhood in Southwest D.C. to build the Southwest Freeway, promising suburbanites easy access and forcing thousands of black families to look for new homes.[6] As white homeowners began to move out of much of the city east of Rock Creek Park, a black working class and tens of thousands of poor, rural, black immigrants began to move into city blocks now informally designated for "Negro" occupancy.

In the mid-1950s, the city's substantial black middle class also began to search for better housing, leaving the neighborhood around Howard University, which had offered gracious homes since the 1890s, for the newer homes and better schools that the Supreme Court's decisions promised to make accessible. Unable to break open the housing market in neighboring Maryland and Virginia suburbs, black middle-class families traveled north from the Howard University area into previously all-white areas of the city, hoping to establish middle-class neighborhoods even as the housing market was being inundated with displaced working-class and poor families.

The racial composition of housing changed neighborhood by neighborhood. Black families began to move up the central Northwest corridor from downtown after school desegregation in the mid-1950s, and within five years, real estate agents had helped to speed a seemingly inexorable transition from white-only to more than 50 percent black in the Manor Park and Brightwood sections. Developed in the 1920s, Brightwood's modest semi-detached housing and apartment buildings had been especially attractive to white Jewish families beginning their move out of the downtown and into an area without restrictions against Jewish home buyers and renters. Manor Park, just north of Howard University, had solid, moderately priced, and relatively small detached houses that had been designed to serve the growing population of midlevel federal and commercial employees during the 1930s.[7]

By 1961, when Janet Brown bought in Shepherd Park, middle-class black families were pressing into Shepherd Park and Takoma, the final neighborhoods up the northern passage before the segregated Maryland suburbs. Shepherd Park, constructed in the 1910s and 1920s for well-to-do white Protestants and graced with spacious, solid Colonial and Tudor-style houses, had finally admitted Jewish home buyers in the late 1940s with the Court's upset of restrictive housing covenants. The area was full of old shade trees and had a reliable federal presence in the Walter Reed Army Hospital campus just at its southern end. To the east was Takoma, D.C., developed at the end of a streetcar line on the edge of D.C. in the 1890s, which had maintained a combination of large, rambling, Victorian houses, well-designed bungalows, and more modest blocks built in the 1920s and 1930s.[8] After 1960, real estate agents were pressuring the all-white residents in these desirable neighborhoods to recognize that the area would inevitably fill with black home seekers.

Within a decade after the housing and school desegregation decisions, the District of Columbia was in the same process of resegregation that affected most cities between the mid-1950s and the mid-1970s.

Instead of being seen as a failure of public policy, however, 1950s resi-

dential segregation was conceptualized as an outcome of free, private decisions. The massive postwar home building of the 1950s was depicted as a
natural fulfillment of pent-up consumer desire to own a home and to live
in bucolic comfort with people like oneself. Having a nice home, living in
a safe neighborhood, and sending the children to a good school was simply a private choice paid for by individual homeowners. Housing developers shrugged off complaints of segregation as the necessary, if unfortunate, result of white families' unwillingness to buy in areas open to black
families.[9] Even though public agencies like the Federal Housing Agency
(FHA) and the Veterans Administration (VA), not to mention a regulated
industry like banking, awarded white-only suburbs preferential funding,
segregation came to be seen as a result of private consumer decisions, not
a consequence of racialized public policies.[10]

A halo hovered over the idea of private housing, the result of the link
between the home and the idealized white postwar family. A stay-at-home
wife, caring for children and supported by a breadwinning husband,
tended a nurturing domestic space.[11] Her husband's purchase of a house
in a neighborhood inhabited by families just like theirs, far removed from
poor and alien people left behind in the cities, secured the family's safety.
This privatized notion of residential security accorded with the idea that
new patterns of racial segregation and inequality were not a public issue
that concerned the average white family.[12]

# Neighbors Inc.

White middle-class families who stayed in cities had to resist the prevailing narratives of neighborhood and family and revive housing as a public
issue. And they had to act quickly. The first wave of turnover in home-
ownership astonished D.C. families, first white and then black, who had
seen Manor Park and Brightwood as secure and attractive areas. By the
summer of 1958, about fifty concerned householders met to see if they
could get control of the neighborhood's rapid turnover from white to black
homeowners. Convened by Marvin Caplan and Warren Van Hook, the
group agreed to form Neighbors Inc., which attracted 175 households by
year's end. Caplan, a white journalist, and Van Hook, a black pharma-
cist, had met at PTA meetings at the elementary school attended by their
daughters and quickly found they shared an interest in protecting the
academic quality of the previously white-only school, which was adjust-

ing to rapid flux in its student and parent populations. Their vision, stated in the organization's founding document, was to "preserve the area as a first-class community of good Americans regardless of race and religion." Quickly the group expanded its purview to include the three contiguous areas between their neighborhood, the Maryland boundary, and Rock Creek Park—Brightwood, Takoma, D.C., and Shepherd Park. They hoped to gain allies in areas that still had substantial numbers of white residents, whose presence could reassure other white families tempted to flee the city and offer a possibility of integration instead of rapid transition from white to black. Neighbors Inc. (NI) founders publicized themselves as "the precursors of a new and more democratic way of urban living."[13]

NI families were hopeful about recruiting other families, because polls showed that residential desegregation was increasingly acceptable to white Americans. In 1956, when pollsters asked white homeowners whether " 'it would make any difference' if an African American moved next door," 58 percent of Northerners said they would accept black neighbors, a rise from 42 percent in 1942, and 38 percent of Southerners agreed, up from 12 percent in 1942.[14] These numbers, while indicating a positive attitude change, represented only a willingness *not* to move out and *not* to protest if a black family moved in next door. Passive acceptance did not indicate a willingness to take positive action. The white leadership of Neighbors Inc. came out of the nation's recent history of organizing to solve public problems. Its founding and most active members drew upon ideals imbibed as they came to adulthood during the crises of the Depression and World War II that looked to public action and government resources to advance social equity and political democracy. President Roosevelt promised in his 1944 State of the Union address that the postwar nation could use its wealth to ensure that every citizen had adequate employment, housing, and education, and the 1944 GI Bill promised such assistance to returning veterans, including large numbers of African American, Mexican American, and American Indian women and men who had served.[15]

Hopes for postwar social democracy darkened when the rise of the Cold War discredited governmental actions other than military as socialistic and social welfare proponents as allies or dupes of the Soviet enemy. Labor unions responded by banishing former Communist Party members or sympathizers, who often had been leading advocates for interracial unions. A white Southern-dominated Congress discouraged liberal political leaders from advocating racial justice when they needed Southern Democrats' votes on other issues.[16] And some black liberals discouraged public discussion of civil rights on the grounds that it undercut the reputation of the United States as a nation qualified to lead the world's democracies in opposition to the Soviet Union's Communist threat.[17]

Still, many union members, military veterans, and liberal members of churches and synagogues held onto an ideal of social responsibility as essential to a democratic nation. In contrast to the postwar ideal of democracy as widespread consumption, these groups held out the New Deal standard of community involvement as the true test of citizenship.[18] A vision of democracy as bargaining and negotiation to achieve fairness, and not simply as a pay scale high enough to buy a house and car, inspired many of the Neighbors Inc. residents.[19] Many had organizing and publicity skills and habits of collaborative decision making gained in civil rights and union campaigns. As they sought homes consistent with their interests and beliefs, they applied their talents to the intentional creation of an interracial neighborhood.

The white co-convener of Neighbors Inc.'s inaugural meeting, Marvin Caplan, embodied many of these qualities and exemplified the personal histories that some other white families brought to the organization. A gregarious, word-loving, Jewish army veteran, Caplan managed to escape his father's Philadelphia butcher business when his Temple University degree earned him admission to the army's Japanese-language unit during World War II. "We became quite friendly with our Japanese American teachers," Marvin remembered, "and for the first time I realized that our government had visited a horrible injustice on hundreds of thousands of people [with internment of Japanese American citizens], wiped out their life's work, pulled students out of college, forced them to sell their farms and their homes for nothing. It was an eye-opening experience that drew me away from accepting [racial discrimination] blindly."[20]

After the War, Caplan worked in Richmond for a Southern Jewish weekly magazine and became part of an enthusiastic band of veterans who met in the local chapter of the racially integrated American Veterans Committee, which supported labor organizing and included in the Richmond chapter African American lawyers protesting segregation in the former Confederate capital. When Marvin and his wife, Naomi, moved to Washington in 1951 for another reporting job, they had lived in a necessarily white-segregated apartment complex full of young families with socialist, labor union, and civil rights politics; Marvin joined pickets to desegregate Washington's downtown restaurants.[21]

Despite these political affiliations, when the Caplans moved from their apartment to a pleasant little house in the north central section of the city in 1957, they didn't intend to integrate a neighborhood. Marvin bought the Manor Park house directly from its white owner and didn't realize that his block was in transition and already being listed in real estate ads as "Colored." But when the Caplans were confronted with a choice to join the suburban flight or to fight for an interracial neighborhood, they drew on a recent history of successful interracial political action and personal friendship; they were unwilling to live in a suburban environment that discouraged both.

Having established an organization and defined its physical ground, Neighbors Inc. had to act quickly to defend its interracial ground. By the late 1950s any racially mixed area was usually described as "in transition," with the assumption that white and black families lived in proximity only briefly as an area switched from white only to all-black. Neighbors Inc. searched for a concept to counter the seemingly inevitable process of transition and found a counter social science neologism, "stabilization." Used by the American Friends Service Committee, a social action arm of the Society of Friends, the term articulated a goal of halting panic selling and buying long enough to enable families to build relationships and confidence that could slow turnover. Richmond friends of the Caplans had been working on projects to stop white flight in California and in Philadelphia, and they introduced the Washington group to work going on in Chicago's Hyde Park and in Philadelphia's Germantown. Neighbors Inc. found it wasn't the only group trying to sustain a middle-class, interracial, urban community.[22]

Heartened that it was not alone, Neighbors Inc. still had to fight for stabilization in northwest D.C. Going to work and tending to children, residents could not volunteer enough hours to compete with the well-financed programs of developers, real estate agents, banks, and federal agencies wooing white buyers to segregated suburbs. Neighbors Inc. needed paid staff, a business manager, and an office to monitor real estate practices in the area and to open up the suburban housing market for black buyers; at the same time, NI needed to cultivate relationships among the white families choosing interracial living and the black families seeking improved housing and schools.

Caplan and Van Hook won a small grant from the local Meyer Foundation, and in the spring of 1959 Neighbors Inc. opened an office and hired Margery Ware as executive director. A Wellesley College graduate and wartime Women's Air Service pilot, Ware had joined the staff of the National Urban League after the war to protect jobs and housing for returning African American veterans. She was a confident, well-educated, independent white woman who moved comfortably in integrated settings and conveyed to reporters and other organizations that a high-status Seven Sisters graduate favored interracial living. Her job was to provide information about housing policies and law, to recruit and direct volunteers, and to represent Neighbors Inc. in its dealings with government agencies and citizen groups. The neighbors would assist by volunteering for essential projects and standing committees.

## Interracial Spatial Integrity

For Neighbors Inc. to succeed, it had to confront the institutions and social norms that assaulted and demeaned an interracial neighborhood and to transform the picture of "interracial" from marginal to acceptable middle-class. First, NI immediately disputed real estate conventions that obliterated evidence of interracial housing. In 1958, the city's leading newspapers, the *Washington Post* and the *Washington Evening Star*, published real estate ads that listed a neighborhood with even one black household as "Colored." Just as the one-drop rule of race had defined a person with a drop of African ancestry as "black," the "Colored" listing presumed that a neighborhood with one black family irrevocably precluded white neighbors. The newspapers' ad listings justified real estate agents' "steering" black home buyers to different areas than they showed white home buyers and accelerated the shift from "white" to "colored" once a black family moved onto a block. The *Post* management defended its real estate listing practice as benign information that spared black buyers the pain of mistakenly looking for housing no one would sell them. But with only two designations, "Colored" or nothing, the newspapers implied that the first was limited to black buyers and the latter available only to white buyers.

In a campaign to end racial steering, Neighbors Inc. collected more than 2,500 petition signatures, enlisted more than forty organizations with the help of the American Veterans Committee, and met with newspaper managers to protest a practice that signaled a majority of the region's housing was off-limits to black home buyers and renters. Neighbors Inc. representatives argued that if the paper sought to give accurate guidance then it need only advertise homes closed to black buyers as "white only." Unwilling to drop the "colored" designation or to add "white" to ads, which would make visible the racial exclusiveness of most of the region's housing, the *Post* temporized.

After almost two years, in the summer of 1960, Neighbors Inc. got a boost from the rising national interest in civil rights. The Democratic Party was chastising President Eisenhower for his tepid support for civil rights as proof of the Republican unfitness to retain control of the White House. Minnesota senator Hubert Humphrey, who had won endorsement of the party's 1948 antisegregation platform, introduced a bill to set a thousand-dollar fine or one-year jail term for any D.C. newspaper or radio or television station that mentioned race in real estate ads. When Neighbors Inc. reviewed newspaper behavior at summer's end, they found that "the Washington daily newspapers [had] quietly changed their policy."[23] Making no announcement that might imply a negative judgment about real estate agents or their own past complicity, the papers simply dropped the word "colored" from ads. It had taken almost two years of Neighbors Inc. protests and the threat of congressional action, but newspaper real estate ads had stopped categorizing neighborhoods by race.

In a second move to redefine the interracial image as middle-class, NI set up regular communication to delineate and defend its physical space. Manor Park and Brightwood continued to transition into solid middle-class and working-class black areas, but the overarching Neighbors Inc. organization held its four sections together in a cross-class, interracial territory with a monthly newsletter and the election of delegates from each section to attend monthly board meetings. Margery Ware published the first NI newsletter in early 1959, with a volunteer committee doing much of the work, and *Neighbors, Inc.* (or *Neighbors Ink* after 1964) went out monthly to households across the area.

A third task, aided greatly by the newsletter, was to protect middle-class standards in an interracial neighborhood. NI countered the popular impression that black neighborhoods were dirty and unruly, even as its instructions conveyed the vigilance necessary to keep an urban environment up to suburban standards. NI advocated on behalf of all four neighborhoods against the constant institutional threat of reduced public services from city governments responsive only to white, middle-class owners, an assault exacerbated by Washington's being under the authority of white Southern senators and congressmen unsympathetic to integration. NI's newsletter educated readers and encouraged them to monitor the decorum and maintenance expected in a middle-class area: garbage collection, street cleaning, leaf pickup, observance of zoning regulations. Within months of its premier issue, the September 1959 *Neighbors, Inc.* asked, "Is the grass on that next door lawn too high?" and provided a number to call to enforce the D.C. code prohibiting grass over four inches. Teaching residents to expect city agencies to help preserve the area, an article in February 1960 reported that of twenty households grumbling about leaves piled up in an alley, two "simply called up and complained. The city came right out and cleaned them up." Ware's office reported abandoned cars and trucks to the police department for removal and asked for special patrols to stop the drag racing on one street.[24] NI volunteers canvassed local opinion and made certain that authorities such as the Alcohol and Beverage Commission knew of local opposition to the commission's approving more liquor stores, in one instance the ninth within a nine-block area.[25]

NI staff and volunteers also managed to block plans to build new freeways to link northern suburbs with downtown, a predictable hazard in interracial areas. In spring 1961, the regional highway commission proposed three possible corridors between the suburbs and city for freeway development, all within the Neighbors Inc. area. Though the National Capital Planning Commission preferred a Wisconsin Avenue route (west of the park) as less costly and disruptive and opposed the District's highway director on this issue, Neighbors Inc. leaders knew that their area was more vulnerable than a white-exclusive one. NI fought to protect its residential area from becoming a throughway for suburban drivers, a threat that finally died in the late 1960s.[26]

Margery Ware also monitored and disputed FHA judgments, which consistently discredited racially nonhomogeneous areas. When an FHA housing inspector rejected a house in Takoma, D.C., and reported to the mortgage company that "the neighborhood is undergoing a transition from single family residential use to rooming house and commercial use," which would make a federally secured loan too risky to approve, Ware wrote the FHA regional headquarters correcting the assessor's condemnatory judgment. The area was zoned only for single-family homes, she informed the administrator, and she queried on what basis the assessor had made a misleading statement. The FHA changed its decision, and a buyer was able to get a federally insured mortgage, but NI had to be ready to battle the predictable opposition of FHA staff to integrating blocks.[27]

Despite NI's hard work, by 1960 the possibility of stabilization as a middle-class interracial community no longer existed in the two southern sections of Neighbors Inc. The clearance of hundreds of city blocks in the late 1950s and early 1960s to build the Southwest Freeway destroyed a working-class neighborhood with a mix of black, Jewish, and Greek residents and pushed thousands of families into a housing market with higher prices than many could afford. White ethnic families might look in the suburbs, but many of the black households, confined to the District, channeled into Manor Park and Brightwood. Neighbors Inc. protested to the District commissioners in December 1959 and asked rhetorically, "Is taxpayers' money being used to carry on a program of rebuilding [in Southwest] which is at the same time producing blight in sound neighborhoods?"[28] To no avail, Neighbors Inc. urged the commissioners to set up a relocation service to assist evicted families. Instead, many of the desperate families surged into the southern parts of Neighbors Inc.'s domain, crowding into small houses, breaking up large ones into apartments, creating a frantic real estate market that pushed longtime white owners to sell, and eroding the middle-class presence necessary for many white families to commit to living in interracial space.

In 1960, the local high school, Roosevelt, a segregated white high school before 1954, had 100 percent black student enrollment. Young white families were unlikely to move into a place where their children would be a tiny minority in school. The Caplans, still in Manor Park and with children in the elementary school, did not move out to Shepherd Park until 1965, and Neighbors Inc. still provided an umbrella for joint action among its four founding sections. The quest for stabilization moved into the two northern NI areas—Shepherd Park, which had only a few black families in 1960, and Takoma, D.C., which still had a white majority in its elementary school. The neighborhoods just beginning the period of transition could be stabilized if a number of white families bought in along with the black and interracial families eager to get good housing. But this simple process would require sustained effort: continued vigilance against institutional pressures, such as blockbusters, that preyed on interracial areas; formulation of an interracial image to attract white home buyers with many housing options; and creation of social spaces to build relationships and trust among varied families.

## Marketing Interracialism

Black middle-class families would buy in the NI area simply to get nice homes. Deciding they would be left a small minority unable to staunch the flow of white families to the suburbs, NI's leaders defined a central problem as recruiting white buyers who had suburban options not open to black middle-class households. Within months of its founding, Neighbors Inc. launched a Housing Information Service to attract white families to the area.[29] In June 1959 the newsletter reported the first white couple buying into Takoma, D.C., in response to a Neighbors Inc. real estate ad headed "integrated neighborhood." The report carried the message that desirable white families would choose interracial spaces if these were properly presented.

To attract white families, NI began to create a narrative of middle-class, family oriented, multiracial achievement and security to compete with the idyll of white suburbia. Neighbors Inc.'s new brochures announced "a vital and lovely place to live," with photographs of commodious tree-shaded houses, the neoclassical public library branch, and school playgrounds. The widely distributed annual reports featured prominent photographs of varied mixes of neighborhood youth at play and at study. A racially mixed crowd of boys rode a playground carousel; black and white boys bent their heads studiously over books at the local library; little white girls played with little black boys and girls; and children raced under the London Bridge arms of day-camp counselors coded as white only by their legs at the edge of the photograph. These images pointed up the absence of black children from the revered pictures of suburban childhood, while depicting a placid, welcoming interracialism to counter media images of racial antipathy roiling the South.

Touting the liveliness of an integrated neighborhood became briefly trendy with the arrival of John F. Kennedy as president in January 1961. Dependent on segregationist Southern Democrats, the administration moved cautiously on civil rights issues, but Kennedy also promised revitalized executive leadership and renewed hope for the liberal cause of integration. Neighbors Inc. moved quickly to take advantage of the new atmosphere. Margery Ware sent letters soliciting newly elected Congress members and newly appointed staff to consider elegant Shepherd Park as a residential choice that provided pleasant housing and congenial neighbors, while also advancing an important national goal. Ware monitored announcements of research scientists, journalists, or judges being appointed to posts in the District and sent inviting information about the neighborhood. House purchases by White House counsel Lee White and White House advisor and soon-to-be assistant labor secretary Esther Peterson affirmed Shepherd Park's connections with the Kennedy agenda. In addition to these white notables, Carl Rowan, a leading black journalist, soon to be appointed ambassador to Finland by the Kennedy State Department, bought a house on the Sixteenth Street edge of Shepherd Park.

NI played to the internationalist orientation of the administration and the imperative of welcoming ambassadors arriving in Washington to represent the nations just gaining independence from colonial rule. Robert and Nancy Good bought into Shepherd Park when he returned from an international study grant in Europe and Africa to head up a Carnegie Endowment program for diplomats from newly recognized nations. With the Goods' State Department connections, Neighbors Inc. hosted a reception for newly posted African diplomats, who were persona non grata in the region's white suburbs. The *Washington Post* featured a front-page photo with its report on the reception "to acquaint diplomats from newly independent nations with the hospitality of the city." An elegant Nigerian woman stood amidst white children and looked down at her own baby, held by a doting "Mrs. James Symington, daughter-in-law of the Senator from Missouri."[30] The report caught the note of social chic, international concern, and child-oriented community that Neighbors Inc. sought to publicize.

In spring 1962, Neighbors Inc. mimicked Georgetown, an elite white area known as the neighborhood of choice for Kennedy administration appointees, and held a "Home and Garden Tour—With a Difference" to show that Shepherd Park could match Georgetown's style and also support a civil rights agenda. In contrast to white-exclusive Georgetown, half the houses on the Neighbors tour had black owners and half, white owners. Four hundred guests paid to see the eight houses that proved that an integrated area could match the standard of Georgetown elegance.[31]

Though Neighbors Inc. succumbed to the belief that it had to show off high-status residents in order to attract white home buyers, it was also creating a new picture of an ideal middle-class U.S. neighborhood. Instead of a suburban ideal of America as white, homogeneous, suburban, and withdrawn from urban and international dangers, Neighbors presented a normative, middle-class image as interracial, cosmopolitan, open-minded, and internationalist.[32] This was a very different image of the white middle class than the one circulated in popular culture and real estate ads.

### Practical Idealists

Today the white families who bought into these ideals and gave them flesh recall hopes more than hardships. They describe themselves as "practical idealists," as one early home buyer put it, a sentiment echoed in every one of my interviews. They stressed the "practical" or the "convenient," I believe, because the NI residents saw themselves as tough-minded and not quixotic; they were not martyrs sacrificing their lives to a civil rights crusade, but middle-class families looking for standard amenities—comfortable houses, safe streets, and good schools—who saw no reason to move out of cities to get them. While everyone emphasized that an integrated neighborhood required volunteer duties, committee meetings, and school monitoring, it repaid the effort with lower-cost housing, urban proximity, interesting neighbors, and a feeling, for the heirs of New Deal liberalism and labor union attachments, of being on the right side of history.

Naming the area a racially nonexclusive one began to attract unconventional white families who believed in breaking down the old restrictive covenants and who also wanted a smart real estate deal. Norman and Janet Brown knew that an imminent baby required them to move from their attractive downtown apartment to a house, but Janet didn't want to leave the center city's vitality. From a young mother in a local park, she learned about Shepherd Park; its large houses were now priced within young families' budgets because of the uncertain market created by white flight. Norman, newly hired as a physicist at the National Bureau of Standards, and Janet, an international relations expert, had already looked west of Rock Creek Park. "We simply couldn't afford it," they remember. When they visited Shepherd Park, they walked into a house that had been on the market for more than a year, because, as Norman recalls, "the woman who owned the house would not sell to blacks. When we walked through the front door that was it; that's the house we wanted. In Shepherd Park, we could afford it because the woman just kept dropping her price hoping for a white customer. So we profited by the segregation problems."[33]

Norman cheerfully tells the story of a white home seller's losing money because of her racism, which worked to his benefit. Implicitly, however, the story distinguishes him as both hardheaded and nonracist, making calculations that didn't include paying a premium to live in a white enclave. (The self-image of financial savvy did not take account of some of Janet's memories, as we will see later, which indicate that she took on extra work to monitor the kids' public schools, a hidden cost to be added to the home purchase price.)

Like the Caplans, the Browns had a previous commitment to civil rights and a desire not to support white segregation, but they had not expected to battle to buy a house. When he looked at the house contract, however, Norman, Jewish by birth though not religiously active, saw that it was "a standard form." He remembers there was "a line that said the deed would be subject to restrictions and covenants of record. . . . [So] I looked up the deed and discovered that it had a restrictive covenant that forbade selling the property to, or allowing the property to be occupied by, anyone who was an alcoholic, a Jew, black, anyone from the Mediterranean area, or some other weird thing [such as pirates, he later said]. I crossed out the line in the form," and the owner accepted his revision.

Norman had become an NAACP member while working for General Electric in Syracuse in the mid-1950s and knew that the Supreme Court had outlawed restrictive covenants in *Shelley v. Kraemer*, though in a sweeping decision that held that restrictive "contracts [could] be legally written, [but] could not be legally enforced," as historian Stephen Grant Meyer interprets the controversial ruling.[34] Caught between the principle that a private citizen could make any contract concerning his property and the constitutional provisions of the Fourteenth Amendment's equal protection clause, the Court, legal scholar Carol Rose explains, did not prohibit contract restrictions agreed upon by buyer and seller but refused to enforce restrictions carried over from previous buyers and sellers, a historical "customary property regime" that assumed that all "white owners would dislike minority neighbors."[35] After a decade's battles over what had become known as "open occupancy," it remained unclear that racial discrimination would not be resuscitated. Throughout the 1950s, the Eisenhower administration had taken no steps to halt violent acts of vandalism against black families who purchased homes in white neighborhoods, for instance. When the Browns got to final settlement, the lawyer passed over a contract that once again read, "subject to restriction or covenants of record." At which point Norman said, " 'No, no, no, no. I crossed this out.' And all [the lawyer] would say to us was, 'I won't sell you a house without it' or 'I won't give you a deed without it.' And the real estate agent said to sign, [because] 'this [restriction] will protect you in the event the Supreme Court ever changes its mind.' "

The Browns asserted the right of home buyers to be free from historic covenants that mandated a racially or religiously homogeneous neighborhood and bought the house without assenting to the covenant.

The NI area's openness to diverse groups proved especially attractive to postwar European immigrants, who were more sensitive to racial segregation and less likely than white Americans to overlook it. Norman Brown told a coworker, Paul Meijer, about his house find. Paul and his wife, Marianne, Dutch immigrants who had come to the United States originally so Paul could take up a postdoctoral fellowship in physics, had eagerly gone looking for a house to accommodate them and their four young children. Marianne had looked at large houses west of the park, the one neighborhood real estate agents were showing to white buyers. When she complained about the high prices, a real estate agent alerted her, " 'If you want a house for the money, you have to stay on the other side of the park,' " Marianne remembers. "Of course, I want[ed] a house for the money."[36] The single-story design of suburban houses, where the small children would always be under foot, was not a style Paul liked, and the old-fashioned two- and three-story Shepherd Park houses allowed the Meijers to send their children upstairs to read and to play in their own bedrooms out of earshot of the adults.

The Meijers had been adhering to the rules of white American house-hunting etiquette, only looking in white neighborhoods, and were relieved when they found an interracial option. Describing herself as a Holocaust survivor who escaped from occupied Paris into Switzerland, Marianne recalls her shock at the segregation they saw when they arrived in the States for Paul's fellowship at Duke University in Durham, North Carolina. The water fountains were still marked White and Colored and the schools were still segregated, and Marianne felt thrown back among social rules that evoked the anti-Jewish regulations of German-occupied Europe. "It's the same thing if you go to school with a [Jewish] star or with a black face. I know what they go through." In North Carolina, Marianne was astonished and delighted that African Americans nevertheless remained kind to white people, as she found when she attended events at black schools in and around Durham.

With the social confidence of a well-educated couple, the Meijers rated intellect more highly than whiteness. "Our friends who thought so highly of the suburbs," Paul recalled, "they live[d] next to businessmen who didn't have the education that a lot of blacks [in Shepherd Park] had. Because [educated blacks] were happy to find a decent house here; they didn't want to live in a slum."[37] The Meijers bought a five-bedroom, five-bathroom house on an attractive street, "totally underpriced," and moved in at the start of 1961. They believed they had struck a smart bargain, made possible by the many white Americans who valued racial homogeneity more than genuine comfort or shared interests.

Another young white couple eager to escape from restrictive rules, Ruth and Mel Stack, moved to D.C. after living in Louisville and San Antonio for Mel's military service. Ruth began working as a public relations writer for the Industrial Union of Electrical Workers (IUE) and remembers, "We had a dog, and the downtown rule was 'No dogs, no children, no pets,' and we couldn't find an apartment."[38] Union friends told them about Neighbors Inc., and the Stacks rented a house with a yard in Takoma, D.C., in 1961. In 1963 the NI Housing Information Service showed the Stacks Ruth's "dream home—four-bedroom, Dutch colonial, with a huge yard and a beautiful tree." They might not have found the house on their own, Ruth believes now, because of "steering." "The real estate dealers would not show you houses [in a racially mixed area] if you were white."

Ruth—who became Ruth Jordan after her divorce and remarriage to Dan Jordan in 1970—had grown up in a predominantly Roman Catholic, Italian neighborhood in northern New Jersey. Her secular Jewish family—her mother in the millinery union and her father an IUE machinist—stood out, and Ruth felt isolated and marginal in school. Even though she did not attend synagogue or practice her ancestral faith, she wanted her Jewish heritage to be unremarkable. For herself and her children, she wanted a place that felt securely diverse.

> I moved [to Shepherd Park] because I wanted to be involved in a committed community, but in an integrated environment with many different kinds of people, including different ages and different experiences, and different cultures. . . . And in fact the neighborhood turned over generationally in a year or two, . . . though some of [the older people] stayed and remained mainstays of that block. Like Mrs. Lambros. . . . She baked Greek cookies, and we had Greek festivals in her house. And she was known as the "cookie lady."

In a space made secure because no group set a dominant tone and pattern, Ruth found her ideal house and embraced a belief that a community could be built around neighborliness, especially caring for children, and learning about other people's traditions. Nonrestrictive, cosmopolitan, diverse—all became not markers of transience, but ways to describe a stable community.

In the years just before the influx of black families seeking nice homes and young white families seeking affordable urban homes, Shepherd Park had been identified as Jewish. The Jewish families who had bought homes there after the anti-Jewish covenants became unenforceable continued to

define the neighborhood, perhaps unwittingly, as white, as the racial categorizing of "Jewish" changed from marginal to fully white. An issue for
NI was whether the Jewish population would stay and become a reliable
ally. One of four synagogues in the NI area, Tifereth Israel, had shifted
its practice from Orthodox to Conservative in 1960. Its newly hired rabbi,
Nathan Abramowitz, said he accepted the job "because this was such a
wonderful opportunity. It's the nation's capital; it's a lovely neighborhood,
a brand-new synagogue building." Arriving in the District from Denver,
Abramowitz found, however, that "there was an absolute panic flight from
the neighborhood at that time. I didn't know that when I came."[39]

He had not sought the fight erupting around him, but Abramowitz,
known affectionately as Buddy, settled in with his wife and children to
make the synagogue a supporting element of stabilization. The young rabbi
had been inspired by his study with Abraham Heschel, soon-to-be ally
of Rev. Martin Luther King Jr., at the Jewish Theological Seminary, and
he led his congregation to meditate on their responsibilities as an ethical
community. For Abramowitz, having a synagogue in the middle of a diverse neighborhood offered an opportunity to enact what he saw as a basic
mandate of his faith, the biblical teaching to value all people. Now a rabbi
emeritus, his voice still gains energy and force when he declares,

> There's nothing more basic in Jewish tradition than the Bible, and
> there's nothing more basic in the Bible than the first page. And
> the first page says it. Period. Q.E.D. End. . . . "In the image of God
> created he him, male and female, created he them." God created us
> equal. We are all equal. We are equally human, equally in the image
> of God.

For Abramowitz, this truth required him to engage, befriend, and collaborate with all the residents in the neighborhood. He became a Neighbors
Inc. board member, offered the synagogue for meetings, and, most importantly, challenged his congregation to live as neighbors in a racially mixed
setting. The rabbi did not identify Jewish with white-exclusive and lead his
congregation out of the city, a path taken by other Northern synagogues,
nor did he stand aloof from civil rights battles in the manner of many
Southern synagogues.[40] Forcefully, Abramowitz taught a Jewish ethic of
fairness and social equality, which synagogue members fortuitously could
practice in an interracial neighborhood.[41]

For some of the Jewish families, longtime D.C. residents who had themselves been allowed to buy into Shepherd Park only as recently as the 1950s, Abramowitz offered guidance for responding to their new neighbors. A brisk, direct, cheerful woman, Mollie Berch grew up in the 1920s and 1930s in Southwest Washington, in a working-class neighborhood with "black people across the street from us and down the street from us."[42] It was an era and a place where races commonly lived alongside each other, though with different positions in the South's racial hierarchy. Even though her family had little more money than their black neighbors—the Jewish wives worked outside the home and couldn't afford to hire domestics to do their housework—official segregation placed Jews on the white side of the dominant racial division. Berch attended Wilson Teachers' College (segregated white), which had occasional meetings with the Miner's Teachers' College (segregated black): "I don't remember being bothered about any of that, . . . because black people came in and out of our store all the time, and we didn't have any maids, and by then [in the 1930s] none of us had any money. The blacks didn't have any money, and neither did the Jews who lived in Southwest."

As was true for young Marvin Caplan and the white women who headed NCCJ camps, the racial segregation of Berch's young adulthood during the 1930s and early 1940s was accepted as the way things were, a fact of life that one might regret but not resist. Like these other well-intentioned young white people, Mollie found that wartime disruption and new housing mobility forced her to think about her own role in sustaining old racial patterns. She married in 1945, began to have children, and moved her growing family into Shepherd Park in the mid-1950s when their old synagogue moved to the suburbs and Tifereth Israel became Conservative, which Mollie and her husband preferred. They also "wanted to be in D.C.," she said. "We were not suburb people." Mollie's job as a teacher at Shepherd Park's Paul Junior High School, segregated white before the 1954 merger of the dual system, made their new housing convenient.

The Berches hadn't expected to be in an integrating neighborhood, though Mollie's classes at the junior high had desegregated after 1954. But she, like other older synagogue members, supported Rabbi Abramowitz's decision to keep the congregation in Shepherd Park and not to follow other Washington synagogues to the Maryland suburbs. Her commitment, she explains, came from the "feeling of we, too, are a minority. . . . We were once slaves. We don't treat people as slaves. That's very much a part of Jewish theology." But abstaining from participating in relations of inequality—the behavior evident in her memories of a rough equality between her white family and its black neighbors in prewar segregated Washington—was not the same as embracing relations of equality and connection. Berch connects her choice to stay in the city with her Jewish faith in *tzedakah*, which translated roughly means "charity." But it isn't exactly charity, Berch explains,

> because "charity" comes from a word that means to move the heart.
> And Jews . . . believe that to move the heart, it could take forever.
> You better pass some laws to do something better. So *tzedakah*
> means you have to do whatever you can to make this a better world,
> . . . repairing the world, making this a better place.

Repairing the world required more than personal kindness. It required creating places where damage and systematic harm didn't occur. Though Berch remained focused on her family and synagogue, she supported a Neighbors Inc. vision of making a neighborhood safe for all its residents.

Abramowitz's resolution to sustain a Conservative Jewish synagogue in an interracial neighborhood provided an anchor for white Jewish families seeking an alternative to suburbia. One young couple, Ed and Ruth Cogen, moved into Shepherd Park in December 1964, a few months after Ed completed his Air Force service and moved to Washington to work in a downtown law firm. He and Ruth chose Shepherd Park, Ed remembers, because

> we were interested in living in a culturally interesting
> neighborhood. We were both from New York City, and running
> off to the suburbs didn't make any sense to us. . . . [Shepherd Park]
> had beautiful homes and trees and big lots; west of the park, it was
> all white at that time, and that was something that we were not
> particularly interested in.

They bought for the convenient, pleasant, and reasonably priced housing and quickly found that its maintenance required not just tending a suburban-style lawn, but nurturing local institutions.

Ed Cogen remembers that they had chosen Shepherd Park without thinking about the local synagogue, but almost as soon as they arrived, Buddy Abramowitz asked them to join and to help keep the synagogue in the city.

> There was a sense that the community was turning black and that the synagogue was going to be an island within this community and not able to attract new members, because most blacks were not Jewish and so you don't have the membership around. What motivated Ruth and me to stay in was what was eventually attracting people from out in the suburbs to move back, the fact that there was this synagogue that was staying young, which was reaching out, trying to attract more families to come in.

Cogen had grown up with activist parents—a father who led a teacher's union and a mother who taught in the public schools—and when he saw "things happening, like in this particular case, families running out to the suburbs, . . . you can either be passive about it or you can try and, in some small way, contribute time and so on." Like many of the early white Neighbors Inc. families, Cogen stressed the practicality of his politics. He argues that the synagogue was very convenient; his family walked one block to services and sent the two children to Hebrew school. "I didn't want to have to schlep the kids out to Montgomery County [for Hebrew lessons], so there was a self-interest in trying to keep the community." The Cogens joined both Tifereth Israel and Neighbors Inc. in 1965.

Black families who moved into Shepherd Park and Takoma, D.C., also saw themselves as practical; often older than their white neighbors, they were looking for the best housing in the most congenial setting that was affordable and open to them. Unlike their white counterparts, the black families had much more interracial experience. They had seen the advantages of white neighborhoods and hoped to gain some of these, but they took pride in their own achievements and felt no need to defer to white neighbors. The black families who joined NI demonstrated to white colleagues the high quality of black neighbors. More importantly, they taught white neighbors about the threats an interracial neighborhood might expect. They modeled self-assurance in the face of hostility.

Now in her seventies, still elegant and thoughtful, Barbara Atkinson moved with her husband and six young children into Manor Park in the mid-1950s to be close to Howard University's medical school, where her husband, Dr. Lewis Atkinson, was training.[43] She had heard that the neighborhood schools, which had just desegregated from white only, were good and wanted her children to be able to walk to school. The Atkinsons could afford a house on Oglethorpe Street in Manor Park, where they were one of the first black families to move in. Barbara loved the house and her carefully tended rose garden, but when the city bought her lot in the early 1960s to clear land for a new middle school, the family moved to Colonial Village in the far northwest corner of Shepherd Park, and Barbara became a stalwart volunteer.

Many of Neighbors Inc.'s white families had grown up in racially mixed city neighborhoods, with occasional connections with African American customers or workers or a few black classmates, but many of the black families had learned to live confidently in predominantly white environments. Barbara felt perfectly comfortable with her white Manor Park neighbors, with whom she shared a gardening passion, because she had grown up in Stroudsburg, Pennsylvania, where she was the only black student in her class. Her parents had moved there during the hard times of the Depression, because her father could find hotel work in the Pocono resort area and her mother could teach. Although Barbara's husband had served in a still-segregated army, he then attended the integrated Howard University medical school, which, Barbara reminded me, had always admitted white students and where "there were quite a few young whites in his class." The Atkinsons took integration for granted and, as professional people, assumed their children needed to learn to live and work with the white majority to have maximum opportunities.

Like the Atkinson family, Joe and Ann Hairston, who had slightly older children, also moved into the southern end of the Neighbors Inc. area in 1954 in search of good schools for their three daughters; the *Brown* decision had thrown their Virginia public schools into disarray. A career army man who had fought in the Ninety-Second Infantry, a black combat unit, during World War II and then piloted planes in Korea, Hairston had battled the army's segregated postings since enlisting in 1940.[44] An officer after the war, he had been dropped back to master sergeant in 1949, when general troop reductions targeted units that could be officered by black men, and he suffered a similar demotion to master sergeant again after Korea. "I began to see that if you're going to get ahead in the world, you have to have a degree in something," Hairston recalls. So he got himself assigned to Ft. Myer outside D.C. in 1954 and completed three degrees by 1961: a BA from the University of Maryland, a law degree from American University, and an LLM from Georgetown University. In 1964, Joe Hairston was a tax attorney for the Internal Revenue Service, and the Hairstons moved to Floral Street in Shepherd Park to be closer to the service benefits available at the Walter Reed Army Medical Center.

The young white families who had wanted nice urban houses without restrictions on the buyers and the slightly older black families who had wanted nice urban houses where their children could live without racial isolation now began to develop relationships with each other. Children were a great social solvent. The move to Floral Street put the Hairstons right across the street from Ruth Jordan, who remembers that she had her first daughter at the same time that Ann Hairston, her older girls already well into their teens and early twenties, also had a baby. "We all began having babies," Ruth laughs, "and we kept saying, 'What is it? The water on Floral Street?' So it quickly became not only an integrated block but an extremely close and tight block, because our children were all the same age." The eldest Stack and youngest Hairston daughter became childhood playmates, crossing the street back and forth between their two houses and families. The shared pleasures were underlined by the shared dangers; families bonded in defending their visions and their homes from the pervasive real estate pressures they were defying.

## Gender Partnership

Neighbors Inc. families depended on relationships to guarantee neighborhood security and family protection that differed from those required in the suburbs. Instead of inhabiting areas isolated from the supposed dangers of the city and depending on husbands to travel to work to earn the income that supported a wife and children, as suburban families did, Neighbors Inc. families depended on husbands who worked and volunteered for community work, wives who raised children and earned incomes, and children who played happily at home and negotiated urban spaces.

In its first years, NI on the surface sustained suburban standards of gender respectability. Women were busy as volunteers and housewives (usually titled in the first couple of years by their husband's name—Mrs. Marvin Caplan, for instance), and men planned and made speeches. To prove that the neighborhood had the same qualifications as all leading U.S. institutions, NI presidents were always white and always men: Marvin Caplan for the first four years, Robert Good for the second stint, Ed Cogen for the third, succeeded briefly to fill out his term by Joe Hairston. Neighbors Inc. women typed and reproduced monthly newsletters, hosted open houses, created a safety net for children to roam between houses, painted classrooms, stitched costumes for school plays, and entertained prospective home buyers. Men served as officers and presented Neighbors Inc.'s public face in negotiations with legislators and safety authorities, while women were, as Barbara Atkinson puts it, "the workers, the doers— the backbone of the organization." Superficially the neighborhood and its public face conformed to the Cold War cultural norms of conventional, middle-class suburban family organization.[45]

Beneath the neighborhood's apparent gender conventionality, however, lay a gender equality and partnership that put it in the vanguard of the long-term postwar trend that saw increasing numbers of wives pursuing careers and contributing substantially to family incomes. In families who chose the Neighbors Inc. area, wives had college degrees and wanted and expected to have professional jobs. Marianne Meijer traveled from Shepherd Park to Catholic University to complete a PhD in French, then to the University of Maryland to teach. Janet Brown earned a PhD in international relations at American University, continued her career as a college professor, and then joined a research group. Naomi Caplan got her children into high school before returning to work as a psychologist, earning essential income, Marvin remembers, to help cover the college tuition for their three children. Ruth Jordan continued to work as a public relations specialist. Barbara Atkinson became the first program director for Reading Is Fundamental and pushed that group to add children's books with African American protagonists to its recommended reading lists. These women bore children and oversaw their care, but they didn't define themselves as housewives. For the white women, having black women as neighbors must have provided some reassurance as they began to take on the kinds of responsibilities for employment and community that black middle-class wives had held for decades.[46]

## Defending against Blockbusters and Advocating Open Housing

The most immediate assault on an interracial area came from real estate blockbusters, and wives often faced the first onslaught. By 1960, realtors— white men and black men— moved on Shepherd Park and Takoma, D.C. Moving block by block, they found a white resident ready to sell or eager to join the white exodus out of D.C., bought the house for a low price, and then sometimes rented it to a large black family to frighten the block's remaining white residents or simply sold it to an eager black home seeker. The postal service delivered two or three postcards to each home daily, and furtive figures slipped flyers under front doors, warning of the neighborhood's imminent decline and offering quick cash. Wives who stayed at home to care for young children especially felt they were under unfriendly surveillance and were annoyed by calls like the ones Janet Brown received. Consistently, messages came to white families to sell out. (Some amusement resulted when a black family received a warning against encroaching black neighbors; when this happened to the Atkinsons, Barbara laughed at being told to fear herself.)

Many of Shepherd Park's white owners were ready to sell without any external pressure, the result of normal generational turnover. The aging owners had raised children and wanted to move to smaller houses. Neighbors Inc.'s task was not so much to stop flight as to attract a diverse array of young families to buy out the old-timers, even as the blockbusters' relentless hectoring of white families undermined hopes of stability.

Margery Ware and the Neighbors Inc. board met with local real estate agents to enlist their pledges to stop blockbusting. Arguing that agents could make money from selling houses to interested white families as easily as to desperate black ones, the board got a lesson in housing economics as agents explained that there were many fewer white buyers looking for integrated housing and that it took much longer to persuade whites to buy in a neighborhood with any sign of "going black." A white family might rent, but the agent's commission for that service was negligible. It took much longer to persuade a white family to enter a racially mixed neighborhood than a securely white one, and the value of the agent's commission decreased as the time without a sale increased. They were not, the agents argued, opposed to integration, but the market forces created by an expanding housing market for white families and a relatively constricted market for black ones meant that it was much more efficient in the Neighbors Inc. area to sell to black customers.

What the Neighbors Inc. members had in their favor, absent legal protections against agents' eager pursuit of commissions, were vigilance, information, good humor, and aggressive surveillance. Paradoxically, even as the neighborhood was beset, those who shared in the fight gained rapport and confidence. Ruth Jordan remembers that "it was a very intense atmosphere."

But one of my joyous moments came when one of these guys was knocking next door, and my neighbor called me and said, "What do I do? This guy won't leave me alone. This is the third night he's been here."

So I called the police, and I said, "I don't know who this guy is, but I think he's a burglar."

And so of course the cops came, and they had him against the car with his hands behind his back. I was thrilled.

This long-remembered victory was a tiny incident in an ongoing war to remove the intimidating blockbusters from the area, which did not gain legal support until almost the mid-1960s, when the District's recently formed Human Relations Commission got the job of halting such harassment.

The other side of the neighborhood's transition was a massive black demand for middle-class housing. In the early 1960s, the entire metropolitan region remained largely segregated and new, reasonably priced housing in the suburbs off-limits to black renters and buyers. So long as the ring around Washington held firm and the barrier of Rock Creek Park unbroken, blockbusters would have eager customers. Unless it could open up the region's housing market, Neighbors Inc. would be trapped in the uncomfortable position of cheering on every white buyer it could interest and offering a more grudging welcome to black families arriving in the neighborhood—not a good foundation for building interracial trust and acceptance. What would it take to crack the region's segregated housing?

Neighbors Inc. members took on three projects to open up the local housing market. In 1961, it joined groups in Prince George's and Montgomery Counties in Maryland, in Northern Virginia, and in Northwest Washington west of the park to form the National Capital Clearing House for Neighborhood Democracy. The coalition of groups from racially mixed or exclusively white areas worked with the NAACP and CORE (the Congress of Racial Equality) to open up white-only neighborhoods to black home seekers through voluntary desegregation. Within the next two years, members of the organizations canvassed their neighbors, passed out fair-housing pledges, welcomed black newcomers to their areas, and staged public demonstrations to embarrass apartment owners who refused to rent to black tenants.

Religious leaders were valuable allies in changing public opinion. The segregation of churches had been so common through the late 1950s that an oft-repeated indictment of these central neighborhood social institutions was that Sunday morning at 10 A.M., when people gathered for worship was the most segregated hour of the week. Now religious leaders admonished their followers to extend the hand of fellowship across lines of color. The National Capital Clearing House publicized admonitions from prominent Catholic, Jewish, and Protestant religious leaders, such as Washington's Catholic archbishop, Patrick O'Boyle, who declared that "Negroes are no longer just a cause. . . . They are our brethren in Christ. When a Negro family moves into our neighborhood, Christ has come into our midst. We welcome them as we welcome him."[47]

Religious leaders had little effect on suburban congregations, however. The best hope for legislative change, given the racial conservatism of Virginia and Maryland, lay with federal authorities. In spring 1962, Marvin Caplan testified before the U.S. Civil Rights Commission about Neighbors Inc.'s inability to sustain an interracial community without governmental help. He argued that many of the black families who had moved into the Neighbors Inc. area might have preferred homes in the Maryland and Virginia suburbs or in Washington's exclusive Georgetown and Cleveland Park neighborhoods, but real estate agents would not take them to such houses or offer them the same terms they promised white home seekers. Raising the emotional stakes, and underlining the equation between the twinned values of religious practice and home buying, Caplan concluded: "The most segregated hour in the week comes on Sunday, but it is not necessarily in churches. It probably comes during the afternoon, when families of both races go their separate ways looking for homes."[48] A presidential executive order that made FHA and VA policies racially neutral could change the moral tone and force open the region's housing markets.

Under persistent pressure from civil rights leaders, President Kennedy finally handed down Executive Order 11063 on Equal Opportunity in Housing in November 1962. It prohibited discrimination in properties federally owned or operated, provided with federal loans or grants, or carrying loans insured by the federal government. "The initiative excluded one- and two-family dwellings that were occupied by the seller because the administration believed broader inclusion would strain its ability to enforce the ban"; the administration avoided widespread noncompliance by applying the order only to housing built after 1962 and to multiple-family dwellings.[49] As a consequence, most of the older white enclaves in and around the District remained unregulated and their large, single-family houses off-limits to African American buyers.

Undeterred, Neighbors Inc. and the National Capital Clearing House followed up on the executive order by pushing for a D.C. ordinance. Testifying in July 1963 before the board of commissioners who governed the District, Neighbors Inc. advocated laws to cover the "transfer and financing of all real property including single-family, owner-occupied housing [because] owner-occupied housing comprises 30 percent of all housing in the District of Columbia."[50] Pushed by the U.S. Civil Rights Commission, the State Department, and others worried about the discriminatory face the capital city was showing the world, the commissioners finally issued an ordinance prohibiting discrimination in home sales after January 1964. The ordinance passed in the face of strong opposition from the House of Representatives Committee on the District of Columbia. Since Congress controlled the District's budget, the ordinance's passage was described in the local press as "an act of municipal courage," though President Lyndon Johnson promised that he would personally protect the city's budget from congressional retaliation.[51] Oversight was assigned to a new Commissioners' Council on Human Relations.

Neighbors Inc. joined other groups, especially CORE, to push for enforcement. Using a technique developed in other cities, Ann and Joe Hairston paired with Ed and Ruth Cogen to compare their success in finding a real estate agent willing to show and to sell them a house west of the park. "Since we were both lawyers," Joe Hairston recalls, "we agreed that we'd ask exactly the same questions, so that we could record the answers and then compare them. . . . Our rehearsal was to make sure that our questions were exact, because if you're going to compare, you need to compare apples with apples."

After a year of real estate agents' figuring out how to circumvent the ordinance, the agents treated the Hairstons with the same courtesy as they greeted the Cogens, and Joe Hairston remembers that he thought their test was going pretty well.

> At the end of the afternoon, my wife and I came home with the feeling that we had not been subject to racism. The agents were all pleasant. But it was when we compared our answers that we found how much different we were. One of the questions we asked is, "Will the owner take back a second trust?" Now, uniformly, my

white friend was told, "I think we can arrange that." Uniformly I
was told it was all cash.

Hairston points out that his seniority as a worker and his larger savings
account should have made him a better credit risk than the younger Cogens—"My pedigree was better than his"—but the Hairstons were offered
less favorable financial terms. The Cogen-Hairston report filed away in
the Neighbors Inc. archives reveals that the difference in treatment was
sharper even than Hairston remembers: The prices agents quoted him and
Ann varied from 25 to more than 50 percent over what they quoted the
Cogens, "super pricing" commonly used to discourage black buyers or to
make them pay a hefty premium for living in a white neighborhood. In
this instance, the Commissioners Council on Human Relations refused to
pursue prosecutions based on the Cogen-Hairston testing data. Because
neither of the couples had actually intended to buy, they did not meet the
status of injured parties required to bring a legal action. They could not
file complaints on behalf of the nameless, and countless, others who actually were seeking housing.[52]

Even as NI's team failed to crack segregation west of the park, it revealed the systemic means through which realtors discouraged black buyers. Until then, NI's white families might have thought black families were
less attractive buyers or hypersensitive. Now the black people were their
acquaintances and told them the precise ways they were put off. Marvin
Caplan marveled, years later, that "Joe Hairston never took it personally"
as he recounted what to him would have been unsettling. NI's white families now knew more about the unreasonable disappointments segregation
inflicted.

As housing segregation persisted in the District, so did school segregation. For middle-class educated families, good schools were a priority. Just
as they fought against blockbusters and closed neighborhoods, NI had to
nurture their own neighborhood schools. While the city's system imagined itself a model because its schools had desegregated immediately in
1954 without violent confrontations, its schools had never been academically strong or effective in educating all the District's children. The expec-
tation for families moving into the Neighbors Inc. area was that schools
such as Coolidge High would remain orderly and continue to offer college-
preparatory courses after desegregation. The system, however, altered rapidly after 1954 in response to enormous changes in school population and

in political backing. White enrollment dropped from almost 40 percent of the segregated system in 1954 to 20 percent of the integrated one in 1960.[53] The schools in the southern tier of Neighbors Inc. all went from white only in 1954 to almost 100 percent black in 1960, as the surrounding neighborhoods filled with black residents.

By the early 1960s, parallel with the area's housing, the possibilities for interracial schools had shrunk to the schools in the northern sections of Shepherd Park and Takoma, D.C.: Shepherd Elementary, Takoma Elementary, Paul Junior High, and Coolidge High School. The middle-class parents of NI, professional people with college degrees and professional degrees and jobs as dentists, engineers, physicists, teachers, journalists, diplomats, union officers, lawyers, and government agency workers, assumed that they could monitor programs, aid principals, and make the schools friendly and academically stimulating for all students, including those whom the school zone brought in from outside the immediate neighborhood. When Shepherd Park Elementary became crowded because black families were claiming their children lived with grandparents or other relatives to get them zoned into a better school, the long-serving white principal's reaction was to detect students she could prove were coming from out of the district and exclude them. White parents joined black parents in objecting to this strategy and moved to solve the crowding problem by redesigning the school. We decided to "make room for them," Janet Brown says. Parents brought in construction materials and on weekends built movable bookcases and carved out two new classrooms from the auditorium and the cafeteria. It was easy, Brown remembers. "Here we were, college-educated people in striving families with well-disciplined children. We all had the same interests, the same values" about aiding all children to get a good education.

At the local junior high, Paul, which had a 50 percent white–50 percent black student population by 1960, parents intervened to create academic programs to raise the educational aspirations of all the students. Nancy Good, who with her husband, Robert, had welcomed African diplomats to the neighborhood, joined Lee White, a top Kennedy administration staffer and member of Tifereth Israel, in creating a special focus at Paul: In the American Democracy in Action program, students at the junior high would have many opportunities to learn about "democracy" and how "positive steps could be taken to achieve stability rather than accepting 'the inevitable'" segregation by race.[54] Using Kennedy administration connections, the program arranged field trips for junior high students to meet leading public officials to talk about citizenship and the operations of government. Field trips to the offices of Attorney General Robert Kennedy vied with visits to see Supreme Court justices William Brennan and Potter Stewart. Teas with distinguished speakers followed school assemblies, and school reporters held press conferences with presidential advisors. Paul Junior High had more than a thousand students; Barbara Atkinson remembers the intense work required to make contacts in government offices, to develop schedules, to supervise groups on field trips, and then to explain enough about government so that students didn't all want "to go to Capitol Hill. [We'd suggest], 'Doesn't somebody want to go to the Pentagon, meet all the Joint Chiefs of Staff?' " A host of parents worked to enable the program's success.

The schools inexorably lost white students, however—by 1964, Paul and Coolidge each had fewer than 20 percent white students—and those that remained became more visible targets for the taunts of the much poorer black kids who arrived from out of the immediate NI area. Many NI parents tried to keep the focus on education, and Margery Ware blamed school problems on "overcrowding." But the white middle-class world outside NI, according to an article in a D.C.-area magazine, was curious about the "dating, even marriage," that could result from "integration at the elementary and pre-school levels," and the specter of interracial sex and marriage became an excuse for some white parents to pull their children out of school or to move out of the area.[55]

By 1963, searching for ways to show off the neighborhood's attractions, to quell white fears about moving among large numbers of black people, and to display its interracial alternative, Neighbors Inc. started an annual summer Art and Book Fair. Unwilling to turn its northern neighborhoods into enclaves like Georgetown or west of the park, the organization designed the Art and Book Fair to be an umbrella for the entire original 250-square-block association, providing for continued collaboration between the predominantly black working-class and poor areas in southern Neighbors sections and the racially mixed middle-class areas in its northern sections.

Affirming the interracial quality of professional accomplishment, the 1963 Art and Book Fair celebrated multiracial artistic production evaluated by authorities in the art world. "One of the first places [in D.C.] with integrated displays of art work," Ruth Jordan claims, the ABF showed sale and exhibit pieces prescreened and selected by National Gallery of Art director J. Carter Brown and by Howard University art professor David Driskoll. Well-known local authors like Pauli Murray, as well as celebrities like Mrs. John F. Kennedy, donated signed copies of their books for sale. The area's international character was affirmed with exhibits mounted by the new African states of Ghana and Nigeria, Pan American Union states of Mexico and Argentina, and faraway Israel and India. Professional entertainment engaged neighborhood youngsters for the three-day festival, and neighborhood women provided an array of food.[56]

On the eve of the first fair, the new international, educated, interracial world envisioned by Neighbors collided with the old elite, segregated, white-exclusive Washington. The planners expected to hold the festival on the Shepherd Park grounds of Marjorie Webster College, a historic junior college for "proper, Southern, white young ladies," as Barbara Atkinson puts it. "But the afternoon before the opening, after we had just about set up the art and book festival," Atkinson remembers,

> we found out that the summer before they had denied a black child admission to their summer camp. Well, Neighbors could not hold anything there. We were expecting Robert Kennedy at nine the next morning to open our festival. So . . . we worked all night long, transporting things from Marjorie Webster up to Shepherd Elementary School and putting up the art and book exhibits.
> And the next morning when he came, we had finished just about everything, and there was a whole crew of us there in the clothes that we came with in the [previous] afternoon, because we had not been home.

The tired workers greeted the president's brother and attorney general, who congratulated Neighbors Inc.: "You have shown the way, that it can be done, that it is possible" to create an integrated neighborhood.

The first, quickly salvaged fair was so successful that it was repeated the next few years, with large multiday festivals in 1964 and 1965 on the grounds of Coolidge High School. Minnesota senator Hubert Humphrey opened the event in 1964 with greetings from President Lyndon Johnson. Mrs. Dean Rusk, wife of the secretary of state, opened the 1965 fair, and Robert Weaver, soon to be the first black cabinet member as head of Housing and Urban Development, gave the welcoming remarks. Other worthies, including Shepherd Park luminaries like Alaska senator Ernest Gruening, Howard University president James Nabrit, Esther Peterson, and Carl Rowan lent their names to a sponsoring committee listed on publicity materials. The fair showed off a democratic space and welcomed a variety of races, classes, and cultures. It was the creation of a confident middle class, enlisting elites, welcoming working-class neighbors, and showing off a middle-class culture of books, art, music, and gracious hospitality.

By 1965, Neighbors Inc. had spent almost seven years building a middle-class interracial neighborhood. The families did not cut themselves off from residents in NI's predominantly black southern sections, which housed many more working-class and poor households. NI invited participation and held out a possibility of mixed-class and interracial cooperation on issues of city services and public programs. With more confidence than doubt, Neighbors relied on strong bonds, and not suburban isolation, to provide safety for families. The weak link for a middle-class neighborhood was schools, and the main question in 1965 was whether NI could sustain schools of high enough quality to satisfy middle-class parents, white and black, who could find other options. Could an interracial urban space sustain the amenities of "middle-class life" still popularly equated with "white suburban"? With Congress passing civil rights legislation, the nation at large seemed to be embracing an ideal of integration; Neighbors Inc. felt confident that its lively, egalitarian, cosmopolitan, responsible neighborhood could continue to be a model for middle-class interracial living.

NCCJ Brotherhood Youth Institute, Camp Kittatinny, New York, August 1962. Courtesy of Walter Chambers.

NCCJ Brotherhood Youth Institute, Camp Kittatinny, New York,
August 1962. Courtesy of Walter Chambers.

NCCJ Encounter, Camp DeBenneville Pines, California,
August 1971. Courtesy of Los Angeles NCCJ Regional Office.

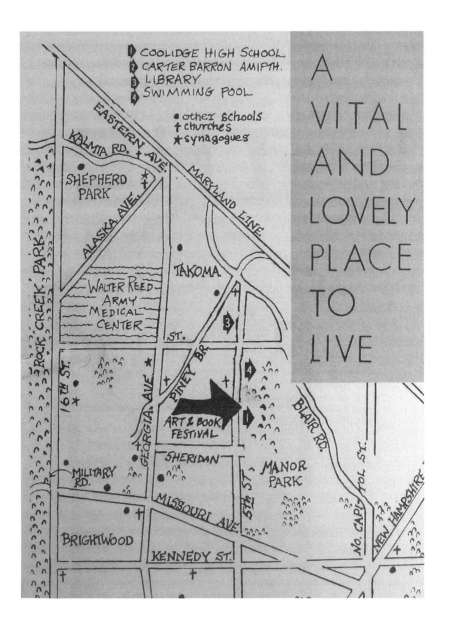

Recruitment brochure, c. 1961.
Courtesy of D.C. Public Library, Washingtoniana Division,
D.C. Community Archives, Collection 110.

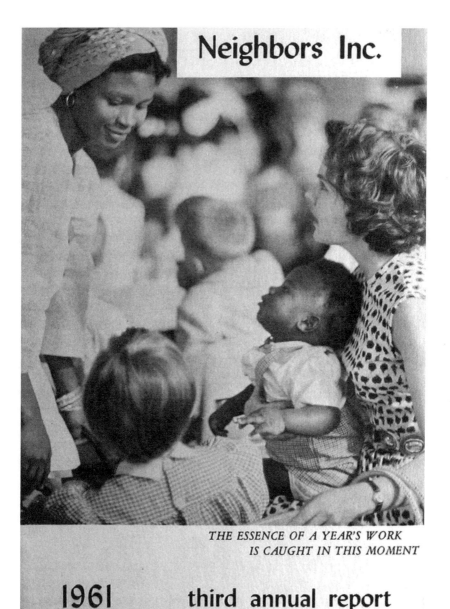

**Neighbors Inc.**

*THE ESSENCE OF A YEAR'S WORK
IS CAUGHT IN THIS MOMENT*

1961      third annual report

Neighbors Inc. annual report, 1961, reproducing the *Washington Post* cover of 15 May 1961. Photo by Vic Casamento. Courtesy of D.C. Public Library, Washingtoniana Division, D.C. Community Archives, Collection 110, and of the Washington Post Writers Group.

"...man's satisfaction in belonging to a community where he can find security and significance..."

Pres. Lyndon B. Johnson
State of the Union Message

# neighbors, inc.

## 6th annual report-1964

Neighbors Inc. annual report, 1964.
Courtesy of D.C. Public Library, Washingtoniana Division,
D.C. Community Archives, Collection 110.

# NEIGHBORS, Inc.

## 9th Annual Report - 1967

Neighbors Inc. annual report, 1967.
Courtesy of D.C. Public Library, Washingtoniana Division,
D.C. Community Archives, Collection 110.

Striking workers at Friedrich Refrigeration Inc.,
San Antonio, Texas, 1964. Courtesy of Paul Javior.

Farmworkers march near Floresville, Texas, 1966.
Courtesy of San Antonio Express-News Collection,
UT at San Antonio's Institute of Texan Cultures.

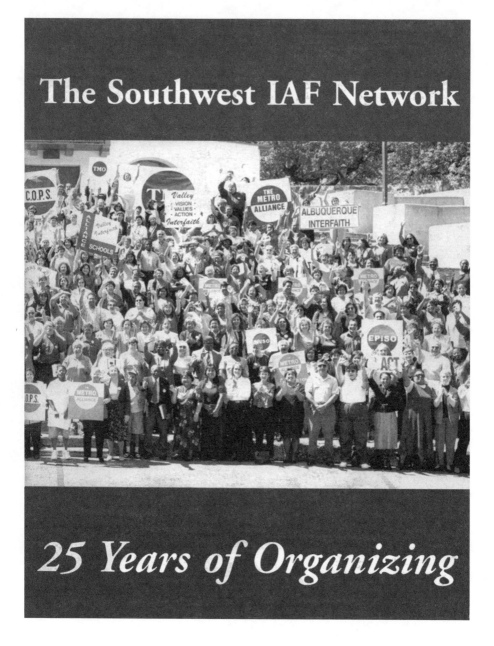

Rally of Texas IAF groups, late 1990s.
Used with permission from The Southwest IAF Network: 25 Years of
Organizing (Austin: Interfaith Education Fund, 1999).

# 4

# Abiding Together

## *Neighbors Inc., 1965–1975*

Integration makes normal those relationships
which once were frightening to many.
*Neighbors Inc. 7th annual report, 1965*

Having and gaining power, being upwardly mobile, living
a little better than one would have expected are in conflict
with the desire to live in a heterogeneous community.
—*Gretchen Schafft, 1976*

Late in 1964, at a meeting of Neighbors Inc.'s Housing Recruitment Committee, a black member of the committee raised the question of "whom we
wish to recruit." If the goal was to seek out white families, then what role
did a black man have in the organization or, indeed, in the neighborhood?
White members defended the committee's focus on white home seekers
with an economic and psychological analysis: In the racially tracked housing market, white families would simply bypass an interracial neighborhood if they weren't given explicit reassurances of welcome. When the
black member argued angrily that he had lived as a minority and expected
white families to be willing to take similar risks, Naomi Caplan responded
on the grounds of the different historical circumstances that white families
and black families brought to interracial living. White families had to be
encouraged to do "something that would be difficult and anxiety producing": being pioneers in an area where they were rapidly becoming an identifiable minority. Analogously, black families, she continued, needed aid to

move into white-predominant suburbs. Since, in the Neighbors Inc. area, white families, and not black, were taking risks, all NI members, white and black, reluctantly directed resources to attracting white households.[1]

The issue of not pursuing black home buyers had come up from the initiation of NI's Housing Information Service. Once the southern sections of Manor Park and Brightwood lost most of their white families, NI focused on the northern sections of Shepherd Park and Takoma, D.C. By the mid-1960s, even those neighborhoods were rapidly gaining black middle-class households and becoming black majority; it was evident that white families would become a minority population, even if a substantial one.

But white families now were also choosing housing in a political climate very different from that of the hopeful late 1950s. The Watts neighborhood of Los Angeles exploded in fire-bombings and police confrontations in August 1965 on the heels of a referendum in which California's white voters had repealed a statewide fair-housing law to open suburban housing to nonwhite buyers and renters. The intensifying U.S. military engagement in Vietnam shifted international attention away from U.S. civil rights and removed pressure on Washington policy makers to advance integration in the capital city.[2] Racial power movements, starting with Black Power, asserted that only group solidarity, not necessarily in pursuit of integration, could gain their members good housing, schools, and jobs. Within three years, a white backlash in response to violent expressions of the anger of nonwhites isolated in inner cities led a national commission to term the country "two nations," spatially divided between black cities and white suburbs.[3] The national picture of economically affluent white suburbs and poor, nonwhite cities effaced the black middle class and made black working-class families on the verge of achieving middle-class status invisible. With the physical and mental landscape starkly divided between urban, nonwhite, and poor on the one side, and suburban, white, and middle class on the other, how could Neighbors convey a promise and reality of interracial and middle class?

Without a general opening up of suburban neighborhoods to buyers of all racial categories, NI's Washington neighborhoods provided precious middle-class housing to eager black home buyers but affirmed the dominant view of the city as "black" space. To counter this trend, NI uncomfortably mimicked some of the behaviors of those who preferred all-white enclaves, steering white families into NI and discouraging black families. However worthy its purpose, NI's action reduced the housing available to black families and benefited white buyers. Forced to give preference to whites, white NI members found it easier to stress their revolutionary desire to break racial lines than to admit the widespread reluctance of other whites to follow their lead. By the mid-1960s, white families were a bare majority even in the northern sections of NI. Even though the residents' education and income levels established the area as middle class, Neighbors now could attract only particular types of white buyers and could reduce only partially the real estate equation of "white" with "middle class."

Eager to attract white interest, after 1965 Neighbors Inc. placed ads in liberal journals like the *Nation,* the *New Republic* and labor and church periodicals. Letters to labor leaders, congressional staffers, journalists, and researchers coming into Washington described the NI neighborhood as "an alternative to white suburbia" and invited readers moving to D.C. to "join us!" The publicity promised "an integrated community [with] urban cosmopolitan living" and listed prominent residents as reassurance of the neighborhood's stability and status. Ads and letters directed interested parties to the organization's Housing Information Service, which would help them locate homes for sale.[4]

Now advertised as an "intown, integrated, interesting place to live," NI appealed to a slightly younger generation than the New Deal–inspired group who had founded Neighbors Inc.[5] The older group of self-described "practical idealists" had expected to fight for the worthy goal of interracial living. The new buyers, who had been inspired by 1950s civil rights activism, took for granted that once an interracial space existed, it would be attractive and secure. These younger families tended to belong to professions and, even if working for labor unions, had less of the collective experience of New Deal and wartime than their immediate predecessors. Influenced by Sixties ideals of individual expression and accomplishment, they were critical of the conformity of immediate postwar housing and suburban gender assignments. Holding what historians Maurice Isserman and Michael Kazin call "a mixed vision of community and individualism," the hopeful young buyers expected they could simply move into the established interracial neighborhood.[6] They were unaware of the hard lesson white people from the New Deal and World War II generation had learned and of black middle-class history: that protecting an interracial, orderly, desirable space required constant struggle.

# Confident Interracialists

Because Neighbors Inc. had solidified an interracial space hospitable to white middle-class people, the white families who bought in after 1965 came into Shepherd Park and Takoma, D.C., explicitly choosing a heterogeneous urban existence in preference to suburban exclusiveness. Gretchen Schafft moved in 1964 to a working-class block in Takoma, which she and her husband, Harry, a physicist, could afford on his salary at the National Bureau of Standards.[7] Gretchen had grown up in Grand Rapids, Michigan, where her parents of Swedish/Norwegian and German/English heritage argued for racial fairness. Her father had joined two civil rights groups, the NAACP and the Urban League, in the 1940s and left one church over its refusal to accept a black child into its nursery school. When the family's next church, a Congregational one, asked families to take in international (meaning European) students for Christmas holidays, Gretchen's mother asked, "Why do you want to do that when there are black students [studying here] who can't go back to the South? We should take black students into our homes." Gretchen had watched her parents advocate integration, and she took for granted that she could now live it. Schafft remembers that, while Shepherd Park and Takoma, D.C., shared many political values, Shepherd Park residents were much more interested in how their houses and lawns looked than were the "hipper" people in Takoma. "Whites in Takoma were very messy," Schafft cheerfully recounts, which for her reduced the pressure to focus on house cleaning instead of studying. Caring for two young children and working on a PhD at Catholic University, Gretchen kept her house open to the neighborhood, and various children played in and out of the space. Gretchen chatted with the working-class white couple on one side, who were "not particularly liberal," and the black family on the other side, one of whose daughters worked as a prostitute. Despite political and economic differences, all these families watched out for each other's children, and the Schaffts found a reliable babysitter in the daughter of a middle-class black family down the street, who became family friends.

The Schaffts' experiences demonstrated to them that the inclusion they valued ethically also bred neighborhood security. Neighborliness depended on acting like a neighbor, engaging and caring for those living around you. Harry Schafft, Gretchen's husband, had been raised an atheist but found his closest friendships with the local Methodist minister and Catholic priest, who organized collections for the neighborhood's poorer families. Harry liked their politics but didn't agree with its religious basis. "One day," Gretchen remembers, "my husband said, 'You know the problem with living in this neighborhood? You can't keep a decent prejudice.'" If Harry could discover that he didn't like some of the ideas of men who looked just like him and, on better acquaintance, that these ideas were not so bad after all, then surely white middle-class excluders could learn that their "indecent" prejudices against nonwhite people were ridiculous, too. The Schaffts' Takoma existence affirmed that simple proposition.

Another set of buyers also rejected the assumption that apparent suburban homogeneity guaranteed comfort and security. Marilyn and Conrad Christiano, both newspaper reporters, had moved to Washington in 1965 when Conrad won a fellowship to spend a year working in Congress to see firsthand how the government operated.[8] Although the Christianos had lived in an integrated area in downtown Rochester, Washington colleagues recommended housing in the suburbs. Conrad remembers that he and Marilyn looked at "these big apartment complexes. And they had pools and they had dishwashers and new stuff, and nice, high security fences. Some of them had guards. But it got to where we couldn't remember where we left off yesterday looking at apartments, because they all looked alike. They were identical." The uniformity offended Marilyn, "an urban type," Conrad says, who in 1967 was devoting her time to their two young children, with a third to come in 1970. She didn't want to live in an isolating place or raise her children in such a setting.

For Conrad, whose father had moved the family from a home in downtown Buffalo to the suburbs in the late 1940s, suburban life also held no romance. The suburbs were the setting for "a very unhappy time in my life. Prejudice there was very thick against people who had vowels on the end of their names, very, very stiff." The Christianos decided to stay on in Washington after his fellowship ended, rented an old Takoma farmhouse, which would soon be torn down for a new elementary school, and in 1968 bought a house right across the street, where they still live.

As in the earlier NI period, European immigrants preferred the easy interracialism of the neighborhood to white suburbia. Maija Hay and her husband, Ray, in 1967 moved from Cleveland to Washington, where Ray worked in an urban-planning firm before he eventually moved into the new Housing and Urban Development Department.[9] "While we were looking at houses, we were invited to a neighborhood party, and we met the whole neighborhood there, and we decided that these really are our kind of people," Maija happily recalls. The Hays "felt very strongly that this racial segregation was having a terrible effect for America," remembers Maija, whose speech still carries traces of her Finnish upbringing. "So when we met people who lived here [in Takoma], there were blacks and whites, and different kinds of jobs—people like mailmen or policemen—and so it was a social and economic as well as a racial mix. There seemed there were more people here who were seriously concerned about social issues. And we felt that was a much healthier environment for the kids to grow." Recalling that friends expected them to buy in the Maryland suburbs or west of the park, Maija remembers the daring of their decision: "We decided we would just go against all the conventional wisdom and buy the biggest house in the neighborhood," a rambling late nineteenth-century Victorian with a stable attached.

The earlier generation of Europeans who settled in the NI area had the Holocaust as its racial reference. For a teenager like Maija growing up in postwar 1950s Finland, however, racial difference appeared an enticing part of new prosperity: "Blacks were considered exotic, musicians and actors, and a lot of Finnish girls really prided themselves if they had a black boyfriend." When Maija married a white American and spent her early wedded years in Cleveland, she learned about U.S. segregation's forced social distance. She and Ray had a black couple as close friends, who introduced them to the Cleveland Symphony's

> Don White, leader of the cello section—he must have been one of
> the first black musicians of that level in an orchestra. Well, he told
> us stories about when the Cleveland Orchestra toured in the South,
> Mississippi and Missouri. And everybody else stayed in a hotel,
> and he had to stay at some Ma Jones back room. And he would talk
> about things as B.C.R., meaning "before civil rights."

White's account helped Maija move from seeing African Americans as rare objects to understanding their everyday humiliations; like the Meijers, she learned about U.S. racializing practices unknown to most Europeans.

Young interracial couples, who were already pushing a national change in attitudes and policies toward intermarriage, which the Supreme Court would not validate until 1967, also assumed that Neighbors offered a welcoming place to raise their children.[10] One couple mentioned by many of the old-timers, Isobel (Peachy) and Robert Murray, first lived in the Neighbors Inc. area between 1962 and 1965 when Bob fulfilled his military obligation as a doctor at the National Institutes of Health.[11] After a brief sojourn in Seattle, the couple returned to Takoma in 1967, when Murray joined the Howard University medical school staff as a medical geneticist. "My husband is black," Peachy says, "and we wanted our children to have the experience of being in the neighborhood with lots of mixed families, and there certainly were at that time, [Takoma] probably much more so than Shepherd Park."

The free-spirited, adventurous young individualists who moved into the area after 1965 quickly began to learn that holding together diverse groups in a heterogeneous neighborhood no longer united by the attacks of blockbusters and divided between its hopes for interracial living and a continuing need for middle-class black housing required effort, organization, and building new relationships. Peachy Murray, having temporarily given up her work as a nurse to care for the couple's four children, quickly became one of the volunteers staffing the Neighbors Inc. office and serving on its committees. She took charge of organizing the monthly Friday-night socials to make certain that families met across the racial boundaries that defined other neighborhoods. "We very carefully tried to spread it around the neighborhood, alternating whether it was a black or white or mixed couple kind of thing. We were very conscious about including everybody." The Friday-night events often featured music and dancing, as well as conversation, and by the late 1960s NI was hosting a well-attended February dance party in the Tifereth Israel community building. As Ruth Jordan later recalled the contrast between the fearfulness and fights of early Neighbors and its later pleasure and confidence, "I danced the Seventies away."

Wives and husbands quickly accepted the Neighbors Inc. premise that a viable community required public involvement outside the immediate family. Like Peachy Murray, Maija Hay found herself engaged to help lead the activities that underpinned neighborhood loyalty and pride. Ed Cogen, Neighbors Inc. president when the Hays moved in, asked Maija to run the Art and Book Festival for 1968. Maija agreed because this was a way to "punch her ticket," a new idea for her. "Until we moved to this house, I had never volunteered for anything, because there always seemed to be other people who could do it." In an interracial neighborhood, however, residents had constantly to build and maintain a network, and Maija felt that her work was "really needed."

The Christianos donated money to Neighbors and went to open houses and by the late 1960s became involved in other neighborhood activities that had developed. Conrad helped lead a Boy Scout troop that had mostly black children; he also offered swimming instruction for neighborhood kids at the Howard University pool and the Takoma Recreation Department pool, which sponsored summer swim teams during the late 1960s and early 1970s. Marilyn, like many other mothers, focused her energies on the Takoma elementary school, where she began to volunteer when her oldest son started first grade in 1968. "There was a constant communication through the whole neighborhood, . . . where you're talking over the problems and what are we going to do about this or that."[12]

## The 1968 Riots

Between 1965 and 1968, Neighbors Inc. looked like a consistent success; confidently it attracted white families escaping suburban segregation, supported open housing in the region, and mounted artistically impressive summer Art and Book Festivals. Then, in the spring of 1968, the city experienced an enormous outburst of anger after Martin Luther King Jr's assassination. Starting on 4 April, as the news spread about King's murder, the District of Columbia endured four days of street unrest and property destruction. Large groups, made up mainly of young black men angry at this confirmation of white U.S. racism, gathered on downtown streets, fire-bombed slum housing, overturned and burned cars, robbed and torched downtown stores, and roamed the streets in large bands that the police could not control or disperse. The military moved in to back up the almost all-white police force and to protect federal government buildings. Washington's conflagrations, matched in many cities across the country, aroused white fears of a war between black and white Americans.[13]

The 1968 riots stand as a major chronological marker in histories of the 1960s, and for some residents the devastation alienated them from Neighbors and the area. Some Jewish families with businesses in the riot areas, who had stayed in Shepherd Park as black families moved in, felt personally singled out and attacked. Many had established and run small businesses in the inner city, and the destruction and looting swept away the shops where they had sold clothing, sporting goods, and food. They believed that their businesses had contributed to the city, enriched people's lives, and avoided price gouging. Many never forgave the black community, which they held responsible as a group for the thieves' behavior.[14]

But the "practical idealists" and "confident interracialists" who had committed themselves to the Neighbors ideal did not interpret the riots as a racial face-off between white and black; the downtown destruction did not affect their confidence in their own relationships and neighborhood. For many of them the hazards and shock of April turned into reassurances that they had made the right decision to join and to sustain an interracial community that didn't allow for easy divisions into "us" and "them." The everyday associations of white parents and children with black neighbors, classmates, and coworkers dissolved some of the self-righteous assurance of labeling and name-calling. Miriam Meijer, Paul and Marianne's eldest daughter, went to class at Coolidge High School the day after King's death, and Marianne recalls that "she was the only white kid in her class. And they did nothing but talk about the riots. And each time a kid would get up and say, 'And the whites did this to us, and the whites did that to us,' they looked at Miriam, and they said, 'We mean the *old* ones.' And Miriam came home and said, 'Momma, it was a good thing I was there, because I reminded them not to judge.'"[15] Maija Hay remembers that she told her younger children not to play in front of their house near the sidewalk, because black strangers to the neighborhood might see only her children's skin color and be angry. But she told her children to play in back of the house just until the city calmed, and she never worried about general safety in the neighborhood. Schoolteacher Mollie Berch recalls that she was driven through the downtown turmoil by a black colleague, who told Mollie to duck down under a coat in the car's backseat and then drove her safely home to Shepherd Park.

Paradoxically, the National Advisory Commission on Civil Disorders, appointed by President Johnson to explain the causes of the Watts outbreak and the riots, or rebellions, that followed, had issued its report only a few weeks before the April events. Among its catalogue of causes— persistent school segregation, urban joblessness, media stereotyping—the commission pointed to ongoing residential segregation as a factor that cut off the nation's black citizens from advantages taken for granted by its white citizens.[16] The solid middle-class residents of Neighbors Inc. were themselves physically removed from the city's worst neighborhoods and harshest conditions, but they were close enough to know that the riots had causes other than simple hatred of white people. Many of the area's black families felt concern for the urban poor, even as they lamented the violence. Many of the neighborhood's white residents also felt sympathetic and, moreover, had been shielded by the black people they lived and worked among. Neighbors Inc. white families felt assured that their choice of residence proved the good sense and necessity of choosing urban, interracial residency.

## The Losing Battle for
## Middle-Class Interracial Schools

For Neighbors' white middle-class residents, the trial of racial self-consciousness came from the public schools. Confident young interracialists and older pragmatic integrationists rode out the 1968 riots. But they feared losing control of the junior high and senior high schools, which were integral to the character and attractiveness of a middle-class existence. Since 1954, when the Supreme Court ruled for school desegregation in the District of Columbia in *Bolling v. Sharpe,* on the same day it handed down *Brown v. Board of Education*, the District school system had suffered from the assault of a white Southern-dominated Congress hostile to school integration and the demands of poor, black, Southern, rural families pouring into the District for better jobs and schools.

Mediocre during segregation, the schools had no heritage of excellence to draw on. Despite a few notable pockets of achievement, much of the public school system had not served students' academic interests during the first half of the twentieth century.[17] Middle-class white children had found adequate schools in their neighborhoods. In the era before meritocracy and education became essential to middle-class well-being, these schools sufficed to send the most ambitious students off to good colleges.

An educated African American elite had operated the selective Dunbar High School within the public system. Run as an elite college prep school staffed by African American PhDs whom white universities would not hire, Dunbar had produced "the first black general (Benjamin O. Davis), the first black federal judge (William H. Hastie), the first black Cabinet member (Robert C. Weaver), the discoverer of blood plasma (Charles Drew), and the first black Senator since Reconstruction (Edward W. Brooke)," while ignoring the dark-skinned, working-class children in its immediate neighborhood.[18] As in other segregated school systems, the D.C. schools had not, before the 1954 desegregation decision, educated a majority of the city's black children; in 1953 fewer than half the black students registered in the ninth grade remained in school through the eleventh grade.[19]

Politically, the District schools relied on congressional funding and oversight, and powerful white Southern Congressmen had no interest in a successful demonstration project for integrated schools. Congressional committees portrayed the city's school system as one that had functioned well under segregation but was now overwhelmed by poor and undisciplined black youth who would destroy white children's education. As evidence, hostile congressmen could point to a local newspaper report of the 1955 nationwide testing results that showed that only three District high schools had high averages compared to the nation at large: Western (in white elite Georgetown), Wilson (west of the park); and Coolidge (in predominantly Jewish middle-class Shepherd Park). A 1956 congressional committee gathered testimony that black students used vulgar language, "bumped" up against white girls in school corridors, and were generally unruly. White teachers expressed concern about the high rates of venereal disease and teen pregnancy among the District's black teenagers and voiced fears that "desegregation would bring white girls down to that level," expressing a worry about the loss of white girls' self-restraint if school contact diminished social distance.[20]

In a cruel confluence of negligence and need, the newly desegregated schools became responsible for a massively increased student population at the very moment Congress reduced support. The African American student population rose from 47,000 to 130,000 in the brief span from 1950 to 1965, while the number of white students fell from 48,000 to fewer than 15,000.[21] Large numbers of the system's 50,000 added pupils came from rural and small-town Southern schools starved of resources in white-run, segregated systems. The parents of the new students had attended similarly ill-served schools, which prepared many only for the near-peonage farm jobs that dominated Southern agriculture until well after World War II. Accelerating white flight reduced the numbers of middle-income households at the very moment that intensifying black in-migration increased the city's proportion of poor households;[22] the tax base available to fund schools declined, and so did the number of middle-class constituents willing to advocate for the schools.

The schools quickly resegregated by income and by race. School attendance paralleled residential segregation. By 1960, most of the schools east of Rock Creek Park had become all black (and Dunbar had lost its distinction as it filled up with neighborhood children); the schools west of Rock Creek Park, which had been white segregated before 1954, remained all white. Staffing assignments held to the preintegration pattern, too;

white teachers and principals often refused to move to integrated or black-majority schools and threatened to abandon their District jobs if they were forced to work in desegregated settings.

By 1967, Neighbors Inc. schools in the northern tier were among the few race-mixed schools in the resegregated public school system. The old black-white division of legal segregation had transformed in thirteen years into a race-class division organized through two structures: residential segregation and school tracking. The tracking system ostensibly offered all students an education appropriate to their ability and ambition. In honors and college preparatory tracks, academic students prepared for college; in the general track, ordinary students took vocational training for employment; and in the basic track, the least capable students gained life skills to function at a sixth-grade level.

Prosperous white families generally lived west of the park in the catchment area of Deal Junior High and Woodrow Wilson High School, which had honors tracks, college prep courses, and parental subsidies for school programs. Most black families east of Rock Creek Park sent their children to all-black schools with overcrowded classrooms, teachers with less experience than those in elite schools, and no honors courses.[23] A 1966 task force on District poverty programs, led by black congressman Adam Clayton Powell, concluded that the "basic" track had become equated with "Black": "It is almost axiomatic that the lower the income level of the high school," disproportionately serving families newly arrived from the South, "the larger the number of pupils working at basic level track."[24] At best, young people with this level of education graduated with skills that fit them only for manual labor and low-wage jobs.

In the northern tiers of the Neighbors Inc. area, Shepherd Park and Takoma elementary schools continued to have a bare majority of white students and middle-class parental intervention. By 1967, Paul Junior High and Coolidge High School, with their wider catchment areas, had 6 percent and 5 percent white students, though a considerably larger cohort of black and white middle-class parents.[25] Would middle-class Neighbors families be able to sustain academic, college preparatory courses in schools where the majority of students came from poor households with no personal experience with higher education and no spare resources to subsidize school services? Would white middle-class families abandon interracial living when it couldn't guarantee the nonnegotiable middle-class requirement of good schools?

A conflation of race and class disguised two ongoing issues. First, schools' achievements were categorized according to racial composition and not available resources, including parent time, attention, and money.[26] An assumption that schools performed poorly *because* they were predominantly black reduced pressure to increase the funding for impoverished schools. But the problem was not only one of low funding. The second issue was ignoring the educational achievements of the black middle class, which perpetuated the idea that "white" and "middle class" were synonymous and that white people had nothing to learn from the black experiences of pursuing education even in a hostile environment. So school integration was easily misunderstood as putting nonwhite students into good white classrooms, with little attention to other salient issues: the ongoing pariah status of racial groups isolated in cities and the unacknowledged reliance on middle-class parents to make up deficiencies in public schools.

Neighbors Inc. first struggled not to conflate race with class. NI won a three-year grant from the U.S. Office of Education to partner its two northern-tier elementary schools, Paul Junior High, and Coolidge High School with teacher-training programs at the nearby University of Maryland. The university could place student teachers in Shepherd Park and Takoma classrooms, expanding the staff to assist poorly prepared students and giving apprentice teachers experience with urban mixed-class schools. The project ended in 1969. Neighbors also filed an amicus brief in a 1967 lawsuit brought by black activist Julius Hobson against the city's school superintendent, Carl Hansen, in *Hobson v. Hansen*. Neighbors Inc. supported Hobson's argument to the U.S. District Court that de facto segregation had replaced the de jure dual system. Neighbors Inc.'s brief angrily denounced the idea that white parents west of the park could cut themselves off from the rest of the city and decide when black students might enter their relatively well-funded and underenrolled schools. The brief argued the positive NI case for interracial cross-class schools—knowledge of the world outside a middle-class enclave:

> It should not be assumed that only the disadvantaged child suffers
> from an "isolated" education. We believe it is equally true that
> the so-called "advantaged" child, the white child from the well-
> to-do neighborhood, receives inadequate preparation for life in
> an integrated community when he goes through his school life
> confined to his homogeneous milieu.[27]

Though NI represented black middle-class families as well as white ones, the brief's argument responded to racial segregation by linking economic advantage and whiteness. In the racial terms of the school debate, NI was not able to articulate support for the academic heritage of the NI's black middle-class.

The District Court's June 1967 Skelley Wright decision, named after the presiding judge, ended tracking, required faculties to be better integrated, mandated voluntary busing of students from overcrowded schools east of the park to underpopulated elementary schools west of the park, and closed an option for Neighbors Inc. students to transfer west of the park to Deal and Wilson. But Wright's decision could only shuffle students and money within the white-minority, middle-class-minority D.C. system, although he held out hope that ultimately D.C. schools would be partnered with white suburban school systems for regional integration.[28]

After Wright's ruling, many Neighbors Inc. families gave up on the neighborhood public schools after elementary school. Many sent children to private schools like Sidwell Friends and Georgetown Day School, options available to black middle-class parents when these schools desegregated in the decade surrounding the *Brown* case. Many of Shepherd Park's Jewish parents chose the parochial option; at one point in the early 1970s, a bus ran between the neighborhood and the Hebrew high school in Montgomery County. Other parents, like Mollie Berch and Buddy Abramowitz, paid out-of-district fees to send children to Bethesda-Chevy Chase High School, located near Shepherd Park in Montgomery County. Some families, like the Caplans, were still able to get children "across the park" to Deal Junior High and Woodrow Wilson High School. When NI's white parents gave up the battle for public schools, they justified their actions by pointing to black parents doing the same. The accumulation of individual choices reduced the neighborhood's attractiveness to white families who considered middle-class schools the bottom line in purchasing a home.

Even though NI's white parents knew that every time they removed their children from the neighborhood schools, they left the schools with fewer resources, the organization gave up its fight, first for the upper schools. Schooling came to be seen as a private family choice to be decided within each home, and often for each child. In his memoir, NI cofounder Marvin Caplan expressed guilt more than thirty years after the event about the family's moving its children out of NI schools. When his older daughter, a standout student and yearbook editor, graduated from Coolidge in May 1968, she warned her parents not to make her two younger siblings suffer "what she had gone through." When his two younger children confirmed that they were being bullied and teased at Paul, Marvin petitioned for them to go across Rock Creek Park to attend Deal and Woodrow Wilson. He characterized the agony of his family as biblical; he had been willing, like Abraham, to "sacrifice a child for his beliefs" but recovered in time to save his younger children.[29] In a secular though equally distressed conclusion, Caplan also recognized in the memoir that giving up the local schools turned Neighbors Inc. from a "vanguard" into a "coterie."

Paradoxically, one of Neighbors' last, fondly remembered interracial battles was over Takoma Elementary School. Animated by the prospect of home rule and greater political power for D.C. residents, Takoma families protested to the now-elected school board that it must devise more up-to-date and community-approved designs for school construction. Parents organized in response to the board's plan to replace the outdated, inadequate Takoma elementary school, built in 1899 and able to accommodate only four hundred of the six hundred students projected for the neighborhood, with the standardized three-story structure of boxy classrooms: an "egg crate" or child "factory," in the middle-class parents' view. Parents picketed the work site after ground was broken in spring 1969. Maija Hay led the family donkey, who bore a sign, "I'm an ass," to convey the neighborhood's opinion of the school authorities. Middle-class black parents united with middle-class white parents, and Dr. Robert Murray led some of the marches with his two young sons in tow. The articulate parents garnered news reports, and, worried about construction-site accidents, the board stopped the work, threatening to scrap all construction. Using their professional skills, the neighbors appealed to the U.S. Office of Education to fund a week-long, community-design meeting. The combative parents won the school construction battle and monitored Takoma Elementary's new replacement carefully.

Relationships built around the school fight confirmed to white parents that many black parents shared their interests. When a black Manor Park mother, Loretta Hanes, complained that "in her area, it was getting so difficult to get anybody to do anything, to get the neighborhood together, and she would like to be in a school where she could be part of it, . . . we devised a system," Maija Hay remembers. "I said, 'Well, I'll take your kids in day care at my house. I'll write a letter to the principal saying that your kids are in day care, and they have to be allowed to go to Takoma' [because most kids went home an hour for lunch]. So her kids and mine all came home to have lunch, so there was a proper, above-board [arrangement]. Loretta became a real activist." The elementary school construction raised morale, but it could not reverse Marvin Caplan's conclusion that the neighborhood middle school and high school no longer sufficed for middle-class families.

By the late 1960s, Neighbors could no longer offer a viable alternative model of urban, interracial, middle-class life to rival the suburban standard. When a local journalist canvassed in 1970, she described declining morale due to the African American suspicion that white residents "believe there have to be white people living here in order to have a good neighborhood."[30] That its failures resulted from the decisions of the white majority to refuse black home buyers in the suburbs and to defend white-majority suburban schools did not excuse Neighbors Inc.'s compromises—recruiting white families and sending children to private schools or public schools in the city's white enclave. Without middle-class schools, the neighborhood could attract a rarefied group who valued integration and could afford private schools if they had children. Nevertheless, Neighbors continued to be one of the rare places where white middle-class families lived as a minority among black neighbors, and it offered tantalizing glimpses of what interracial neighborliness might accomplish.

## Taken-for-Granted Interracialism

After 1968, Neighbors presented itself as holding together a laudable, stable neighborhood where middle-class households, white and black and racially mixed, could live together amicably. Without effective public schools, however, NI had become over-refined—an alternative that appealed to white political liberals and liberal Jews attracted to neighborhood synagogues and still offered some of the sparse middle-class housing for black families in the region. NI's white residents focused more attention on the political causes of the era—the Vietnam War and women's rights—than on the cause of interracial living, which seemed, in the case of NI, to have accomplished as much as it could.

Political liberals had identified Shepherd Park/Takoma as one of the only neighborhoods in Washington to live out civil rights principles. Howard Wachtel, who is white and a nonobservant Jew, moved to the city in 1969 to teach economics at American University and knew of Shepherd Park through his associates in the Americans for Democratic Action.[31] "By the time I moved in, the neighborhood had stabilized, unlike the exodus of a decade ago," Wachtel recalls. He rented and then bought a house from its first-generation Italian American owner, who had retired and moved out of D.C. when the 1968 flames burned out sections near his barbershop. Howard loved the house's "magnificent dark, old wood and big dining room," ideal for an "intellectual salon" and for hosting out-of-town friends coming for political demonstrations. Aware that NI fought against more liquor stores opening on the commercial strip on Georgia Avenue and monitored trash collection, Howard nevertheless remembers, "I had the sense they were past the big issues"; the diverse people around his block took integration for granted.

By the mid-1960s, young Jewish antiracists identified Shepherd Park as a secure neighborhood for a white family that wanted to live civil rights beliefs and also belong to a Jewish community. As a young teacher, Barbara White became conscious that pleasant white people who didn't speak about segregation did not always share her values about racial equality.[32] Teaching piano to students in an area just north of Georgetown (an elite district west of the park), Barbara had only one black student among many white pupils. When she organized a student recital, "they all came in their party clothes and every single white kid did a double take when he or she saw that black kid. And I knew some of the parents, so I didn't expect this kind of double take, and I thought, 'Boy, if I ever get married and have kids, I'm moving to Shepherd Park.'" By 1969, she had married Howard White, an Orthodox Jew. When they decided to start having children and Barbara's pregnancy test came back positive, they "started looking in Shepherd Park for a house."

In the late 1960s, the Shepherd Park/Takoma Park area had four synagogues to serve the dense Jewish population that had been able to buy houses from the late 1940s on, after the home sellers stopped paying attention to covenants that excluded Jews. The Whites first tried services at the synagogue at Thirteenth Street and Eastern Avenue, where "the rabbi and his family lived right on the corner. They invited us over for lunch! . . . And everything is perfectly pleasant, and then she talks about 'them,' and we knew very well what 'them' meant. It meant blacks. So we didn't like that. But we had not made a decision as to where we're going to go. . . . Then we got a phone call [from friends at Tifereth Israel]. 'Buddy [Abramowitz] was in trouble.'" Like the Cogens four years earlier, the Whites joined Tifereth Israel to help the rabbi.

Although the argument at Tifereth Israel arose partly because of the rabbi's insistent criticism of U.S. policy in Vietnam, the disagreement also reflected a division between the older Jewish congregants who had filled TI when the neighborhood was racially segregated and the newer members entering a community dedicated to integration. The small-business owners and government civil servants who had predominated in the congregation and been distressed by the 1968 riot were giving way to a highly educated professional class; these opposing groups put up contending slates of officers for synagogue governance in 1969. With the votes of new families like the Whites, a slate that included past Neighbors Inc. president Ed Cogen won the election and began recruiting members who wanted to keep the synagogue in the District. (Marvin Caplan's family joined TI that year.) Within the year, Barbara White was in charge of putting out TI's biweekly bulletin; one 1970 issue noted the first religious observance held for the entire neighborhood, with a hundred non-Jewish neighbors coming for a family service.[33] TI announced both its distinctive presence and its desire to be in fellowship with its neighbors.

Personal relationships could both strengthen white-black connections and strain them. NI's newsletter circulated some members' interest in interracial adoption just as the organization of black social workers condemned the practice. Barbara and Howard White adopted a black child just a few months after their daughter was born, "adopting from the motive of, these kids aren't getting homes." Barbara decided to adopt so quickly because she was an older mother at thirty-three and thought, correctly, that she would be able to nurse her baby son while still lactating with her daughter of a year and a half. Her father-in-law, who had grown up in a tight Jewish community in Bensonhurst, New York, "just broke off relations, almost completely." Her husband had worried that his father would not accept a black child but had not expected so extreme a reaction. When Barbara's son was about four, her father-in-law died, and her mother-in-law welcomed the adopted black son. But in 1972, when black social workers condemned the practice of interracial adoptions of black children, the issue divided the neighborhood, though proponents were not all white or opponents all black. The congregation at TI, where the White's son went to Hebrew School and had his bar mitzvah, supported Jewish identity for a number of black children adopted by TI families.[34]

# Shared Gender Norms, Distinct Heritages

In the earlier era of NI, activist wives had defied suburban ideals and shown that a new kind of public-spirited woman was an equal partner in an interracial community. Both immigrant Jewish and middle-class African American women had historically expected to participate equally with their husbands in caring for family and neighborhood—to hold jobs, to meet with neighbors, and to work on public issues. In the context of the late 1960s women's movement, however, these activities took on new meaning, marking women as equal partners in family and community decision making. The newer ideologies of the white women's movement paradoxically mixed with the older ideologies of community obligation to favor a view of women at odds with that of white suburban domesticity.

The District's job structure encouraged women's working. By 1970, the District reflected a correlation between a relatively high family income level and an unusually high level of employed wives, a pattern not yet common in the rest of the nation, where high family incomes usually decreased wives' presence in the labor market. Washington exceeded almost every U.S. city in the proportion of employed women, including households with employed husbands and wives and those with employed mothers raising children as single parents.[35] For the Shepherd Park and Takoma neighborhoods, the consequence was more egalitarian households, with less pressure on husbands to define themselves solely as breadwinners and on wives to comport themselves primarily as housekeepers. Shared work and community responsibilities aligned white families with what sociologist Bert Landry labels a "dual-worker ideology" that emerged among middle-class black families after Reconstruction. In these families, women needed to earn income and men needed to support community services, sharing rather than dividing gender roles. Landry argues that the "dual-worker ideology . . . united rather than separated the public and private spheres."[36]

Two distinct groups in which women claimed shared leadership were the Conservative synagogue, Tifereth Israel, and the middle-class African American community affiliated with Howard University. Each of these provided an anchor for middle-class white and black families that allowed the establishment of secure identities and the discovery of shared interests.

The TI congregation diverged from some predominant patterns of postwar Jewish Americans, notably in not moving to the suburbs, in having high rates of wives' employment, and, perhaps as a corollary, in priding itself on its egalitarian makeup. Tifereth Israel's urban interracial synagogue offered a vision of Jewish possibility different from that of many contemporary synagogues that were building large suburban structures in emulation of white Protestant church programs.[37] TI aligned itself philosophically with many Jews who did not accept residential segregation and suburbanized domesticity for wives. At Tifereth Israel, members sought to sustain Jewish distinctiveness, emphasized the social duties taught in the faith, and refused the segregation that defined life for other white Americans, including suburban Jewish families.

Their employment and activism in the neighborhood allowed Jewish women to expect more authority in the synagogue, which became the first "in the Washington area," says Abramowitz, "to have complete equality for women to participate in services. Complete equality. Which meant that every part of the service was open to them just as it was open to men. We were the first to have bat mitzvah that was completely equivalent to bar mitzvah." But the synagogue was not radical, Abramowitz asserts. "At the same time we maintained the service itself, the Hebrew nature of the service, as a completely traditional presentation that was about equivalent to an Orthodox presentation. So we were both right wing and left wing, depending on the issue. If it was a social issue, we were on the left. If it was an issue of liturgy, we were on the right. . . . We were not one-dimensional."[38]

By 1974, the new leadership had attracted more congregants and paid off the synagogue mortgage. "We reached $180,000. . . . 100 [different] participants gave," Rabbi Abramowitz remembers. "The largest single contribution was $5,000. [Unlike other synagogues with one major donor,] in our synagogue the goal was to have the broadest possible base of support, . . . so that the synagogue would be a democratic institution. And not run by one voice." The egalitarian practices of Tifereth Israel had created a new path for its congregants. The synagogue anchored white families in NI, but families whose whiteness included interracial residency, working wives, and liberal political consciousness.

Balancing the self-conscious community of white residents was a self-reliant black community similarly characterized by interracial comfort, employed wives, political intelligence, and accomplishments usually invisible to white America. Prominent achievers, like the eminent lawyer and Howard University president James Naibrit, bought houses on the Sixteenth Street border of Shepherd Park in the mid-1950s, part of an influx of well-to-do African Americans that earned those blocks the name Gold Coast.[39] The Gold Coast designation obscured, however, the much larger group of middle-class black families who saw the Neighbors area as a place where they could find solid houses and maintain the standards of education long valued by the black middle class.

Brenda Atkinson-Willoughby, the third of Barbara Atkinson's six children, was one of the first black children to attend each of her previously white-exclusive D.C. schools and graduated from Coolidge High in 1969.[40] She was conscious, she remembers, that her father and mother had been to Howard, and her maternal grandmother, too. "And that was my heritage. And while we believe in integration, I certainly had a lot of pride in that history of family, of an African American family that was entrenched in education." Brenda sustained the family tradition by attending historically black Fisk University. Though some of her siblings chose historically white colleges, they and their white NI friends all knew that higher education was not a white preserve.

The black middle class had developed dense social networks unknown to most white Americans. "My kids' social life was not just in the neighborhood," Barbara Atkinson remembers. "There were things like the Jacks and Jills [a black social organization], made up of kids from all over the city, but it also has chapters all over the country. And so when it came to parties and dating, [my children] met people not just in their neighborhoods and not just in the schools." Supported by her family and this larger social network, Brenda and her siblings had a racial array of playmates and friends in Scout groups and in Junior Neighbors, an organization formed for young people to hold their own events and to raise funds for NI. In Neighbors, white families learned about a black middle class that, as Brenda put it, would not "devalue their property or weaken the school."

## Reaching Out in the Wake of the Riots

In the wake of the 1968 riots and defections from public schools, how would a middle-class interracial neighborhood conduct itself? The first impulse was to respond inclusively; in a fall 1968 report, NI asserted that "we solve our problems best by solving those problems common to all."[41]

For the next few years, NI used its knowledge and influence to advocate for services that middle-class households took for granted, especially in aid of the mixed-class southern tier areas of Manor Park and Brightwood. One of the most basic city issues was recreational programs for young people. Neighbors advocated consistently for public programs and facilities for children who did not have large homes and yards to play in. A 1967 budget request to the city's commissioners included funds to hire Roving Leaders to work with teens in every area of the city, to operate swimming pools throughout the summer and recreation center clubhouses during the winter, and to keep meeting spaces open in schools after the regular school day ended. The group helped raise funds for the Woody Bartges Boys Club (named in honor of the pastor at the Evangelical United Brethren Church) for work mainly in the Manor Park neighborhood, where teen gangs began to appear in 1967. In winter 1968, Neighbors sponsored a Neighbors Knights football team in a citywide Recreation Department league for young men beyond high school age and funded the First Annual [Thanksgiving] Chitterling Bowl, where the Knights defeated the Black Panthers team at the Coolidge High School stadium.[42]

NI supported projects that assisted low-income neighbors living nearby, for example, backing applications for public funds to operate daycare centers at local elementary schools and near the junior high school and a request for variances to operate a preschool center at Takoma Baptist Church, where Joe Hairston was a trustee. In 1971, the group approved the construction of two rent-subsidized housing projects, one built by a local black Baptist church on Sixteenth Street, though warning against the "over-concentration" of subsidized housing that might threaten a black-majority area.[43] In 1973, parents of a Shepherd Park Elementary School student who had died of leukemia led nearby residents in establishing a foster home run by For Love of Children, a group created in 1965 to push for the closing of the custodial institution that Congress had paid to house the District's homeless and dependent children. And in 1975, Neighbors Inc. sought support for the National Children's Center School, housed near Coolidge High School, where mentally retarded young people could learn skills to hold a job and to live in group homes or halfway houses.[44]

Neighbors Inc. remained vigilant against the depredations city governments often overlooked in neighborhoods classified as nonwhite. By 1970, the group was aiding tenants in Brightwood's many low-rise apartment buildings who were fighting landlords over adequate maintenance of the aging units. Helping somewhat poorer neighbors would, in this instance, protect the area's housing stock by alerting landlords they could not charge high rents without caring for the area's safety and appearance. In 1972, Neighbors was called on to help pressure the city to maintain the neighborhood infrastructure in Manor Park. The congressionally dominated city government had required homeowners to pay for repairs to water pipes that connected individual homes to the city-maintained central pipes that ran down the middle of residential streets. When the connector pipe to her Fifth Street house broke, Loretta Hanes argued that it was unfair for a homeowner to have to pay for breaks caused by heavy bus and car traffic over which she had no control; she phoned her friend Maija Hay for help. Neighbors Inc. investigated who was paying for line breaks and discovered that the resident repair policy hit poorest neighborhoods the hardest. Neighbors advocated for public responsibility and a "small increase" in every homeowner's water bill to create a fund, like an insurer's risk pool, to aid homeowners hit "unexpectedly with very large bills."[45] Ultimately the first elected city government, which took office in January 1975, passed legislation holding homeowners responsible only for breaks within their property lines and gave some compensation to families who had been forced to pay repair bills in previous years.[46]

Zoning fights to protect adequate parking and to regulate liquor stores and other property uses that diminished the visual order and safety of a middle-class residential area replaced blockbusting fights. NI's Neighborhood Services committee opposed allowing a local bank to store repossessed cars on a vacant lot and fought against various proposals after 1968 to build high-density, high-rise apartment buildings near the Silver Spring, Maryland, boundary and its new subway station. Manor Park and Brightwood regularly asked for help to fight off the incursions of all-day commuter parking on their blocks and an irresponsible business owner's proposal to sell liquor at his "five and dime" store. NI hectored city agencies to ensure adequate trash collection and the pickup of stray dogs.[47]

As a majority black area, Neighbors continued to attract the attention of planners seeking to locate transportation facilities to assist suburban commuters. By the early 1970s, planners had substituted a regional subway plan for the freeways that had earlier threatened the Neighbors area. Neighbors Inc. supported the principle of public transportation and the convenience of a station stop in Takoma Park, but not the five-hundred-car parking lot proposed to make Takoma a major access point for the downtown service; the neighborhood had worked out its position in hours of discussions at monthly open houses.

Apparently under the impression that the opposition came largely from the local black population, one of the subway's developers asked Maija Hay to use her large Takoma house for a public presentation. He asked, she remembers, if I "could call some of the neighbors together," because whenever the Planning Commission announced a meeting, he said, the people who came were " 'always a bunch of radicals.' And I said, 'By all means.' "

> So I called everybody, and I probably had fifty people, and it looked very middle class. It didn't look at all radical. [But one resident], rock-solid, looks like a conservative, started talking and told him exactly what the neighborhood thought of the people from the suburbs driving in, polluting our streets, creating traffic jams, tear[ing] down housing from the tax base, just so the Metro would have a cheap parking lot. After one speaker after another, he said, "Well, I get the gist of it. This is a no go."

A polite hostess to the end, Maija replied, "I'm sorry, I tried my best," and she savors the memory of middle-class politeness defying bureaucratic expectations that white residents would side with white officialdom.

In 1971, Maija's husband, Ray, organized a Neighbors Inc. offshoot, Plan Takoma, which began a five-year struggle to protect Takoma's low-density, mixed-income housing from the harmful effects of subway construction. Zoning battles always held the potential to move beyond community self-regulation to exclusionary protectiveness. In Neighbors Inc.'s most expensive and high-profile zoning case, some prestigious members along Sixteenth Street, led by Patricia Roberts Harris, soon to be Housing and Urban Development secretary, used Neighbors to face off against a pair of researchers who had bought the defunct Marjorie Webster Junior College campus and sought to use it for drug therapy and counseling programs. For almost two years, and especially intensely in 1972, the fight occupied much of NI's organizational planning and energies, even as many began to complain that the case was taking attention away from other necessary work. The school's new owners charged NI with racism in opposing the shift from a "college formerly for upper class white girls [to one for] men, blacks and some poor students, like most other junior colleges." Joe Hairston, speaking for the Neighbors Inc. board, pointed out that "racially mixed communities are very subject to zoning changes" that harm an area and reduce property values. In this instance, the NI board argued, the for-profit school could succeed only by taking federal funds to operate a drug-training center for former addicts; the issue was not race, but bringing drug users into the neighborhood.[48] NI ended up paying out thousands of dollars to an elite law firm to represent it in a case important mainly to its wealthier members, white and black, in upper Shepherd Park. The result was that many residents withdrew, at least temporarily, from Neighbors Inc.

## Holding on in Urban Public Schools

As Neighbors Inc. devolved into a property protection group, albeit one with an interracial social conscience, a few families continued to live out the dream of a fully functioning neighborhood, which included high-quality public schools. This group's resourceful, energetic defense of this central middle-class institution provides a picture of what might have been had NI had the political backing and outside resources to remake the District schools.

Some middle-class black families did not have the money or the desire to abandon the good public schools they had expected to find in NI. Jenice View's parents bought their Takoma home in 1969 in what they considered a "racially integrated community trying to do good things [and] with solid housing stock."[49] Her father had moved back to the District to work in the laboratories at Walter Reed, while her mother did clinical work for the Department of Welfare. They first had a house in an anomalous, histori-cally black cul-de-sac west of the park near the Civil War–era Fort Reno. In the months after the 1968 violence following Martin Luther King Jr.'s as-sassination, however, the Views became fearful of the drug sales that were beginning to take place around the affluent, predominantly white schools their children would attend west of the park and looked for housing in the less elite and better-organized Takoma, D.C. They became friends with their neighbors, the Christianos and the Schaffts, and Jenice's father and Conrad Christiano jointly led the local, predominantly black Boy Scout troop. Jenice, who would graduate from Takoma Elementary School in 1969, babysat for the Christiano and Schafft children and became friends with Peachy Murray's son in her school class.

The Views and a few other middle-class Neighbors Inc. families, a list of names invoked as admirable and a bit eccentric if they were white, kept their children in the public schools through the late 1970s. These white parents learned to distinguish the discouragement of low-income black children from the ambitions of middle-class black children. They recognized the effects of class but also came to appreciate that being a middle-class black person was a heritage and challenge different from having middle-class white options.

Marianne Meijer was proud of the resourcefulness of her two older children, who stayed at Coolidge until Dan graduated in 1971. Adamantly unwilling to have her children in segregated schools, as Jewish children had been segregated during World War II, Marianne expected her children to cope with being the white faces that might be visibly middle class and liable to shakedowns from poorer kids. The oldest, Miriam, hid her money—not in her shoe, as her mother guessed, but in her books, where the other kids wouldn't think to look. The next in line, Dan, simply didn't carry money. He wore old clothes and never had any cash, and all the bullies gave up expecting to get anything off him.

Dan Meijer found that middle-class resources existed in the D.C. school system and that the system's slightly chaotic operation suited his nonacademic temperament.[50] In the final two years of high school, Dan could plan his own schedule, staying out of school many hours to repair old televisions and radios and stereo sets—"start his business," as he describes this preparation for the electronic repair company he founded. In senior year, he spent every afternoon at a course taught on the D.C. public school system's brand-new computer at the old Armstrong Adult Education High School. Busing over, Dan found only black students from Eastern and Cardozo, and the black teacher "told me not to come because I'd be the only white, and he didn't think it would work out. That made me even more determined because my parents paid the same taxes as everybody in the city," he remembers, so "I wasn't going to be excluded."

As the academic side of black power emerged, Coolidge students followed the model of Howard University undergraduates and demonstrated for new courses on black history, black writers, and Swahili language, preparation for serious study of Africa. Dan Meijer found the new discussions freeing. When he presented a World War II assignment about his Jewish mother's escape from German-occupied Paris into the safety of Switzerland, the young man who had started the campus's Black Student Union turned to him and said, "I didn't know that other people were discriminated against." Dan felt appreciated and able to reciprocate with interest in black history and in Africa. Marianne Meijer pulled her children out of Coolidge only after the school dropped the algebra courses necessary for college entrance. She petitioned successfully to send her two younger children to Woodrow Wilson High (west of the park) for the requisite math courses.

White parents continued to enroll children at Paul Junior High, searching for talented teachers and bargaining with the principal. They found talented black teachers at Paul who confirmed their beliefs in the merits of an interracial system. Marianne Meijer remembers "one teacher at Paul was extraordinary, a math teacher, a black, middle-aged woman— if you saw her, you would think she was just a housewife. And that woman was such a fantastic math teacher, the kids fought to be in her class. I once said to the kids, 'How come she never has discipline problems?' And they said, 'Mom, they all want to be in her class, and if you don't behave she kicks you out.'" Janet Brown's slightly younger children also valued this math teacher, whom they called "Mrs. Algebra Brown" to distinguish her from a teacher of another subject, "Mrs. English Brown."

White, middle-class parents saw Mrs. Algebra Brown as a paragon of competence, middle-class discipline, and proof of the advantages of integration. She was also a dedicated black teacher unwilling to abandon the working-class black children who did not have parents helping them out. Janet Brown recalls that by the early 1970s, this extraordinary teacher had as many as forty-two students in her classroom. She managed the large group through learning collaboration. "She kept a box of problems, and advanced kids would work by themselves while she taught the others. And [then the advanced students] would correct and explain problems to the other kids." When Janet asked Mrs. Algebra Brown why she couldn't help other teachers improve their classrooms, the teacher pointed out that "if she made too much of her own ability, it would look to her colleagues as if she was 'putting it on.'" The school system had no way to reward and recognize a first-rate teacher except by sending her to a safe white school, and Mrs. Brown wasn't leaving. But she managed only by isolating her classroom within the school. Janet describes how "she locked the door to keep the chaos in the hall out of her classroom—latecomers came in the window—and [when students tried to disrupt school by setting off] fire alarms, she wouldn't leave."

The school disruptions did not result from the race of the students, white parents learned. And the experience of black middle-class students affirmed this judgment. Jenice View's parents moved into Takoma in 1969, in time for her to finish sixth grade at the elementary school before going onto Paul Junior High in 1970. With the vestiges of tracking, she ended up in classes mainly with white kids. Black kids in the school taunted her,

"You talk white; you think you're white." In the close-knit neighborhood elementary school, teachers and parents had protected her, reprimanded the hostile kids, and mediated with their parents. But when she moved to Paul, "black and white [kids], who were all middle- and upper-middle-class kids, who were doing very well academically, were the target of the bullies."

The threats to middle-class children, whether white or black, persuaded Barbara Atkinson to get her children out of Coolidge High. "There was some violence," she said, "and one of my daughters got caught up in it, running away from the fight, and got her teeth messed up. And then my son had been approached to give up his lunch money and his spending money. And the first time it happened, I sort of ignored it, but it happened too many times."[51] Barbara had represented Neighbors Inc. at school budget hearings during the 1960s and had aggressively petitioned the central administration for good treatment for the first black students entering the previously all-white Coolidge High; when she asked, the system approved transfers across the park to Deal Junior High and Woodrow Wilson. The small group of white kids stood out visually, which made them even more vulnerable to the resentment of students for whom the schools promised no help and little attention. "If I were a black kid, and a poor student at Paul, I'd probably be a bully, too," Janet Brown remembers thinking.

Carefully monitoring their children's teacher, middle-class parents found that school administrators would yield to their requests in order to sustain some middle-class backing for the system. For NI parents, the primary urgency after 1971 was getting their high school children transferred from Coolidge across the park to Woodrow Wilson. "In those days," Janet remembers, "a principal could transfer kids if there were good reasons." Her elder daughter had taken three years of language at Paul, but "there was no German at Coolidge, and there was such good math at Paul that she was ready for an advanced math class," so the principal authorized a transfer to Wilson. After observing that her older daughter was so well prepared that she found Wilson courses easy, Janet asked the junior high principal to authorize her younger daughter and son to skip a year and transfer to Wilson "early." Faced with demands from Janet and other parents, he approved transfers for children from twelve families, many of them black. The middle-class children from the NI area advanced together.

Even though Paul Junior High kept a small number of middle-class students for a few more years, by the mid-1970s parents perceived that the principal and teachers had lost control of the school. Marilyn Christiano's oldest child, Tim, was attending Paul in 1974, and she got a chance to substitute teach in the spring. "And the day before, the assistant principal had been thrown out the window and taken to the hospital, and you had to lock your door because some guy was wandering around with a baseball bat. The kids in the class stole everything out of my purse." Christiano blamed the principal's poor leadership, but her decision was, "Quick, we've got to get Tim across the park." The next year he started at Deal. Ruth Jordan's older daughter, Rebecca, was scheduled to start junior high in 1975, and by then Paul was famous for its tough kids.

> I grew up in a very tough neighborhood in Brooklyn. It wasn't a racial thing, but it was very intimidating, and I really didn't want my kid's life to be filled with the terror of, "Am I going to be robbed of twenty cents? Am I going to have my bus fare?"

Ruth told the central administration that her daughter needed a campus closer to her after-school dance classes in Georgetown and got approved for Deal (and later Woodrow Wilson), where her younger daughter would follow a few years later.

By the early 1970s, the Neighbors students who remained in the public schools generally went across the park to Wilson High or downtown to an experimental high school, School without Walls, opened in 1971. A citywide magnet school that taught academic classes in the morning and placed students in internships in the afternoon, Walls offered a racially mixed school that appealed to intellectually motivated kids. Peachy and Robert Murray's two boys attended Walls, and the two Murray daughters went to Wilson. The Brown daughters alternated between Wilson and Walls, as did Jenice View, whose mother thought Walls too oddball to prepare Jenice for college admission.

These middle-class families strategized together to support good teachers, find academic opportunities, and maintain a middle-class stream within the public schools. The parents believe that their children thrived when they had attentive teachers and unconventional options. The younger of Janet Brown's daughters found a special program in photography, movie making and printing, federally funded vocational training, at the Lemuel Penn Center. Mira Brown and a friend from the neighborhood became bike riders and made round trips between Shepherd Park, the northwest D.C. campus of Wilson, and the northeast D.C. campus of Lemuel Penn, becoming adept at photo and print production and learning bicycle maintenance, too. Four years later, Ruth Jordan's daughter started at Walls. Her future changed when she interned at Walter Reed with a leader of the black PhDs group that had volunteered to mentor students in the D.C. public school system. He pushed Rebecca toward the sciences. Ruth Jordan remembers that the research director phoned to compliment her parenting. " 'I know,' he said, 'a lot of people don't think of girls in the sciences, but I really want to recognize that you've been encouraging Rebecca.' "

For white middle-class families, the integrated schools offered safety and care that did not entail segregating from the city or from dark-skinned people. The city gave young people the chance to be on their own and to see a variety of people. Paradoxically, many parents now recall, they judged the city schools to be safer at that moment than the suburban ones. In the drug-oriented 1970s, dealers preyed on well-off students and schools, and parents estimated that students at the urban schools didn't have enough money to attract the drug pushers. In the demanding but reasonably safe world these parents had carved out, their children felt reverse snobbism toward kids who went to private schools or to schools in the suburbs.

Staying in the public schools helped white children unlearn the implicit racial curriculum of de facto segregated suburban schools—that normal white people lived in enclaves to protect themselves from dangerous black people. Ruth Jordan wrote in 1977 about her daughter Rebecca that she learns "that her black classmates read books and discuss them, like to draw and play music, have pictures on their walls of grandmas and great-great-grandmas in high-necked dresses with a look of long ago, like ours in the family picture that hangs on our dining room wall."[52] Jordan was describing the families her children knew well, the Hairstons across the street and the Atkinsons, and also her daughter's middle-class public school classmates.

But by the late 1970s, white parents pulled children even from the public elementary schools in the NI region. In research for an anthropology dissertation, Gretchen Schafft observed Takoma Elementary School in 1974 and 1975. By the mid-1970s Takoma was a mixed-income, middle- and working-class neighborhood, 36 percent white, with an elementary school 95 percent black.[53] The elementary school fought for by NI parents in 1969 had been built without "egg crate" classrooms. As Gretchen now recalls, the plan was a mistake, designed by the whites, . . . who dominated everything. I don't think we ever listened to anybody who was black in the meetings. . . . It never occurred to me at the time, but I remember at the end one black woman got up and said, "You haven't heard anything we've said. And we have said that our kids will never learn if there are not walls in the classrooms."

By the time the school opened, the open spaces proved hard on all the children, but especially the white ones, as Gretchen began to see in her research. As a small and visible group, white youngsters stood out, and "the kids were all exposed to anybody who wanted to run by and feel their hair or call them 'honky,'" the disdainful term children were learning from black separatist politics. Expected to achieve academically, white children were often selected by teachers (the school had begun hiring black teachers only in the early 1970s) to tutor black children with less solid academic backgrounds. Even though many of the middle-class black pupils also achieved and were selected as classroom monitors, they could blend into the majority as white children could not.

The white children adapted to a more complicated, though still protective, world. Schafft described the neighborhood's pattern as one of social segregation, broken up by the monthly Neighbors Inc. parties, occasional connections in Boy Scouts or church groups, and the school Safety Patrol. The significant number of biracial children in the school, who functioned in both black and white social networks, acted as "brokers" to keep the white children from being ostracized and isolated. Friendly adults, typically black adults who had grown up in largely white environments and were at ease in both social networks, linked children in their charge. In this setting, the white children became bilingual, adopting what Schafft called Black English Vernacular as well as the Standard English dialect their parents spoke at home.

Schafft concluded that being a minority, regardless of one's race, was difficult, and that African American students being asked to integrate schools would need help, as the white kids did in Takoma. Popular media seized on her results as proving that integration wouldn't work, Schafft remembers. "Black kids were going to school and saying to my kids, 'Oh, your mother's the one that wrote that stuff and your mother says that we hate you,'" Schafft recalls. Worried that their sons would be harassed on account of the reports, the Schaffts moved just over the District line into Silver Spring. A few years later, Gretchen's older son asked to go back into the city for high school to " 'graduate with my friends from D.C.' So we paid tuition for him to go to the [interracial] D.C. School without Walls," she says bemusedly.

By the early 1980s, when the youngest Christiano finished up at Takoma Elementary, he was, Marilyn thinks, the only white child still in the school. She worried that his school experience "was not what anybody would think of as a normal situation. [But when I asked him,] he said, 'No, I don't think most kids see me as white.'" He was one of them and, as he told his mother, "If I have any problems, I got enough friends" that would stick up for him. The handful of white children in the schools had proved their membership in a category that was not white.

# Neighborliness

In 1969, Neighbors joined the network of National Neighbors, an association of thirty self-defined interracial neighborhoods.[54] Joe Hairston became the first National Neighbors president and, afterward, NI's delegate to the annual meetings. National Neighbors' diverse communities, formed in different historical contexts and with different constituencies, all challenged the popular narrative of the segregated suburbs as the model for U.S. life. Joe Hairston summarizes the shared ideal as "fair housing" as opposed to "open housing," the principle that people should be able to buy housing wherever they can afford. Instead, he says, "the Neighbors' concept is living your beliefs" in human equality and connection. It worked on the principle, Hairston says, that "you should love your neighbor as yourself. And you can't love that neighbor from afar. To really love that neighbor, you have to be close to them."

Neighbors Inc.'s white families chose the path of neighborliness in the belief that middle-class families could construct an interracial existence with shared values of good homes, good schools, and good families. When they faced two harsh realities—that other white middle-class areas would not open up housing to black families and would not open their schools to integrate urban children—then NI's families settled for living as a middle-class interracial community, but one always searching for white home buyers and regularly removing children from the neighborhood schools. Neighbors Inc. as an organization and a place could not counter the overwhelming market and political pressures of the white suburbs or counterbalance their mythic image of safety and exclusiveness.

NI's white families, however, did not leave. For some, the distinctive ethnic identity and affiliation as Conservative Jews let them accept the position of a racial minority, while their interpretation of a Jewish social ethic affirmed concern for all neighbors. For others, the benefits of urban living and dual-family jobs made any strains worthwhile. For many, living in accord with principles that rejected all human discrimination and, specifically, not living in suburbs that advanced racial separation were essential to their self-image. As they befriended black families and mixed-race families, they became even more committed to a whiteness that nurtured and protected all the residents of a democratic, integrated neighborhood.

# 5

# The Limits of
# White Anglo Benevolence

## *San Antonio, 1948–1968*

> Not so many Anglo Catholics hate their brothers of
> Mexican descent and those who do are not so virulent
> [as they were twenty-five years ago]. But there are many
> Anglo Catholics who are silent in the face of grinding
> poverty, atrocious health conditions, incredibly bad
> housing, malnutrition among children, general lack
> of education, and widespread starvation wages.
> —*Archbishop Robert Lucey, San Antonio, 1965*

In 1948, an unprecedented coalition of African American, Mexican American, and Anglo American liberals contested two local school elections in San Antonio, Texas. A group of youngish, New Deal–oriented men and women, inspired by New England–educated Unitarian minister Bill Lovely, formed the predominantly white Organized Voters League to pursue the more democratic governance the postwar years led them to expect. If they could mobilize enough white voters to work in coalition with the civil rights efforts coalescing around the NAACP and the League of United Latin American Citizens (LULAC), then the city's majority might elect a more active and responsive city government.

The daring effort succeeded. The first black candidate elected in Bexar County since Reconstruction, G. J. Sutton, a funeral home director on the black East Side, gained a seat on the community college board. He shared his triumph and voters with the first Mexican American victor of a citywide contest in the twentieth century, lawyer Gus Garcia, already well known for filing a federal suit against de facto school segregation of

Mexican Americans, who won a school board seat.[1] "Minorities Combine" warned the headline in the 4 April 1948 *San Antonio Light*, alerting its readers to the union of Mexican American and African American neighborhoods and ignoring the white participation in the "combine."[2] Journalists would not credit the idea that a white citizen could approve an alliance between "Negro" and "Mexican" that would disrupt the old order of white-dominant politics.

The city's two white-owned newspapers had predicted disastrous consequences if nonwhite groups gained government offices. Only white candidates would "keep our schools FREE FROM RACIAL STRIFE," admonished ads in the *San Antonio Express* on 2 and 3 April 1948, and "serve the welfare of the ENTIRE COMMUNITY." Mexican American and African American officials held "minority" views grounded in selfish concern for their "race," a partiality, the ads implied, that white politicians transcended, expressing a view common to the papers' readership that white people had no special status or interest that would prevent their rationally pursuing the equal welfare of all citizens.

In Texas, racial distinctions permeated political power and governance at the start of the civil rights era.[3] In San Antonio, whites had a near monopoly on public offices. Ever since white U.S. immigrants had won independence from Mexico and conservative Democrats had reestablished white authority during Reconstruction, white politicians and voters had directed the state's affairs. The white Democratic Party protected its power through occasional bargains with black and Mexican voters and through racial appeals to mobilize socially dominant white voters.

After the 1948 multiracial victory, elite power holders quickly reasserted their governing authority in San Antonio. Because the city had a bare white majority in 1950 (54 percent), almost equaled by Mexican Americans (39 percent) and African Americans (7 percent) combined, it took a few years to work out an effective mechanism for guaranteeing the return of a white-run government. First, San Antonio's white business owners created a city manager reform government that promised, as one historian of postwar Southwestern cities puts it, "efficiency and lower taxes, clear lines of authority and administration, and government by 'better men' rather than 'politicians.'" When the new charter did not result in the election of an acceptable mayor, a group headed by the president of the Chamber of Commerce formed the Good Government League (GGL) to select slates of candidates trustworthy because of their past business success or civic activities. The GGL selected the great majority of city office-holders from the mid-1950s to the mid-1970s—with the notable exception of Henry B. Gonzalez, elected to the San Antonio City Council by a briefly resurgent minority-white liberal coalition in 1953.[4]

During the next two decades, the interracial coalition promised by the white liberals of the Organized Voters League remained a distant hope. Only a few white citizens—those in a statewide labor-liberal coalition opposed to ongoing racial segregation, and a local Roman Catholic bishop and some of his young priests—concerned themselves with the interests of San Antonio's large Mexican American working class and its lack of political representation.

## Racializing Mexican Americans

The city that white business owners claimed for their own in the early 1950s was one of the larger and poorer in the United States. Although military installations mushroomed there during World War II, San Antonio functioned like a small town and its leadership prided itself on low taxes and minimal city services.[5] In response to interracial populism at the turn of the twentieth century, the landowning and business wealthy designed a political system to circumscribe the majority's use of power. Limiting the legitimate exercise of government power to policing, enforcing contracts, and building infrastructure for business development, the dominant racial group, conceived as white, could carry on life unconcerned with the possible demands of minorities, who had no cultural authority or institutional leverage to push for an enlarged idea of the society's obligations.[6] White authority justified political dominance through a political position that equated liberty with low taxes and a limited public sphere.

In the 1940s, two systems of racial differentiation and domination distinguished white Texans from their nonwhite coresidents: the Old South's black-white segregation system and the Southwest's Mexican-Anglo colonial economy. Legal segregation classified all residents into "Negro" or "White," required separate schools, enforced "Colored" balconies and "White" ground-floor seating in movie theaters, allowed department stores to prohibit black shoppers from trying on clothes before buying, authorized race-defined hiring and training for jobs, and, even after the Supreme Court downgraded them, overlooked racial covenants that barricaded white neighborhoods against black home seekers. But the GGL acted to dismantle official, legal segregation against African Americans, or at least not to implicate the city government in its defense. With the military a major local employer and with a relatively small African American population, San Antonio acted quickly to avoid giving offense to the newly desegregated military and to nonwhite geopolitical allies training at San Antonio bases for the international war against Communism. The city desegregated public schools, swimming pools, and golf courses and passed a resolution encouraging the voluntary desegregation of restaurants, hotels, movies, and other privately owned facilities. When the U.S. military received complaints from Asian trainees who were denied service at San Antonio restaurants, GGL backers, local religious leaders, and civic groups like the League of Women Voters led a private campaign to end restaurant segregation. Similarly, an interracial group of local college students held weekly stand-ins at the downtown Majestic Theatre to protest the Colored entrance and upper-balcony seating, and black ministers led marches to publicize the segregated service at local department stores. By the mid-1960s, much of the apparatus of black-white segregation had vanished, and San Antonio, despite continuing job discrimination and de facto housing and school segregation, claimed a reputation as a racially tolerant city that had suffered few civil rights demonstrations and no violent protests.

Even as the black-white system of legal discrimination eroded, the bare white majority maintained its authority over the near-majority Mexican American population. Since state laws did not require their racial classification and automatic segregation, people of Mexican ancestry were sorted by others and sorted themselves according to a different set of rules. Mexican Americans had been officially defined as a distinct racial category only once, in the 1930 Census, but well-to-do Mexican immigrants who had fled the 1910s revolutionary upheaval raised a huge outcry, the Mexican government protested, and the Census Bureau abandoned the "Mexican" designation. In law, a Mexican-ancestry person was white. In practice, as a common saying went, "Money whitens"; a Mexican-ancestry person could be white but usually was not.

Most "Texas whites regarded Mexicans as a 'mongrelized' race of Indian, African and Spanish ancestry," historian Neil Foley states.[7] Rich, bilingual Mexican Americans, some of whom had held land grants when the United States incorporated Texas in the 1840s or who had arrived with money after the revolutionary Mexican wars of the early twentieth century, carried white status and stressed their distinctiveness by naming themselves "Hispano" to emphasize their European pedigree. By contrast, whites became "Anglos" in the Southwest. Paradoxically, "Anglo," as a term meaning non-Mexican, was not limited to English-origin or even English-speaking individuals. Conflating the diverse cultural mix of central Texas, "Germans, Czechs, Wends, Irish, English, Polish, and French," whatever language they spoke at home, all became "Anglo." The usage "whitened" all European ethnics, in Matthew Frye Jacobson's terms.[8]

When a small Mexican American middle class emerged in San Antonio in the 1930s, it sought to negotiate more respect for Mexican Americans but often found itself forced to choose between assimilation to Anglo life or confinement within Mexican American limits. The dichotomous racial categories constrained a middle class hoping to retain integrity as an ethnic group while also enjoying the legal privileges that defined full citizenship for Anglo whites. Living in or near working-class neighborhoods on the West Side and South Side, speaking English as well as Spanish, worshiping in Catholic churches, and celebrating festivals like Mexican independence, *Diez y Seis,* and Day of the Dead, the Mexican American middle class founded its own civil rights organizations—LULAC in 1929 and the GI Forum for returning World War II veterans in 1946—to gain civil equality and funded lawsuits to challenge the de facto segregation of Mexican Americans, especially in schools. The emerging middle class named itself "Latin" instead of appealing to the European heritage implied in "Hispano," and historian Mario T. Garcia argues that this group "did not turn their backs on their Mexican-Indian (mestizo) character, [even though they] believed they qualified as 'whites.'"[9]

Money, language, and political participation constructed the white-Mexican racial distinction.[10] A white person had a well-paid supervisory or managerial job, lived in a nice clean neighborhood earned by his hard work, spoke English, and had no hindrance on voting or office seeking. A "Mexican"—rarely hyphenated by white Texans as even partly American—was identifiable by his poor, dirty, uneducated state due to natural laziness, improvidence, and the inability to speak English. The vivid material differences in income, education, residence, and language distinguished the majority of Mexicans from Anglos and created a pervasive contrast that whites could construe as the natural result of racial differences.

Political decisions about public services created many of the material conditions that separated the Anglo from the Mexican. In the postwar era, wealthy Anglos lived comfortably in exclusive areas on the city's North Side with paved streets and well-constructed water and sewer service. In the large houses and elegant blocks, a low-wage, dark-skinned workforce cooked and cleaned, clipped the lawns, and cared for the children, who attended well-financed public schools in exclusive school districts. Mexican Americans inhabited modest homes to the south and, especially, west of downtown, where muddy streets, absence of sewer connections and piped water, and lack of storm sewers and flood controls exposed residents to disease and filth that made "the West Side" synonymous with "poor" and "backward."

The existence of the impoverished, unhealthy West Side marred the picture of progressive good government the city government wanted to project, and some of the most shameful West Side conditions aroused Anglo women to civic action on behalf of the poor.[11] In tandem with the Chamber of Commerce, from which the GGL leadership would emerge a few years later, the middle-class white League of Women Voters (LWV) chapter focused on public health, voter education, and civic improvement. Perhaps inspired by a 1946 West Side tuberculosis outbreak that received national attention, well-educated North Side LWV members undertook an investigation of West Side sanitation.

Acting as social scientists, dozens of the League's members left their well-ordered houses and impeccable neighborhoods to walk door-to-door along unpaved streets in the city's Mexican American ghetto to count toilets and survey plumbing. Fay Sinkin, who made the project a centerpiece of her late 1940s League presidency, remembers the shock and also the new sense of responsibility:

> We went out to count pit privies. Do you know what they are? A pit privy is a hole in the ground. Instead of having bathrooms, that's what they had, and the people were living in corrals. Now they're usually for horses, but there were people living in corrals [long rows of single rooms, like horse stalls, built around a shared central area]. And each family was paying eighteen dollars a month, and they only had pit privies for bathrooms and no running water. They had to buy water from trucks that roamed the West Side. . . . And we counted—you won't believe it—twenty-five thousand privies.[12]

Sinkin, who had recently married a San Antonio businessman and moved from her hometown, New York City, had not imagined that rural sanitation conditions could exist in a city. As she remembers these shocking findings, Sinkin recollects that other San Antonio residents hadn't known about unpaved streets and open sewers in their city, either. "We all lived in enclaves. And went to school in enclaves." With their evidence meticulously collected, the League women went to the mayor, expecting him to recognize that their research demonstrated the need for appointing a city sanitary engineer. When the mayor responded that such a person would be "super*fluo*us," as Sinkin remembers the imperfect pronunciation of the ignorant pre-GGL mayor, the women organized to press an amendment to the city charter to remove the Health Department from the mayor's supervision. In 1950, the business community, through the Chamber of Commerce, called for more sewer hookups and urgency increased with a 1951 *Look* magazine exposé of West Side squalor. Only with GGL control in 1954, however, were the women's demands finally incorporated into a public policy that saw sanitation as a prudent public expense. Over the next decade, the Water Board replaced a majority of the West Side privies with residential water lines.[13] Street paving, however, the GGL did not see as a public necessity. The city paid only one-third of the cost for paving in poor residential areas. When Mexican American families couldn't afford the two-thirds private cost, the streets remained unpaved.[14] The Anglo governance pattern had been set: Men would lead the government and women would counter its worst human deprivations.

School districts tightly paralleled residential patterns in San Antonio, and sharp differences in schooling underlay racial assignments. Instead of the city-suburban pattern of school racial divisions common elsewhere, Texas's system was "an extraordinarily large number of school districts—over one thousand—[which] create[d] islands of property wealth sheltered from the demands of nearby concentrations of students."[15] San Antonio contained fourteen independent school districts divided roughly along lines that separated Anglos from Mexican Americans. Some districts, such as Edgewood, Harlandale, and San Antonio Independent School District (ISD), served mainly Mexican Americans, and they functioned with substantially fewer tax dollars for books and buildings than did predominantly Anglo districts such as Alamo Heights and Northeast ISD.[16] (Before 1954, nearly all African American students attended the "Colored" division of schools in the San Antonio Independent School District and with the end of de jure segregation in 1955 integrated into this majority Mexican American district.) Within the San Antonio ISD, schools divided between academic ones in Anglo neighborhoods and vocational ones in Mexican American and African American areas. Catholic high schools were not of much help to the Mexican American majority, because few Mexican American families were able to pay even the modest tuition.

Prudently paying for the basic services needed to avoid unfavorable publicity, the GGL acted on an implicit ideology that the public benefited only from low taxes and business development and that any problems of the poor were private concerns. Urban historian Amy Bridges sees this as the typical pattern in postwar reform-minded Southwestern cities, where "the relatively short wish list of the affluent and middle class edged aside the longer lists of other communities. Less comfortable citizens also wanted low-income housing, social services, and public hospitals. . . . Southwestern city governments left them to county government, private charity, or the market."[17] In San Antonio, specifically, policy analyst Heywood Sanders concludes that "the city's older neighborhoods were effectively ignored until the 1970s, [and] parks, libraries, and recreation facilities" were treated like "frills."[18]

The GGL focused on building business infrastructure, along with a reputation for efficient government. They sponsored bond issues to expand the airport and to build highways and sewer and water line connections for new housing tracts and related shopping complexes. They worked with the military to assure the continuation of payroll benefits from the five bases around the city. They supported low wages that would enable some small manufacturing plants to operate profitably. They set out to bring in a few prestige institutions and in the mid-1960s attracted a new branch of the University of Texas Medical Center and an offshoot of the University of Texas, the BA- and MA-granting University of Texas at San Antonio, both built on the far North Side well away from Mexican American areas. Finally, to seal San Antonio's reputation as a world-class city, the GGL and its business supporters raised funds for the 1968 HemisFair, a world's fair to celebrate the United States, Mexico, and Canada, and, coincidentally, to construct the downtown infrastructure for an expanded tourism industry.

Two systemic elements enabled the GGL's control. Contenders for city office, unlike those for county government offices, had to mount at-large campaigns, which advantaged Anglos, who voted in higher percentages than did African and Mexican Americans. Before 1966, the Texas poll tax and, from 1966 until 1971, an annual registration renewal requirement discouraged and substantially reduced participation of lower-income citizens. The condition for GGL victories was voting rates at lower than 12 percent of the eligible population during the 1950s and well under 20 percent through the 1960s and into the late 1970s. Throughout the 1960s, moreover,

whenever nonwhite citizens mounted campaigns to claim a share in decision making, the GGL moved swiftly to activate the racial fears of white
voters and to avoid any repeat of the 1948 interracial win.

The city's politics, society, and culture, divided relentlessly along racial lines, left few openings for egalitarian interracial efforts in the 1950s
and much of the 1960s. Persistent Anglo prosperity and Mexican American poverty encouraged benevolence as the most humane connection.
Paradoxically, benevolence sustained racialized inequalities; its failure
persuaded some white San Antonioans of the necessity of uncomfortable
political assertiveness, as we will see.

## Archbishop Robert Lucey and the
## Appeal to Anglo Benevolence

Although some remnants of 1948's interracial coalition persisted in statewide civil rights efforts by Texas's small group of white liberals, the most
prevalent Anglo association with San Antonio's Mexican American West
Side came through the Roman Catholic Church. Archbishop Robert Lucey,
who led the region's Roman Catholic faithful for almost thirty years, from
1941 to 1969, saw his role as bringing the needs of the poor to the attention
of the powerful. A fiery orator and powerful physical presence, Archbishop
Lucey used his grand house, chauffeured limousine, and elaborate vest-
ments to claim a place among municipal and national political leaders.

Archbishop Lucey had trained at a California seminary in the 1910s
and worked there and in New Mexico as a priest before being appointed
bishop of Amarillo in the midst of the Depression 1930s.[19] His career had
seen a remarkable change in Catholic doctrine as the Church responded
to a new urban industrial social reality in the 1890s and to the international economic and political crises of the 1930s. Lucey had imbibed Pope
Leo XIII's 1891 encyclical, *Rerum Novarum* (On the Condition of Labor),
the inaugural text of a Catholic social analysis of modernity, which Pope
Pius XI commemorated and strengthened in the 1931 *Quadragesimo Anno*
(On Reconstructing the Social Order). The earlier official statement of
Church policy argued that labor organizing was necessary to enable
workers to negotiate with powerful employers, and the later reiterated a
need for citizen associations in place of the statist responses—Fascism and
Communism—to the global Depression.[20] Lucey had supported Frank-

lin Delano Roosevelt's New Deal, especially its protections for labor organizing.

In San Antonio, Lucey found a parish divided between well-to-do Catholic Anglos who too often lacked charity and poor Catholic Mexican Americans and immigrant Mexicans who too often displayed passivity. The Church had offered some aid to its needier parishioners in the 1930s. An Italian-trained Jesuit, Fr. Carmelo Tranchese, had successfully fought for New Deal funds to build public housing for the city's poor—Mexican, white, and black—and had gained approval for a San Antonio Housing Authority. The West Side Apache-Alazan Courts—public housing complexes—were just being completed when Lucey arrived in the city, but this victory for public funding was not repeated during the 1940s and early 1950s. The brief attention to public housing was an aberration made possible only by the New Deal's strong external pressures and funds before the 1950s Anglo business ascendancy.[21]

Archbishop Lucey himself was immediately embroiled in the emergency of World War II, which triggered a new contest over the rights of workers, especially politically marginal nonwhite workers, in wartime. Southwest growers proposed to keep food prices at a reasonable cost by importing large numbers of Mexican farmworkers to replace Americans moving to military service or war production; in 1942 Congress authorized the bracero program to import Mexican labor. Lucey responded with an effort to counterbalance the growers' political dominance, lack of concern for workers, and use of the program to cut farm wages for Mexican American citizens: He persuaded his fellow clergy to form a Bishops Committee on the Spanish Speaking (BCSS), placating New Mexico Hispanos by not using the term "Mexican" and also encompassing another group of Spanish-speaking poor, Puerto Ricans coming to the mainland for war work.

At its founding meeting, Lucey and his handpicked conferees adopted resolutions grounded in Catholic principles of social obligation that they expected to reduce human separation and mistreatment of nonwhites. Their resolutions opposed segregation in schools, advocated union organization of Mexican American workers, proposed abolition of the poll taxes that discouraged Mexican Americans and African Americans from voting, and encouraged teachers and all seminarians to learn Spanish to communicate more effectively with Mexican American students and parishioners.[22] (Following his own recommendation, Lucey took intensive

Spanish summer courses in Mexico in the mid-1940s and from 1950 on required his San Antonio seminarians to become bilingual.)

The changes envisioned in the BCCS recommendations were necessary, Lucey implied, to teach Anglos to see Spanish-speaking persons as fellow humans; then Anglos might stop behaving as if they were the master race, almost like their German enemies. White citizens had lynched and kept African Americans in political and economic slavery, he reminded listeners in a conference speech titled "Are We Good Neighbors?" Although Anglos hadn't treated "our Mexican people" as harshly, they had used legal authority to silence and impoverish the "honest, industrious, and hard working" Mexican American and the unprotected bracero. Greedy employers fought union organization so that they were free to impose "miserable wages," passed laws to deny "public relief" to the poor and unemployed, and refused to hire truant officers who might keep Mexican American children in school. "If some Mexicans seem to be inferior," Lucey argued, "it is because we [Anglos] have made them so. God gave them rights and gifts like all the rest of us but we have degraded them."[23]

Even as Lucey articulated a vision of God-given human worth, he was not immune to the Southwestern image of Mexican Americans as temperamentally in need of guidance. In a 1944 speech, Lucey identified himself with the Anglo audience and appealed for sympathy for a mythic Latin people.

> We [Anglos] are a commercial and industrial people. We admire success and the building of great fortunes. The Mexican loves home life, children, music and laughter. By our tests he is sometimes impractical and even improvident. But he has much to contribute to our way of life. A generous injection of music and beauty into our hard-headed commercial culture would give it a measure of richness and fullness which it does not now possess. . . . Doubtless by giving justice to our Latin Americans we shall enrich ourselves.[24]

Lucey's sentimental image of Latino charm and Anglo efficiency may have been intended to enlist his audience's sympathy, but it also revealed an unself-conscious assumption that he and people like him would make the decisions about social change. Throughout the next twenty years, Lucey consistently spoke out for Catholic social justice positions, and the archdiocese's priests and nuns provided much of the attention and aid that San

Antonio's Mexican Americans received in the 1950s and 1960s. But the easy cultural appeals to Anglo charity and the urgent economic needs of Mexican American poor nevertheless conspired to produce acquiescence to policies that offered a bit of relief and left intact the racial norm: white people controlling public life.

## Controlling Poverty Program Funds

Anglo politicians in Texas systematically opposed social welfare expenditures. Poor people might receive charitable aid, but they were not entitled to government assistance. To mitigate what he regularly referred to as the "barbarism" of the Texas establishment, Lucey protested "the deplorable lack of social services in the state of Texas," as he put it in a 1948 meeting on catechism classes. In 1952, as San Antonio's leaders were rewriting the city charter, Lucey lobbied for adding a welfare clause that would authorize the use of city funds for public assistance programs, even if no such programs were on the near horizon.[25] He entered the fray again in 1959 to argue for the city's accepting federal public housing aid. In preparation for a citywide referendum, Lucey's office sent local priests a suggestion to preach on the Sunday preceding the vote, reminding parishioners that federal housing funds would replace slums with "durable and decent (not luxurious) housing."[26]

Archbishop Lucey's political connections and prestige brought Lyndon Johnson's War on Poverty to San Antonio in 1965. When the newly legislated Office of Economic Opportunity (OEO) announced a first round of federal grants, Lucey authorized Fr. John Yanta to draw up an application. Yanta's effort won federal funds for a new entity, the San Antonio Neighborhood Youth Organization (SANYO), which would keep poor kids in school by paying them the federal minimum wage of $1.25 an hour to tutor younger children and to run summer and after-school recreation programs, a project the BCSS had imagined twenty years earlier.

Local business leaders and the state's governor responded angrily to this federal "intrusion" into local politicians' and employers' control of the wage scale, an intervention that would raise incomes in predominantly Mexican American and African American households. Conservative Democratic governor John Connally immediately protested imposing the federal minimum wage on Texas; it might be all right for jobs in interstate commerce, but its extension to local jobs would disrupt the Texas economy. When Yanta announced that SANYO would certainly pay the federal $1.25 minimum wage, the San Antonio Independent School District's board president denounced the plan. Because, he warned, many fathers and mothers earned wages that were much lower, paying teens so much money would undermine parental authority as well as "upset the economy of this area." To avert these dangers, the archdiocese's weekly newspaper, the *Alamo Messenger,* reported on 5 March 1965, the school board would not allow the program to use any of its buildings.

The activist priests running the *Alamo Messenger* entered the debate to point out that of Texas's 3.7 million workers, 1.5 million earned less than $1.25 an hour and 500,000 earned less than $0.75 an hour. In per capita income, Texas ranked thirty-fifth nationally. Half of San Antonio's families met the federal standard of hard-core poverty, and the school district, Yanta recalled, was one of the prominent groups that paid wages as low as $0.80 or $0.90 cents an hour.[27] By late June, the state had given up the wage battle, and the school board had reconsidered and donated schools for SANYO use.[28]

If the archdiocese's victory over wages left the San Antonio power structure initially scrambling to reassert its rule, it quickly recovered. The GGL announced the formation of a local authority, the Economic Opportunity Development Council (EODC), which would henceforth dispense federal poverty funds. Washington's OEO headquarters initially withheld approval because Mayor Walter McAllister's plan envisioned a majority of EODC appointees coming from the mayor and the local business council. This plan violated the poverty program's requirement of the "maximum feasible participation of the residents of the areas and the members of the groups" eligible for assistance. Quickly adapting, Mayor McAllister started 1966 by winning OEO approval for a plan to elect one-third of the governing council from neighborhood groups of "the poor" and scheduled those elections for May. Archbishop Lucey entered the political fray to point out that the designated "neighborhood groups," such as the San Antonio Housing Authority, the public schools, the United Fund, and even Las Palmas Town Council, "a sort of Rotary Club of the West Side," were all instruments of the GGL and hardly representative of the families who needed aid.[29] Recalls Charles Grace, a county commissioner in 1965, the GGL idea was: "Hell, those people are dumb. They don't know what the hell they're doing. We're going to run the programs."[30] Given the GGL success in presenting itself as the competent guardian of public funds, Mayor McAllister probably felt confident that white voters would back him.

In 1966, however, the courts put an end to the techniques Texas had long used to discourage nonwhite voters. In early spring a federal court invalidated the state poll tax, which Texas had retained after the 1964 Supreme Court ruled poll taxes unconstitutional for federal voting. The state announced a twelve-day registration period in March when people disqualified by their past failure to pay the tax could get on the voter rolls. Eager to sign up voters who might help in the May EODC election, SANYO encouraged its teens to canvass their neighborhoods with registration forms, and these energetic young people recruited more than thirty-six thousand new voters in just under two weeks. On the presumption that such a large number of "Mexicans" could not possibly be eligible to vote, the city attorney challenged the lists and found that the SANYO volunteers had erroneously registered only sixty illegal aliens. The *Alamo Messenger* defended the effort as "a magnificent example of the poor— SANYO enrollees—helping their poor brothers to help themselves through the precious right of the ballot."[31] City officials excoriated Yanta for using the SANYO enrollees for a "political" purpose and then sent out official-looking letters that warned of harsh penalties for voter fraud, a tactic that scared off many of the first-time registrants.[32]

After discouraging Mexican American voters, the GGL mobilized Anglo voters to defeat the head county commissioner (titled the county judge), Charles Grace, who had exercised his oversight of county government to disallow the GGL's early efforts to pack the EODC board. Judge Grace was a San Antonio native of impeccable Anglo background: military service in World War II, law degree from St. Mary's University, and unremarkable work as a county judge since 1954. But he was part of the small band of New Deal–inspired liberals who supported civil rights in San Antonio, and his populist interpretation of OEO regulations made him a traitor to Anglo interests.

More than thirty years later, Grace still remembers the venom and fury with which the GGL turned his reelection campaign into a battle over racial dominance. Someone sent out anonymous but official-looking invitations to downtown business owners: "There is something happening in the city, and we need your presence here to help us solve this problem." One of Grace's friends went to the meeting and reported that Gerald McAllister, an Episcopal minister and son of the mayor, got up before the group and said, "Boys, we've got to do something. If we elect Charlie Grace, every Nigger and Mexican's going to take over this town. They're going to run us whites out." A slightly more subtle message was broadcast to white vot-

ers in a campaign of television ads and selectively mailed handbills showing images of the downtown skyline with a black hand hovering above
the city and a photograph of Grace seated next to Albert Peña, another
county commissioner and well-known Mexican American advocate. In
the television ads, a strong voice intoned: "The liberal element and militant
minorities of our city are making a grandstand play to take over Bexar
County. You cannot let this happen." The message, longtime Texas liberal
and writer Mary Beth Rogers concludes, was that Mexicans in government
were dangerous, and Charlie Grace would side with them in a fight for
racial control of city government.[33] On Election Day, North Side Anglo
voters turned out in large numbers and voted Charlie Grace off the county
commissioners court, the county-level equivalent of the city council.[34]

The Anglo business victory was a compelling illustration of the political reality that Daniel P. Moynihan pointed out in his study of the poverty program's ineffectualness. Congress had required poor people's participation in an effort to "ensure that persons excluded from the political
process in the South and elsewhere would nonetheless participate in the
*benefits* of the community action programs," instead of having most of
the money go to the friends and followers of local politicos, as had happened in New Deal programs. "It was taken as a matter beneath notice,"
Moynihan continued, "that such programs would be dominated by the local political structure."[35] Archbishop Lucey might have hoped to shift some
political authority to the Mexican American neighborhoods, but the GGL,
like local elites across the country, retained control over the new monies.

The GGL had proved its political power and proceeded to assert control
over the local OEO. SANYO continued to win grants from Washington,
but SANYO and Yanta ceased to challenge the city's Anglo authorities. By
1967, Yanta conceded that SANYO had aided the 1965 voter registration
campaign only because "it was a special emergency. It's a different situation now."[36] Yanta had hoped to develop leaders "among the people of our
impoverished neighborhoods," but he had to beg Lucey for refreshments
to serve the SANYO neighborhood councils, since federal funds couldn't
be used for this basic element of community organizing. The poverty program was thoroughly domesticated—providing desperately needed funds
to improve family income, education, and literacy in the poorest areas of
the city—and firmly under the control of the Anglo business elite. By 1970,
the federal program reduced funding and backed away from any pretense
of organizing the poor, the SANYO neighborhood centers and their allied organizations folded into seven pilot corporations, and emphasis on

business development displaced the early focus on education, income enhancement, and citizen action. Anglo direction of poverty funds sustained the racial assignments of competent benefactor and Mexican American petitioner.

## Striking Mexican American Farmworkers

Anglos also had a vested interest in a low-wage agricultural workforce. South Texas growers counted on a docile workforce, aided since the late 1940s by the bracero agreement between the U.S. and Mexican governments that authorized U.S. growers to hire Mexican laborers. The program had begun in 1942 to let Mexican workers fill in for Americans going into military service and war-related work, including high numbers of Mexican Americans called up by South Texas's Anglo-run draft boards.[37] But initially the Mexican government had not allowed its citizens to work in Texas because of the state's systematic segregation of Mexican Americans and Mexicans and its generally poor treatment of farmworkers, housed in shanties without running water or sanitation and kept in line by police authorities, including the Texas Rangers. After Texas worked out an arrangement to monitor the treatment of workers whom Texas growers had continued to bring across the border illegally, in 1949 the Mexican government allowed bracero workers in Texas.[38] The bracero (literally, "arms") program continued through and past the Korean War. Justified as necessary to keep food prices low in the high-consumption postwar economy, the program allowed growers to hire Mexican workers for as little as thirty or forty cents an hour. When the program finally terminated in 1964, growers pushed the secretary of labor to certify regional "labor shortages" so that they could continue to import Mexican workers.

Archbishop Lucey assigned Fr. John Wagner as the public advocate for farmworkers when he appointed Wagner chief of staff for the Bishops Committee on the Spanish Speaking in 1958.[39] Wagner came from a devout Southeast Texas Czech farm family (with a Germanized name) that lived on the margin of Anglo whiteness. "We spoke Bohemian at home and Spanish with the neighbors," Wagner remembers, "and I learned English at school," where he was classified "white" in Texas's triracial system. Wagner learned Christian caring from his family, who took responsibility for their Mexican American neighbors. "My dad was their doctor, their sheriff, their priest, and everything. . . . I never heard my dad say no. . . .

He'd have big crops, and somebody would break in or steal most of these crops [and he'd say,] 'Well, God gave it to me, what the heck.'" Like his father, Wagner expressed sympathy for Mexican American poor and wrote a column, Breakthrough, in the *Alamo Messenger* "because I was looking for a [white, middle-class] breakthrough to some appreciation and acceptance of the Hispanic people," as he puts it.

When the end of the bracero program made it possible for U.S. farmworkers to begin to control the labor supply, the Church supported labor organizing. Cesar Chavez and the recently created National Farm Workers Association (NFWA, which became the United Farm Workers, UFW, in 1967) began to organize California grape pickers in 1965. The union combined workers' wage demands and civil rights claims for the Mexican Americans who predominated in the fields.[40] Faced with staunch resistance from the growers, farmworkers set off in a mass march from Delano to the state capitol in Sacramento in early spring 1966. Evoking the Christian liturgical calendar, the marchers walked through the Lenten season preceding Christ's crucifixion and arrived in Sacramento for an Easter service of resurrection. A devout and determined people inspired by their Mexican ancestry, they marched under banners that pictured the Virgen de Guadalupe, Mexico's patron saint. They had sacrificed often enough, the marchers implied, and now they expected to win. Hundreds of union and civil rights supporters joined the march at various stages.

Fr. John Wagner flew to California to join the strikers' walk and to report the story to his San Antonio readers. Like many sympathizers, Wagner saw something new in the assertive organization of the farmworkers. The march, Wagner wrote in his column,

> has given to us the first real concrete example of Mexican American
> farmworkers uniting in an effort to do something for themselves.
> They have endeavored to do this by one of man's most basic
> rights, the right to form associations for the improvement of one's
> condition.[41]

At the Sacramento rally, middle-class supporters and an interracial array of laborers followed the Mexican American lead, Wagner wrote. "Everywhere the cries of 'viva' came from not only Mexican Americans, but also from the Negroes and Filipinos, and the clergy, Protestant and Catholic."[42] Acting on Catholic principles of building associations to equalize the power of employer and worker, the workers planned meetings, mobilized allies, and drew public attention to their view of the labor bargain

As his estimation of Mexican Americans rose, Wagner's opinion of dominant Anglos, including himself, fell. His own California march, Wagner felt, was a "pilgrimage of penance," a recognition that he and the Anglo-led church had lived at ease when their neighbors had not.[43] "What has been my role as a priest with the poor in the past?" Wagner asked. "How much of a victim have I become to the luxuries of 20th century living?"[44] Wagner recognized that he needed to work with Mexican American workers instead of speaking for them, even if such collaboration required moving out of his comfortable position as expert.

How Anglos would respond to a Mexican American farmworkers' union soon became a Texas issue. On 1 June 1966, melon pickers at La Casita Farms in Starr County in the Rio Grande Valley declared a strike and announced their intention to form a union allied with Chavez's NFWA. La Casita Farms, certified by the Department of Labor to hire Mexican workers because of a supposed local labor shortage, paid fifty to sixty cents an hour, well below the federal minimum wage in agriculture of a dollar an hour, for the stoop labor of picking melons. Mexican workers, facing even lower wages on their side of the river, took the jobs, and hundreds of Starr County families went on the road each year for better wages in Illinois, Michigan, Wisconsin, and Washington fields before returning to Texas in the winter. Those who didn't leave and worked at the wage scale set by the local Mexican economy lived in extreme distress: one-third earned less than $1,000 a year; 70 percent made less than the $3,000 poverty rate; 20 percent of the population was illiterate; and most residents didn't graduate from elementary school.[45] Starr County was one of the poorest in the United States.

Powerless to stop farm owners from hiring Mexican workers to undercut striking U.S. workers, the valley farmworkers turned their energies to winning a state minimum wage law that would require employers to pay an "American" wage of $1.25 an hour to any farm laborer in Texas. To gain public support, the group adopted the California tactic of a sympathy-winning long march. The strikers declared their independence by setting out on the Fourth of July to walk four hundred miles through the blistering summer heat from Rio Grande City to the state capitol in Austin. They planned to meet Governor John Connally on Labor Day to explain why, despite Connally's opposition to federal wage standards, the state needed an agricultural minimum wage.

Unlike California's unionists, who built on a Mexican American organizing tradition from the 1930s, Texas farmworkers came as petitioners
dependent on Anglo goodwill. En route to Austin, the marchers arrived in
San Antonio in August for a welcome from the archbishop. After Lucey led
a mass in Spanish  at San Fernando Cathedral downtown, he delivered a
homily that lamented the historical passivity of Mexican Americans, who
had "suffered in silence the injustices heaped upon them either by individuals or by a badly organized social order." Even as he praised the new
spirit of the marchers "to stand up and defend themselves," he was personally embarrassed to be associated with their timid goal.

> It is with a large measure of reluctance and regret that we endorse
> and approve your demand for an hourly wage of a dollar and
> twenty-five cents. No sane man would consider *that* a fair wage
> in these days when the high cost of living requires a much better
> return for your labor, and we join you in desiring that this
> inadequate wage be granted to you only because you have known
> the sorrow of cruel wages in the past and this objective of yours is a
> step in the right direction.

Lucey made it clear that "this explanation and this apology to the nation
are necessary *because I have approved* this brutal wage scale," which he
would not think adequate for himself.[46]

Lucey then intervened with Governor Connally as one powerful Anglo
to another, secretly advising him to meet these "human beings made to
the image and likeness of God."[47] Connally's sympathy was not aroused;
he announced that he would not change his plans to be out of the capital
on the holiday weekend, and then he set out to overawe the pilgrims. Driving from Austin in his air-conditioned Lincoln Continental to intercept
the marchers, Connally lectured the strikers that marches resulted in "riot
and bloodshed." They should return home and trust the governor, who had
already "attempted to do everything that we know how to do," including
Head Start programs, schools for migrant workers, and poverty funds applied to adult education.[48] The governor then drove off for a country weekend, leaving the tired and sweaty marchers unimpressed and resolute.

When the marchers finally arrived in Austin, they transformed the
public space of the capital—"more members of these minorities [con-
gregated in] downtown than one native of the city has ever seen there at

one time before," marveled a writer for the liberal *Texas Observer*. But it quickly became clear that the workers would simply serve as a backdrop for Anglo liberal/labor men to rebut Connally and display their goodwill. Texas AFL-CIO leader, Hank Brown, advocated a minimum wage, and strike leader Eugene Nelson listed the demands of farmworkers. Ralph Yarborough, whose 1957 U.S. Senate election had marked a brief victory of Texas white liberal Democrats over the conservatives who ran the state party, lauded the marchers as "the heroes of Texas" whose march began "an epoch in farm life and the lifting of people from poverty in this great state." As one Anglo supporter said that day, he came to march "just to add another body to the Texans who are showing that they are willing to add themselves to somebody else's cause."[49] Better wages were a "cause" for Anglos, not a need.

Though Mexican American farmworkers occasioned the event, they were not center stage. Henry B. Gonzalez, the middle-class Mexican American who had won a San Antonio City Council seat, then moved to the state legislature and finally, in 1961, to the U.S. House of Representatives as an advocate of nondiscrimination, counseled the workers to stand up and claim their citizenship. Cesar Chavez briefly addressed the group with greetings from the California farmworkers, and the Catholic priest and Baptist minister who led the march recounted the horrible need in the valley. No farmworker spoke.

One way to claim citizenship might have been a biracial workers' coalition. Forty black farmworkers had marched in solidarity from Southeast Texas, and the day had concluded with the crowd's singing the civil rights anthem, *We Shall Overcome*. Even though LULAC and GI Forum participated in the march, middle-class Mexican Americans did not want their cause equated with African American tactics. A few years later, a Dallas-based organizer for the AFL-CIO, Pancho Medrano, remembered that the Mexican American middle class wanted " 'no demanding or picketing or marching. We are above that.' Especially the LULACs; they say, 'we have more pride or education than that. You leave this to the Negroes.' "[50] The Mexican American middle class was uncomfortable with behavior associated with people unable to claim social and political power.

Although Archbishop Lucey and his activist priests argued that, as Wagner put it in his *Alamo Messenger* column on 9 April 1965, "the Popes for years have made it very clear that everyone who works has a right to a living wage," the legislature voted down a state minimum wage. By the fall of 1967, the valley farmworkers' strike petered out as growers, faced with a court-ordered cut in work permits for Mexican pickers, raised wages slightly. Workers who had spent a year without employment, been jailed for small violations by Texas Rangers, and been blacklisted from jobs by growers came back into the fields.[51]

At least one of Lucey's staff placed the blame not on a failure to organize Mexican Americans, but on insufficient moral training of the Anglo clergy: "Many of our priests lack an understanding of, and an empathy for these causes of justice" and need to be reassigned from "silk stocking areas" to poor parishes on the South West and West Sides.[52] For the moment, the Catholic Anglo faithful heard only the message of charity, ignored the words about justice, and, like the rest of Texas's white middle class, continued to enjoy cheap food.

## Labor Union Organizing

When the third challenge of the civil rights era to the Anglos' monopoly of city government and their assumption of a quiescent labor force came along—labor union organizing of San Antonio's factory workers— once again the archdiocese offered the only significant Anglo support for changing the racialized economic order.

As a Roman Catholic New Dealer, Archbishop Lucey had supported the 1935 National Labor Relations Act (NLRA) that created a National Labor Relations Board (NLRB) to monitor employer antiunion practices and to protect organizing unions who were promoting workers' interests against the enormous power of large employers. He applauded the opening the federal legislation gave for the new Congress of Industrial Organizations (CIO) to organize unskilled workers previously ignored by the craft-based American Federation of Labor (AFL). When he arrived in Texas, Lucey expected unions to be able to raise wages and improve working conditions there as they were doing in much of the nation (mostly outside the South).

After substantial labor gains during the massive industrial production period of World War II, when many nonwhite workers, aided by the federal Fair Employment Practices Commission, escaped the unskilled, low-wage jobs that had been cited to validate their inferior racial status, the business backlash was harsh. Business leaders attacked the previous decade's labor gains and gained congressional passage of the 1947 Taft-Hartley Act that constrained union actions and allowed states to pass right-to-work legislation. In Texas, employers won a law that prohibited the union shop (where new hires automatically joined if the union already had a bargaining unit in a plant) and protected workers who crossed the picket lines of strikers. The economic and political powers in the state were vehemently antiunion and regularly denounced unions as corrupt, hostile to American individualism, and loyal to the kind of collective action that nurtured Communism (despite unions' purging Communist members in the postwar period).[53]

San Antonio lacked the big industries like aerospace, oil refining and petrochemicals, and machine tool plants, where unions had won collective bargaining contracts in Houston and Dallas; in San Antonio, only the building trades successfully unionized and produced traditional, Anglo-exclusive craft unions. Mexican Americans made up the majority of the poorly educated, low-wage labor force. Just before and after World War II, they worked in food-processing industries like pecan shelling, extractive industries like limestone quarrying for cement, and small industries including garment making, cigar rolling, and metal fabrication and window sash manufacturing. The best many working-class people could hope for was work on the military bases that ringed the city and that expanded during World War II and the Cold War military buildup. Even here, the federal requirement to pay no more than the "prevailing local wage" kept the demands of unionized federal workers at the ceiling set by the low wages paid the local Mexican American majority. Archbishop Lucey summed up the situation in the late 1950s: "The U.S. mint in Denver sends its nickels to San Antonio and its dimes to Dallas because we are not organized down here."[54]

In the antiunion climate of the 1950s, the archbishop regularly aligned the Church with labor unions. In speeches to Catholic lay leaders, he often quoted Pope Leo XIII's *Rerum Novarum* to remind them that "inadequacy of his strength, learned from experience, impels and urges a man to enlist the help of others. . . . Such is the teaching of the Holy Scripture: 'It is better therefore that two should be together, than one, for they have the advantage of their society.' "[55] Lucey's rhetoric, buttressed by the Catholic Church's international stand against Communism, argued against the narrow-mindedness of the Texas business ethic. First, paying workers as little as possible created the conditions of social injustice, poverty, hunger, and illiteracy that provided a fertile ground for Communism. Second, the business dogma of low wages and maximum profits grew from the same barren materialism as Communist ideology, Lucey pointed out.

> Have justice and charity a place in business life? If you say "no," you fall into a Communist trap. Those who insist that "business is business" or that the "profit motive" rules all, have joined with Karl Marx in his assault on human freedom; . . . we *have* to do what we do because of inexorable economic forces. Are we really such slaves of competition, of money-hunger, or desire for gain and comfort?

The Catholic Church didn't expect businesspeople to give up profits, but it did require that employers accept routine negotiation with workers about how profits would be divided. Justice required that worker organization balance business power, because "only by uniting for bargaining purposes shall [wage earners] obtain their just share of production. Only through strong unions shall they possess any security in their jobs. And with so many large enterprises, only the democratic union can give most wage earners a voice in the decisions which determine their work lives."[56]

Convinced by the mid-1950s that antiunionism and low wages doomed San Antonio's workers, Archbishop Lucey dispatched Fr. Sherrill Smith to take an economics MA at the Catholic University of America in preparation for leading an archdiocesan Department of Social Action. A Northwestern University business graduate and ex-navy pilot who had joined the priesthood after military service, Smith combined religious devotion and daring. He returned to San Antonio in 1957 just at the moment that the Texas AF of L merged with the Texas CIO to present a united labor front, and he became a constant presence at union meetings and on picket lines. A tall, lean man in black garb and white clerical collar, Smith visibly embodied the Church's backing for workers trying to form unions.

In the late 1950s, for the first time since the legendary pecan shellers' strikes of the 1930s, the working poor got some AFL-CIO backing to organize unions in the small industries that employed about 15 percent of all San Antonio workers. A much higher percentage of Mexican Americans, who were predominantly if sometimes nominally Catholic, worked in these plants. One of the few unions willing to take on organizing in low-wage industries was the Industrial Union of Electrical Workers (IUE), which had some assurances of help from Henry B. Gonzalez, now a state representative and anxious to do something to ease the widespread poverty of the West Side. The IUE began to organize at Ed Friedrich's air conditioning plant.

For San Antonio, Friedrich had a relatively large employment roll of five hundred workers. An early manufacturer of commercial refrigerators and grocery display cases, by the 1950s it was building air conditioners for the postwar housing market. Friedrich divided its work assignments to fit the city's racial hierarchy. "The whites," Friedrich employee Ruth Harris remembers, "were a mixture of German and Polish. The owner of the company was German, [so] you went German and then Polish and then black, and the Latino was down at the very bottom. Sometimes it was vice-versa; the black was at the bottom."[57] Like every other plant in San Antonio, Ruth continues, Friedrich's "didn't have unions; they paid whatever they pleased. They gave you raises and told you to shut up and don't say anything so the guy next to you wouldn't say anything [and ask for a raise also]."

Ruth Harris got an opportunity to become more than a hard-working aggrieved wage earner when the AFL-CIO sent in an organizer. Daughter of an Anglo military man and a Mexican American mother, Ruth attended San Antonio schools and, like many of her Mexican American classmates, quit after ninth grade. In rapid order she married, had two children, left her husband, and found work at Friedrich, which hired a lot of Mexican American women in the departments that polished and trimmed, welded, and spray painted the various parts stamped out for home air conditioners. Energetic and responsible for her family income, Ruth felt anger at the owners' meanness. The aging founder of the firm symbolized their penny-pinching ways. "Old man Friedrich," Harris recalls, would

come and sit in a chair and, with a hammer, start pushing all the old nails out of boards, saving them in a tin can. This is the man, the owner of the factory, so tight and chintzy that he had to save the old rusty nails, to be reused again and recycled. And he didn't let somebody else do it. He did it himself. [The Friedrichs] had a big farm out here with the long-horned steers, and he's sitting there on a bench knocking nails out of boards, and it used to really aggravate us. Instead of making us feel bad, it aggravated us, because this old man was rich and didn't want to give us anything. He kept everybody at the lowest level he could.

Friedrich's attention to the materials at the plant and his inattention to the workers galled Ruth, and she went along to early union meetings. Although the NLRA offered legal protection to industrial workers, the Friedrich employees met secretly to avoid retaliation. Under NLRB rules, employers could not fire workers simply because they wanted a union. But, Paul Javior, Ruth Harris's coworker at Friedrich, explains:

> You don't want to give yourself away until you have a substantial number of supporters, because if the company is aware that someone's trying to organize a union, they just come up with some phony excuse and terminate [fire the worker]. You protect yourself with a button, because the employer will fire you and the first thing they'll do, they'll say, "Well [I was firing for bad performance;] I didn't know that person belonged to the union."[58]

A worker who went in wearing a button that declared support for the union had some protection against the usual employer intimidation of simply dismissing any worker brave enough to advocate a union.

Getting up the courage to wear buttons and risk losing a job was hard, and Ruth Harris recalls how the union organizer prepared pro-union workers to take the necessary time to persuade coworkers. He told them, Harris remembers, "I'm not selling you pie in the sky. You're gonna have to do this on your own. You're gonna have to work hard at it." The workers knew they could manage hard work, so if a union took hard work, they could produce. "We weren't afraid of work back then," Ruth affirms. In some sections of the Friedrich plant, Mexican American women predominated. Though they were hard workers, they were also proud and held themselves aloof to hide their limited English fluency. Because she spoke English and Spanish at home, Ruth had the language skills to become the spokeswoman for the women and even some of the Spanish-speaking men. "A lot of them couldn't speak English, were embarrassed to get up and ask a question, so I asked the questions, and as a result, I kept getting pushed forward."

Coming into the workforce after military service in Korea, Paul Javior refused to consider himself an Anglo when that meant identifying with the racialized privileges of the employer class. Like Wagner's family, Javior's had spoken Spanish with its Mexican American neighbors, and by the time Paul was in school in the 1940s, he contested his small town's de facto school segregation by playing on the Spanish-speaking side of the playground with the Mexican American kids. In the South Texas racial scheme, Javior chose an ethnic identity over a racial one. "My ancestors came from Silesia, Poland, so actually I'm a Slovak. I'm not a Anglo. I'm not a WASP, that's for sure. They're discriminatory, they're prejudiced in general; that's a bad statement, 'in general,' but I've had that experience in my lifetime." When he got the job at Friedrich, he was told to keep his head down and he would presumably move up the ladder to just below the Germans. Instead, he figured, "If I'm going to have to work in this place forty-three years I might as well do something about it to get decent pay and a decent retirement," which meant aligning himself with the plant's Mexican American and African American workers.

Almost all of the plant's workers ultimately joined the union. But they still had to break the longstanding pattern of protecting their job, however poorly it paid, and walk into the factory wearing union buttons. When the organizer asked the workers to go in with buttons, "everybody looked at each other, and nobody wanted to," Ruth recalls,

> so the women, we stood up and we said, ya, we'd go in there wearing union buttons. We were looking at the men, and they weren't doing anything, and we thought we had bigger balls than they did. We just were tired of being pushed around, and we just decided that this was it. So we went in wearing union buttons, and the men went with us.

Paul Javior, in contrast, remembers the men going in first. But whichever gender took the lead, every worker who marched in defied the prevailing image of docile Mexican American and African American workers.

After winning the contract, the union asked Ruth, a Mexican American woman, to be president, but she refused the position because she did not feel qualified yet. "I didn't want to be president. I didn't know what to do, but chief shop steward, I knew what to do. I knew how to argue with the supervisors and how to argue with the personnel director." She became the chief steward for the plant, went to union seminars, found helpful mentors and teachers on the NLRB staff, and learned labor law and bargaining procedures. And then she taught her coworkers to demand benefits that raised their long-term security and opportunity. "We knew nothing about health insurance. . . . Since that time it's been used over and over again, but at first they thought, 'Money's what I want.' . . . We were trying to show them that not everything was dollars and cents, as such, that insurance was dollars and cents when your kid got sick, that seniority was dollars and cents, and a job promotion." By the early 1960s Ruth Harris was a staff organizer for IUE.

Archbishop Lucey took union campaigns as occasions to remind Texas employers that they had no more legal rights or higher moral claims than their employees, and Smith stood with the workers as the archbishop's representative. In a time when public use of Spanish was still discouraged and Spanish speakers were marked as marginal people, the Church implicitly affirmed the legitimacy of Spanish in local organizing. Smith, who had followed Lucey's direction to become bilingual, counseled workers about Catholic labor doctrine. In 1962 he wrote to striking garment workers:

> The Catholic Church teaches her members that they have a right from God to join labor unions, and that to take part in honest union activity is a good thing. Such activity may be *necessary* to obtain justice in wages and working conditions. . . . If you're a Catholic (and you've listened to the sermons at Sunday Mass) you heard the priest talk about the workers' right to a living wage and the workers' right to join labor unions. . . . If you have any questions, I'll be happy to answer them at any time (in English or Spanish).

The reverse side printed the same message in Spanish, and Fr. Smith closed with a salute: "Que el Senor sea con Ustedes en sus Trabajos" (God be with you in your work).[59]

In 1964 Harris was trying to persuade workers at George C. Vaughn Lumber to sign union cards and to wear buttons into work, and Smith stood beside her as she passed out union handbills to the men going off shift. A Vaughn representative wrote to Lucey querying the Church's involvement in agitating workers, especially since the Vaughn shop treated its workers fairly. Lucey replied with a disquisition on Catholic labor doctrine. "Workers," he wrote, "have a natural right as well as a civil right to join a union of their own choosing . . . and this right is natural, that is to say, bestowed by God."[60] Lucey closed with his usual friendly signature, an invitation to accept the Church's view that employers must bargain amicably with workers.

Employers would fight, however, to keep the almost seigneurial power granted in the racialized class system. One of the major confrontations occurred at the factory of prominent business owner Marshall Steves, who had only recently been selected by his peers to head the building of HemisFair, the GGL's pinnacle project. A number of Mexican American workers in plants Paul Javior had successfully unionized asked him to help out their relatives working at the Steves Sash and Door plant. "[The IUE was] an electronic union," Javior remembers. "We wouldn't normally be organizing a wood mill, but we felt obligated to do something for these people. . . . The highest-paid employee in the bargaining unit, that had been there for thirty-two years, was making like a nickel more than minimum wage, [and the workers were] 99 percent Hispanic, 10 percent female. Not a single black." The IUE signed up workers and won election for a bargaining unit in 1965, but Steves refused to recognize the union. When negotiations broke down completely in the summer of 1966, just as the valley farmworkers were marching toward San Antonio, the Steves workers went out on strike and added to the feeling that a Mexican American revolt was underway. The workers picketed throughout the fall, Javior remembers, and one day the owner confronted him on the picket line and explained Anglo supremacy: "My family's worth $150 million. How much is your family worth?" Steves asked. Javior responded with a new message of the value of people working together: "Well, my family's got seven hundred thousand members in it." Javior laughingly recalls his reference to the nationwide membership of the IUE.

How could numbers be converted to power? After months of standoff, the union organized a Christmas demonstration to highlight the difference in values between the Mexican American workers fighting low wages and a wealthy local employer unwilling to bargain with them. The march began at the building site for HemisFair, near downtown. "Why [do] we gather at the HemisFair?" Paul Javior asked. "This group and their sympathizers gather here to let the community know the type of civic leaders we have in this community." Steves's intransigence and Scrooge-like lack of Christian generosity deprived workers of incomes that might let them join the holiday festivities and shop alongside other citizens. Strikers and their friends walked through a bustling downtown to Smith's church, which sat in the shadow of San Antonio's most prestigious department store, and celebrated a mass for fair wages.[61]

Steves workers won a contract in spring 1967 when the press revealed that the plant had surveillance cameras placed in company bathrooms to monitor workers on toilet breaks. Steves had overreached the public's accepted limits on employer control, and the company finally signed a contract.

In the summer of 1967, the threads of union organizing, Mexican American deprivation, and SANYO assertiveness came together when the city garbage workers, nearly all of them Mexican American men, went to the city council to demand pay raises. Led by Humberto Villalpando, who had learned leadership skills and neighborhood pride in one of the SANYO councils, the garbage workers almost unanimously called in sick to protest erratic work assignments that had them working only six hours on some days and ten hours, with no overtime, on others, and to demand the Anglo council reconsider its stance of no pay raises.[62] As garbage rotted in the July sun, the city manager announced mass firings, and workers besieged city council with signs reminding voters that "America is rich, but *we* are poor." Mayor McAllister tried to bully the workers. He ruled that staying away from work meant they had voluntarily quit their jobs. Each worker would have to reapply for his old job and trust the kindness of the city authorities to get it back. Finally, in a continuing skirmish, the council agreed to rehire strikers and to give a pay raise, but to take away the sick leave days the workers had accumulated before the strike. The victory of a $1.70 an hour wage for seasoned workers was seen as a Mexican American victory over Anglo leadership and not as a benefit for the entire city.[63] Lucey's call to Anglos to join with Mexican Americans to seek social justice was still largely unheeded.

## The Disappointment of Assimilation

The 1966 farmworkers march and the staunch Anglo animus against any improvements for Mexican American workers raised doubts among middle-class Mexican Americans who pursued whiteness as a strategy for gaining equality. The promise of interracial harmony through assimilation faded amidst battles over public responsibility for poverty and low wages. Cultural theorists Avery Gordon and Christopher Newfield argue that assimilation "encourages functional ranking of various cultures and ignores the way supposedly neutral institutions are pro-white."[64] One of the consequences of mid-1960s poverty program/labor battles was to make the prowhiteness of assimilation visible to some middle-class Mexican Americans.

Andy Hernandez remembers how, as a sociable and studious youngster, he attracted the attention of teachers who wanted to cull him from among his Mexican American classmates.[65] His father's job at Kelly Air

Force Base and his mother's work as a school board secretary lifted his family into "upper working class," he says. They were able to buy a nice home on the East Side in the 1950s as white families fled and left behind a marginal neighborhood of poor blacks, whites, and Mexicans. Andy stood out in the elementary school, and he learned quickly that Anglos would interpret his intelligence as elevating him from other Mexicans.

> I remember getting into a fight and going to the principal's office, because I was always a pretty good student in school. I remember her saying, "I'm very shocked you got into a fight. You're not like the rest of those Mexicans." And that for me was a kind of an awakening, because I said, "No, I am them." They used to separate you out. If you succeeded then it wasn't that you succeeded because you were Mexican American; they said you were *not* Mexican American that you succeeded. "You're like us [Anglos]."

Despite Andy's refusal to identify as Anglo, his parents knew the neighborhood high school couldn't prepare him for the college education that would move him fully into middle-class status. In the mid-1960s they bought a small house in a predominantly Anglo neighborhood near Jefferson High School, the only San Antonio ISD high school with a college preparatory program. At Jefferson, Andy and his outcast Mexican American and Jewish classmates ridiculed the white kids' exclusive sororities and fraternities and started a club that required a "rejection letter from one of the other ones" to become a member.

In the mid-1960s, the farmworker march took the fun out of playing with racial identity. "The march brings in[to politics] a lot of the working class, middle class who were not struggling [economically] in the way the farmworkers are, for whom the farmworker movement symbolized the struggle of all Mexican Americans for their respect and their dignity in their work," Andy recalls. He began to move to more conscious action in opposition to Anglo political exclusion of Mexican American interests.

Some Mexican American adults—what historian Mario T. Garcia labels the ethnic-oriented "Mexican American generation"—also felt disillusioned.[66] Slighting the farmworkers' march, Anglo politicians revealed their unconcern for Mexican American interests. Raised by a widowed mother in the West Side *corrales*, Joe Bernal and his brothers had earned high school degrees at the predominantly Mexican American Lanier High School and played on its renowned basketball teams. Bernal served in

World War II and used his GI benefits to earn a Trinity University degree in education. By 1966 Bernal's was a success story; he was so respected as principal, youth coach, and Boy Scout leader that the GGL had tapped him as its candidate for the state senate in 1964. When the valley farmworkers sought better wages and treatment, Bernal thought he had attained a position where he could help. Joining with newly elected Barbara Jordan, the first African American woman in the Texas legislature, Bernal optimistically introduced a state minimum wage bill in 1967, only to see it sent to subcommittee for review and sidelined.[67]

Bernal's worldview changed when he made a fact-finding trip to the Rio Grande valley to investigate complaints that the Texas Rangers were harassing farmworker pickets and strike sympathizers. The Rangers' famous (or notorious) leader, Captain A. Y. Allee, had promised to enforce order, which he interpreted meant arresting local workers, labor union officials, and strike supporters. Bernal, an athletic 5'7", confronted the towering 6'4" Allee, whose cowboy boots, Stetson hat, and holstered pistol carried the historic authority of the state's public protectors. Allee accused Bernal of butting into legitimate law enforcement and poked him in the shoulder to make the point. Bernal told the Ranger "not to touch" him and, after a fearful night awaiting retaliation, flew back to Austin to report the intimidation. Bernal's image went from "affable, amiable representative," he recalls, to crusading "Chicano man."[68]

Reflecting on the vicious attacks on those trying to help poor workers, Bernal constructed a new life narrative at odds with his earlier assimilation success story. When Bernal went into military service, he had tested well and been accepted into a special army program to develop engineers. During the training at Texas Tech University, he learned that other young men arrived from high school with slide rules to solve difficult equations and with skills in trigonometry, sometimes calculus, courses his high school had not offered. "There weren't enough from the community to have prep courses for college, because the feeling in the community was, 'You go to school and you go to work,'" Bernal figured out, "because back then a high school diploma was as important as a BA or BS degree" for jobs. Working-class Mexican American parents didn't think that college was a realistic possibility for their children, and school authorities didn't require college prep math in any high school outside Anglo neighborhoods.

Even with a college degree, Bernal recalls realizing in the late 1960s, the informal racial tracking of the public schools limited his job opportunities. In the early 1950s, "you could look around the school district at that time and there were no blacks and no Hispanics." His former elementary school principal advised, " 'Well, Joe, what I really would like for you to do is maybe have another year [teaching out in a country school district] and then come back and perhaps we could hire you.' She would not hire me." Bernal trustingly followed her suggestion and taught students of Polish ancestry in a country school, then found a job in the Edgewood district, one of the poorest of the myriad San Antonio districts, and finally bypassed central administration to get hired at his old elementary school in the West Side barrio. In the early 1960s he applied to be promoted to principal, only to be asked by the San Antonio ISD personnel director, " 'Joe, are you Catholic?' I said yes. And then he said, 'Why don't you go and become a principal in one of the Catholic schools?' I said, 'I'm a product of the public schools, and I've been a public school teacher now for ten years, and I think I'm ready to be a principal.' 'Well, you ought to try one of those Catholic schools.' And that was my sendoff." The San Antonio ISD would not appoint a Mexican American principal.

Anglos continued to show no willingness to give up exclusive power. By 1968, middle-class Mexican Americans who had believed that joining white institutions was a path to acceptance and interracial power sharing were ready to try another tactic.

## The Limits of Benevolence

Archbishop Lucey's Catholic priests were scrutinizing the interracial approach of benevolence with similar doubts, especially as the beneficent archbishop made clear his own unwillingness to reduce hierarchical authority. Before his death in 1963, Pope John XXIII had convened the Second Vatican Council, which met between 1962 and 1965. The revolution of Vatican II was to articulate a vision of the Church as "the people of God," bound not by hierarchical chains of command but by shared faith and purpose. As one of the official delegates, Archbishop Lucey voted to approve the council report, which called on the powerful to share responsibility. "The joys and the hopes, the griefs and the anxieties of the men of this age, especially those who are poor or in any way afflicted, these too are the joys and hopes, the griefs and anxieties, of the followers of Christ, [and Church faithful are required] to give witness to the truth, to rescue and not to sit in judgment, to serve and not to be served."[69]

Archbishop Lucey was a poor candidate to accept any diminution of his accustomed prerogatives. The archdiocese marked 1966 with elaborate celebrations of the milestones of his powerful life—his seventy-fifth birthday, his silver jubilee as archbishop and golden jubilee as a priest. Lucey believed that he used his power prudently to instruct the rich and to aid the poor and that the archdiocese's priests were the agents of his intentions. He did not anticipate that his judgment might conflict with that of his priests.

But in 1967, Lucey found himself in conflicts much like those of the growers and employers he had once reprimanded. When workers approved union representation at the chancery office, the archdiocese's *Alamo Messenger* newspaper, and the main Catholic cemetery, Lucey dragged out negotiations. When Fr. Sherrill Smith confronted Marshall Steves and Steves protested the Catholic Church's incitement to worker organizing, Lucey removed the priest from his post as director of social action. When Smith and Fr. Bill Killian, editor of the *Alamo Messenger*, traveled to the valley in early 1967 to bring publicity to the foundering farmworker strike, Lucey reprimanded the priests. Many of the archdiocese's priests formed a senate in January 1967 to gather for discussions about their work; when the forum criticized the archbishop's reining in of Smith, Lucey reassigned outspoken priests to rural parishes away from San Antonio.

In the newly democratic Catholic context, Lucey had the stagnant air of an aging and unresponsive patriarch. In September 1968, fifty-one of Lucey's disenchanted priests—the "young Turks," as he dismissed them—petitioned Pope Paul VI to replace the archbishop with a man more amenable to consultation. After a diplomatic pause, in 1969 the pope accepted Lucey's resignation and appointed Fr. Francis Furey, a less imperious character, as archbishop.[70]

In the years between 1948 and 1968, San Antonio demonstrated that an Anglo willingness to accept civil rights claims to fully democratic participation was not an inevitable, natural progression. Despite ending publicly backed segregation of the city's African American population, Anglo leaders remained firmly in control and prepared to beat back efforts to increase Mexican American economic or political power. Many of the archdiocese's priests and nuns, and a few Anglo liberals and labor organizers, might advocate on behalf of Mexican Americans, but their pleading only reaffirmed Anglo views of their own competence and of Mexican American neediness. The rare Anglos, like Paul Javior and some Catholic priests, who worked with Mexican Americans to learn new skills and to assert themselves, often conceived themselves as marginally Anglo, when

"Anglo" meant "dominant." A number of the middle-class Mexican Americans who had trusted in assimilation to erase hostile racial barriers now shifted their hopes to concerted, racially conscious Mexican American action against Anglo hegemony.

The Anglo men who ran the city entered 1968 full of confidence. HemisFair opened, tourists came, the GGL celebrated San Antonio's new international renown, and the question posed by the promising 1948 election remained: How could Anglos accept Mexican Americans, now the demographic *majority*, as legitimate equal participants in the processes of negotiating public goals and governing the city? Who would create new sites of interracial cooperation, and how?

# 6

# A Victory of Multicultural Collaboration

*San Antonio, 1969–1983*

> We cannot open up to others without offering to them some of
> what we are and receiving from them some of what they are.
> Yet in this process no one ceases to be, but all are enriched.
> All have to die in their *exclusivity*, but no one will simply
> die. On the contrary, all will become richer in the process.
> —*Virgil Elizondo,* The Future Is Mestizo, *2000*

In the late 1960s, some San Antonio high school students walked a picket line in front of a local grocery store, alerting customers not to buy grapes from farms whose owners would not bargain with a workers' union. Andy Hernandez, a brash, smart, talkative young Methodist, participated regularly, attracted by the girls sharing the picket line, especially the young woman he would ultimately marry. Andy's Protestant faith and politics began to coalesce in the "huge religious orientation" of the farmworkers' struggle, though he candidly admits that the powerful trio of "Christ" and "cause" was completed by "chicks," the "three Cs" of his rising Mexican American political consciousness.[1]

But Hernandez also found he had to counter the impulse of the Mexican American middle class to see itself as already assimilated into whiteness. At a Methodist summer camp meeting sometime after the picketing, a youth pastor aroused enthusiasm by closing a prayer service with the racial power cry, "Viva la Raza." The girl Andy had liked got up to speak and reprimanded the speaker: "The Bible says that in Christ there's no Greek or Gentile, no man or woman, so we shouldn't divide ourselves along ethnic lines." Andy confronted her and asked,

"Do you think Mexicans are lazier or dumber than Anglos?" "No,"
she said. "Then why are they poor—why are we poor and the
Anglos rich? Maybe it has to do with how things are set up. You're
right that in Christ there's no Greek or Gentile. But in Christ there
is [both] Greek and Gentile, and they should be treated equally."

The denial of the worth of the people who worked the fields led Andy
to a different interpretation of the biblical injunction: not to see everyone as the same, but to value the distinct histories and ancestries of all
humanity. Andy had a model for respectful collaboration in the Rio
Grande (Spanish-speaking) Conference the Methodist Church had established, separate from the Southwest (Anglo) Conference. His new self-
consciousness affiliated him and many other young middle-class Mexican
Americans with the new Chicano movements, which rejected any ambition to join white America by leaving behind a racialized identity.

## Chicano Consciousness

Frustrated with the persistent Anglo rejection of public policies to increase
Mexican American incomes or political access, a group of students at San
Antonio's St. Mary's University organized to take action. A Catholic liberal arts men's college and law school on the West Side, the school had
served generations of local Anglo and well-to-do Mexican and Mexican
American men (especially after World War II when many attended on the
GI Bill), admitting women students in 1962. Five of the students (quickly
known as Los Cinco in a group that took pride in its Spanish-English bi-
lingualism) founded the Mexican American Youth Organization (MAYO)
in 1967 and the Mexican American Unity Council (MAUC) in 1969.[2]

The Chicano movement in San Antonio rejected assimilation as a
matter of course and reclaimed a demeaning and racialized name, just
as young African American and American Indian activists were replacing "Negro" with "black" and affirming a "Nation of All Tribes." But the
principles of the local Chicanos followed two different paths: "oppositional
consciousness" to any Anglo authority; and community building. To Anglo minds, both threatened a loss of power and of reassuring assumptions
about Mexican American inferiority amidst the heightened domestic tensions of the Vietnam War, urban and campus riots, and, coincidentally,

rising crime rates. Anglos in San Antonio, as in other cities, saw racial power as the violent finale to the more benign civil rights movement.[3] MAYO intended to arouse a quiescent community to anger and action, especially to protest voter exclusion and the miseducation of Mexican Americans. One visible success came with South Texas high school students, who resented poor academic programs and a curriculum that taught only Anglo achievement. In spring 1968, students walked out at San Antonio's Sidney Lanier High School and in Edgewood to protest self-serving Anglo school governance. Student demands emphasized three major points: "the instituting of college preparatory courses, the establishment of culturally relevant courses, and the elimination of the 'No Spanish' rule forbidding the use of Spanish on the school grounds." Students wanted more, as one of them wrote years later, than "a stable life of hard work, limited mobility, and a traditionally well-played football schedule."[4] MAYO disrupted the norms of teaching an Anglo worldview and of limiting academic programs for Mexican Americans. To halt the demonstrations, the San Antonio School Board agreed to most of the student demands.

Influenced by black nationalists such as Stokeley Carmichael and Malcolm X, José Angel Gutiérrez, one of Los Cinco, also focused on mobilizing voters in South Texas towns where Mexican American majorities had the numbers to win control of local governments previously run by Anglos.[5] Gutiérrez adopted a rhetoric that opposed all Mexican Americans to all white Anglos, even though Gutiérrez, like Carmichael, understood white domination as an institutional process and not a biological imperative.

Another of Los Cinco, Willie Velásquez, offered a counterpoint to Gutiérrez's conception of militancy. In the mid-1960s, the Ford Foundation, a major philanthropy supporting antipoverty work, sponsored an investigation of Mexican American poverty, poor education, and political exclusion and pledged funds for Southwestern projects. Inspired by Mexican writer José Vasconcelo's concept of the "cosmic race" of Mexico's mixed peoples, Velásquez imagined a positive social order arising from a combination of the region's cultural values and heritages.[6] With a calmer tone and less notoriety than Gutiérrez, Velásquez won Ford Foundation money for a new group, the Mexican American Unity Council (MAUC), to organize barrio residents, improve schools and job training, and register voters, revising some goals of the SANYO poverty program that Anglo authorities had squelched a few years earlier.[7]

Velásquez and MAUC drew on the ideas of Saul Alinsky to revive the participatory ideals of the mid-1960s poverty legislation. Alinsky had developed principles of community organizing in the 1930s, bringing together labor leaders and Catholic priests to motivate poorly paid, working-class white residents in one of Chicago's meatpacking neighborhoods to assert their interests as citizens. In *Reveille for Radicals,* published in 1945 and reissued in 1969, Alinsky laid out the principles of a "radical democrat" in the tradition of Tom Paine and Thomas Jefferson. He blended political astuteness with religious references, praising Moses and Saint Paul as "two of the greatest organizers who ever lived," and attracted a band of serious young men raised in Catholic traditions.[8] Eager to think about energizing an excluded citizenry to crack the barrier of Anglo control, Los Cinco invited Alinsky to St. Mary's in 1967; two years later, the newly funded MAUC began to send staff to Alinsky's Industrial Areas Foundation (IAF) in Chicago to train as community organizers.

Arnold Flores, who had already spent three years fighting the employment practices at Kelly Air Force Base to break up a job hierarchy that kept Mexican Americans at the bottom, attended the IAF school as a MAUC trainee in 1969.[9] He began to develop an organizing program that relied more on building community competence and less on arousing oppositional Chicano consciousness. "We had a lot of barrio people who . . . had only one approach: raise hell, raise hell, raise hell," Flores remembers. Like Willie Velásquez, who became a friend during this period, Arnold sought to reproduce the successful community-based labor organizing embodied in earlier successes of A. Philip Randolph's African American Brotherhood of Sleeping Car Porters and Cesar Chavez's Mexican American United Farm Workers. Flores went to work for the Service Employees International Union (SEIU) to bring the Mexican American janitors and service workers who cleaned the schools and municipal buildings into the union.

Flores himself had tried the assimilation model of individual upward mobility when he returned from Air Force service to San Antonio in the late 1950s and got hired at Kelly Air Force Base, one of the city's largest local employers. He discovered that Anglo bosses at Kelly oversaw an employment system that kept Mexican American workers confined to the lower tiers of jobs and pay. Mexican Americans stayed in jobs just below any executive or supervisory position in the federal GS ranking or in blue-collar jobs not covered by civil service rules.[10] Flores saw that Anglo bosses used educational requirements for racial tracking, that is, when Mexican Americans had only high school degrees, the upper-level jobs required college degrees, and when Mexican Americans took courses to upgrade their qualifications, then new promotion requirements were added, such as specific work experience previously unavailable to Mexican Americans. Although Flores won the three-year litigation in 1968, he knew he had to leave Kelly, where his dogged investigations offended supervisors.

Working with SEIU, Flores now tried Alinsky's model of uplifting a community through pursuing its self-determined interests. Flores discovered that public school janitors' biggest frustration was working in schools and not being educated themselves. He shamed the superintendent into putting together a GED course. "I said, 'How dare you? You ought to be ashamed of yourself. You have the physical facilities, you have the teachers, you have the books, and you do not do anything to try to educate your janitors.'" The San Antonio ISD accepted Flores's challenge, and seventy-five of the three hundred janitors who started the course completed the requirements for graduation, Flores recollects. When a number of the janitors got GED degrees, Flores arranged a ceremony, and the men dressed up and "one brought his children and his grandkids. And then we realized how important it was to them, how they had felt inferior" when their poor education confirmed Anglo expectations of Mexican American ignorance.

Flores confronted the institutional means by which the Anglo school authorities sustained the idea that Mexican American janitors did not merit increased responsibility or higher wages. Because the union required promotion from the ranks, the schools would buy new equipment, like air conditioners, and then use the janitors' unfamiliarity with it as an excuse to hire outside the union ranks. The union won commitment to job training to elevate workers' skills to maintain the new equipment and persuaded the schools to buy recognizable uniforms, instead of having the janitors work in old, shabby clothes brought from home. Like the garbage workers who had struck in 1967, the janitors' union struck for higher wages in 1970 and challenged the old idea of Mexican Americans as a passive, uncomplaining labor force. They marched to City Hall, their placards proclaiming, "Mr. Cheap Wages Died Here." The compliant Mexican American low-wage worker was dead, too.

Whether in MAYO's oppositional actions or in MAUC's self-assertion, the new Mexican American was pictured as male. At the same time

MAYO sought respect for Chicano culture and people, its emphasis on opposition required a militant, martial mode. Standing up for the people merged into the hypermasculine imagery of a nation in an increasingly bloody and unpleasant war in Vietnam and evoked seductive images of machismo. At MAUC, the young men bonded after work at neighborhood bars, traditionally masculine spaces congenial to the political conversations carried on long after the women had gone home from the more egalitarian workplaces. St. Mary's had only recently admitted women students, the young men had little experience with women colleagues, and the rhetoric of nation building called up images of strong men protecting their women in hostile territory.

Mexican American women's historian Vicki Ruiz has pointed out that many young women worked in Chicano organizations and served as staff to write and print political notices, get out marchers and voters, provide information to the media, and plan projects. But these young women were not the public representatives of the movement, and their participation could be construed as that of the stereotypically domestic and subdued Mexican female. A few years in the future, Chicana feminists would begin to critique the movement's sexism, but in the late 1960s, smart young men saw themselves as leading a crusade, and it was up to others to fall into line and follow them.[11]

The masculine militancy of the organizers created images frightening to Anglo voters and easily manipulated by opponents, who, by the late 1960s, included local congressman Henry B. Gonzalez. Gonzalez's middle-class family had fled the disorder of the Mexican Revolution in 1911, and he had been able to attend the University of Texas and St. Mary's Law School before entering military service in World War II. During the 1950s and through the mid-1960s, he had lambasted the narrow-mindedness of San Antonio's Anglo elite, invited in unions to organize low-wage Mexican American workers, fought against the state legislature's efforts to maintain African American segregation after the *Brown v. Board* ruling, and advocated for San Antonio poverty funds. Like his friend and ally Archbishop Lucey, Gonzalez radiated an aura of intelligent compassion and care for those weaker than himself. Like Lucey, Gonzalez expected to have his leadership respected. He was not about to accept either the primacy of young men who had been his acolytes or their ideas of nationalist separatism. In a contest for male leadership, Gonzalez, as a popular longtime member of Congress, had many advantages.

In spring 1969, Gonzalez attacked Los Cinco and criticized the Ford Foundation for awarding its tax-free dollars to spread racial hatred in the guise of political advocacy. In a MAYO press conference to counter Gonzalez, José Angel Gutiérrez only inflamed Anglo fears. He provocatively answered a reporter's question about how to end gringo dominance of Mexican Americans: "You can eliminate an individual in various ways. You can certainly kill him, but that is not our intent at this moment." Gutiérrez's earlier analysis of ending gringo power had made clear his institutional approach: "A *Gringo*," he had written, "is one who talks of justice, liberty, freedom, democracy, equality, and the Bill of Rights, yet systematically denies 12 million Spanish-speaking people in the U.S.A. meaningful participation in the affairs of this nation."[12] But when the media reported his plan to "kill the gringo," Anglo listeners understandably heard a physical threat. Through the summer of 1969, Gonzalez attacked the racism of Gutiérrez and MAYO on the floor of Congress and successfully pressed the Ford Foundation and other agencies to withdraw support from MAYO and its MAUC offshoot or lose their tax-exempt status.[13]

Buoyed by Gonzalez's vehement criticisms, San Antonio Anglos joined a sharp backlash against Mexican American political power. In 1971 Pete Torres, who had won two city council terms as a West Side independent, ran for mayor and lost. In 1972, with the Mexican American vote divided between the Democratic Party and a newly formed Raza Unida Party (RUP), Joe Bernal and Albert Peña Jr., who had held a position of power as county commissioner since 1956, lost reelection campaigns—Bernal to Anglo businessman Nelson Wolff, and Peña to former Gonzalez aide Albert Bustamente. "It was," Andy Hernandez recalls, "the collapse of the Chicano progressive electoral base. . . . If we'd have won, I'd have built off Joe Bernal. We'd have run candidates, we'd have done the voter registration stuff, but everything was gone. We had nothing left." Anglo voters had come out in large numbers to make certain that Mexican American political advocates lost any hold on city governance.[14]

Chicano rhetoric and demands had hardened lines of racial difference by basing Chicano positions on "oppositional consciousness" to Anglo ones.[15] In San Antonio in the early 1970s, Anglos still controlled money and employment and could turn out voters if the contests were defined as Chicano versus Anglo. Local Anglos had shown they did not intend to lose their ability to define a minimal public sphere and to let inertia sustain the educational, economic, and residential differences that continued to structure unequal possibilities for Anglo and Mexican American citizens.

# Community Organizing

After the 1972 setback for Mexican American political gains, some Mexican American activists focused on organizing the Mexican American community instead of castigating Anglo authority.[16] Some Anglos, especially those affiliated with the Roman Catholic Church in San Antonio, shifted the Church's approach to helping the poor and working class toward aiding organizers.

Intellectual and institutional changes in the global and local Roman Catholic Church were essential to this new orientation. In 1963 Pope John XXIII had asserted in *Pacem in Terris* that "all men are equal by reason of their natural dignity" and that governments exist to protect and promote basic human rights, announcing what one scholar labels the Catholic "human rights revolution."[17] The Second Vatican Council (1963–1965) followed the pope's lead in its final statement, *Gaudium et Spes* (Joy and Hope), which envisioned human development as a basic goal and conceived the individual as a social being whose health depended upon good-working families, neighborhoods, workplaces, and politics, where decisions were made through inclusive discussions and wide participation. As Archbishop Lucey had found to his discomfort, Vatican II could be evoked to justify greater lay participation and less hierarchy in Church governance.

In San Antonio, Lucey's successor, Archbishop Francis Furey, carried some of the new principles into support for increasing the organizational and cultural competence of his Mexican American congregants. The Irish Catholic son of a Pennsylvania coal miner and a no-nonsense administrator, Furey had succeeded Lucey in 1969 with the tasks of smoothing over the battles between Lucey and his unruly priests and caring for a parish numerically dominated (70 percent) by working-class Mexican American families. Acting in the spirit of the Vatican II injunction to bring the poor into the core of the Church and to invigorate lay participation, Furey promoted promising young Mexican Americans and directed his budget to social services and the development of lay leadership.

In 1970, the archbishop hired Joe Bernal as executive director of a new archdiocesan office, the Committee for Mexican American Affairs, to develop a health clinic, food stamp access, and leadership training on the West Side. As director, Bernal tried to energize Mexican Americans politically and to engage Anglos in the cause of extending democracy. "The complex problem facing the Mexican American," he wrote in his third annual report, "is truly a problem of the total community. When a portion of society hurts because of injustice and discrimination, everybody suffers its consequences, resulting in our American democratic ideals and way of life becoming limited only to a select class."[18]

Furey moved to incorporate Mexican Americans into leadership. In 1970 he appointed Fr. Patrick (who reclaimed the Mexicano "Patricio" for a while in the early 1970s) Flores to the position of auxiliary bishop, the first Mexican American elevated to bishop in the United States. Furey also supported Mexican American claims to unique cultural insights. In 1972 he budgeted funds for a scholar and native son of the West Side, Fr. Virgilio Elizondo, to create a Mexican American Cultural Center, which offered bilingual pastoral training and invigorated scholarly study of the influence of the Southwestern and Latin American indigenous cultures on Catholic worship. And Furey gave Church backing to increasing political participation. At Joe Bernal's recommendation, in 1973 the archbishop helped fund a new project directed by Willie Velásquez for citizen voter research and education and interceded for additional funding from the national Catholic Church's Campaign for Human Development. The project, which would evolve into the Southwest Voter Research and Education Project in 1975, began to investigate why more than half of eligible Mexican American voters weren't registered and, coincidentally, gave Andy Hernandez his first political research job.

Archbishop Furey also backed IAF-inspired organizing in place of the depleted Chicano movement. In 1973, one of the young men who had been part of the intellectual-political milieu at St. Mary's University and disappointed by the 1972 political defeats, Ernesto Cortes, returned to the West Side to apply organizing principles he had studied in Chicago.

Ernie Cortes, as the young organizer was usually known, had grown up in a comfortable South Side middle-class home that maintained family ties to Mexico and embraced an ethnic identity: "American of Mexican descent." Bookish and precocious, Cortes graduated at sixteen from Central Catholic High, a school with a strong academic tradition and a heritage of training elite Anglo and bright Mexican American young men.[19] Cortes won admission to Texas A & M (one of a handful of Mexican American students on campus in the early 1960s) to study chemical engineering. His dazzled A & M professors opened their libraries in economics, medieval history, and literature to him, and Cortes graduated in three years with an English major. In 1964 he headed to UT-Austin for graduate study in economics and quickly joined the civil rights activists at the campus YMCA-YWCA. The group protested segregated local bars, compiled lists of nonsegregated off-campus housing, sponsored a civil rights lecture series that included Mexican American issues, and also read and argued theology.[20]

In 1966, Cortes left graduate study to aid the farmworkers' fight in South Texas. When the strike failed, he returned to San Antonio, got hired by the U.S. Civil Rights Commission to write a research report on job discrimination at Kelly Air Force Base, joined the staff at MAUC to plan local economic development, and read and argued about social empowerment with the MAUC/St. Mary's activists. He cultivated successful local Mexican American politicians, but when the 1972 election swept many of them out of office, Cortes followed the path of Arnold Flores and other MAUC staff to Alinsky's IAF institute in Chicago because, he recalls, "IAF had a reading list."

As a thinker, Saul Alinsky emphasized a process of democratic self-development and engaged public decision making; he did not start with an ideal and seek followers, but started with people and conveyed techniques for their working together. The organizer, he taught, has

> no fixed truth, no final answer, no dogma, no formula, no panacea. . . . The banner of the free-society organizer emphasizes the question mark. He challenges and tests his own beliefs and findings. Irreverence becomes important because it is essential to questioning. Curiosity becomes compulsive. His most common word is "why?"[21]

Alinsky had sought organizers able to inspire ordinary people to claim public spaces and roles, not to oppose the powerful but to bring their own citizen interests into the public arena. Organizers energized and inspired people to take brash public actions that confronted and embarrassed the powerful so as to gain a place at the negotiating table. Saul Alinsky died in 1972, and when Ernie Cortes soon afterward joined the group, now led by Ed Chambers, the two began to think through religiously salient aspects of Alinsky's determinedly secular thinking. Jewish by birth, Alinsky had not affiliated with a synagogue, but religious thinkers had perceived links between his work to develop a conscientious citizenry, Christian principles of equal human worth, and political systems unlikely to succumb to the totalitarian populism that had roiled Europe in the 1930s and fueled World War II.[22] When organizing in Chicago, Alinsky had found Catholic parishes and labor unions the institutional allies that engaged communities.

Cortes and Chambers now more explicitly appealed to a religious ethic for political engagement and looked to neighborhood parishes and churches as an organizing base.

Cortes carried back to San Antonio an ideal of a collaborative community, in contrast to the Chicano movement's more hierarchical pattern of a few leaders and many followers. For an organizer, Cortes believed, building citizen competence came through respectful attention to each person's history, values, and interests—slow time-consuming work that enabled individuals to gain the self-confidence to work through agreements with other, similarly empowered persons.[23] Cortes needed a sponsor to support him during the time-consuming work of meeting the solid, working-class Catholic West Side citizens whom the city's Anglo business leaders had chronically ignored. He also needed a group that would give him credibility when he asked people to take the time to talk with him. The Committee for Mexican American Action formed, made up of priests, ministers, and scholars, some of them Anglos whose motives had been altered by the powerful messages of Pope John XXIII and of Vatican II and the Protestant embrace of responsibility for valuing all humans and fighting racism. They paid Cortes from church discretionary funds and aided him with parish connections. This new effort of interracial cooperation rigorously disavowed benevolence as a motivator of purpose or of behavior in this effort.

One of the few Anglo members of the committee was Charles Cottrell—Charlie, as he is widely and affectionately known. Cottrell spent his early childhood on San Antonio's South Side before going to live with his German American grandparents in the rural Hill Country north of San Antonio; there he converted to Catholicism at age fourteen and attended a small-town church with a goodly number of Mexican American parishioners.[24] After earning a BA at St. Mary's and a PhD at the University of Arizona, Cottrell took a one-year teaching post in 1966 at Texas A & I in Kingsville, where he met students who soon became part of the emerging Chicano leadership. In 1967 Cottrell returned to teach at St. Mary's and joined the intense political discussions of Los Cinco. He supported Mexican American political aspirations because of his childhood affections and because of his political values, which would lead him to become an expert on voting rights cases.

Charlie Cottrell's approach to political transformation came partly from grappling with Currin Shields's *Democracy and Catholicism in America*, published at the end of the 1950s on the eve of the presidential campaign that raised the issue of papal influence on candidate John Kennedy.[25] Cottrell had written his dissertation at the University of Arizona under Shields, whose influential book argued that Catholic thought was compatible with democracy but antithetical to classical liberalism, which Shields defined as the protection of an individual's freedom from external control, especially the authority of governments. Modern liberals of the New Deal sort, however, had accepted the need for some basic governmental regulation to protect union campaigns, to spend public funds to provide adequate schools, sanitation, basic housing, and medical care, and to end segregation, on the grounds that some government intervention was necessary to open up the opportunities necessary for each individual to thrive.

Catholic thought as of the late 1950s, according to Shields, diverged from both classical and modern liberalism on two points: the concept of the individual and the role of the state. The Church understood humans as "persons," not as isolated "individuals." "Association," not solitary "liberty," was the foundation for each person's unique nature, which developed in relationships in family, school, neighborhood, labor union, sports team, and church club. In these "subsidiary" institutions below the level of the state, persons dealt face-to-face to develop personal skills and capacities, including those needed for self- and group governance. The 1931 papal encyclical *Quadragesimo Anno* had laid out the principle of "subsidiarity," decision making at the smallest feasible organizational level, at the same time it invoked "social justice" to name a shared responsibility for the equitable distribution of power and goods in a society.[26] These were principles that Archbishop Lucey had advocated, though always alongside a "natural" hierarchy he had expected to head. The ideal of developing persons and political competence through association and local decision making supported political strategies at odds with winning elections and claiming "rights" through litigation. Pope John XXIII and the Second Vatican Council further developed the conceptions Shields described. Drawing on Jacques Maritain, the council restated the fundamental paradox that each person possesses a unique divinely formed self, which nevertheless can be developed only through connections with others. The Pastoral Constitution on the Church in the Modern World (*Gaudium et Spes*) issued at the close of the council's three-year series of meetings emphasized the "dignity of all persons" that was to be protected and enacted through social life and political organization.[27] The council's embrace of political efficacy as a part of human dignity required what Charlie Cottrell called "civil engagement democracy," both as recognition of human personhood and as a means to develop the capacities of governance.

What could "civil engagement democracy" look like in practice? How could Mexican Americans gain recognition for themselves, their families, and their neighborhoods and become legitimate participants in public culture and decision making?

Ernie Cortes used Catholic connections and IAF techniques that put new relationships at the center of personal and political change for San Antonio's Mexican Americans. First, with the implicit backing of the West Side parish priests (including Fr. John Wagner), who gave him names of local parish leaders, he spent time talking with West Side men and women. In these conversations, Cortes had to drop the Mexican American Action from his committee's name so as not to offend their values. "If I had come around like that," Cortes remembers, "no one would have talked to me. These weren't loud-mouthed radicals like the Chicanos. They were responsible people raising families, paying mortgages. So I'd say I was from this committee, and they'd talk with me."[28] Meeting in "one-on-ones," eliciting another's life story and telling some of his own in return, Cortes met with hundreds of West Side residents over the next year, asking about their interests, listening to the needs they expressed for their neighborhood, and filling out note cards to catalogue the information. Cortes's respectful attention and probing questions enabled previously excluded Mexican Americans to rethink the stories through which they had understood their lives.

Andres Sarabia, for instance, had achieved a comfortable, respected life; he owned a modest middle-class home near downtown, held a solid civil service job as a computer expert at Kelly Air Force Base, and was a lay leader at Holy Family Catholic Church, where he coached Catholic Youth Organization teams, led the local Boy Scout troop, organized the church fund-raising festivals, and served as parish council president.[29] A military veteran and model Mexican American citizen, Sarabia had never participated in politics. "What Ernie did was to learn my story, learn what had happened to me in middle school, and in high school, and in the college, and at Kelly." Sarabia rethought his life narrative in terms of the historical social options for Mexican Americans. His parents had moved to San Antonio from Chicago, and his Midwest grade-school background was strong enough that he could skip some elementary school grades in Texas.

> But going into the middle school, it was a different mentality. We were Mexicans, and when we're getting ready to graduate, they

brought us into the auditorium and told us that since we were Mexican, we should go to either Tech High School or Lanier High School, because they were both vocational schools. And since we were Mexicans, we would be laborers for the rest of our lives. So I went to San Antonio Tech and took electric shop.

When he graduated from San Antonio Tech, Sarabia found that no employer would hire him without a union card, and the Anglo-run union wouldn't give him a card unless he had a job. "So I did what the majority of young Hispanics in my age group did; I went into the army." The military provided alternative resources, and when he completed service, Sarabia got a job at Kelly Air Force Base and applied to the junior college to take computer classes "to prepare myself for the future." But the junior college refused to admit him because his three years of electrical "shop" courses carried no academic credits; he had to take a GED exam to prove he was prepared for college work. When he went to get his high school transcript, he discovered that he had been near the top of his class and might have had some academic potential, but no one had ever told him.

His aptitude did earn him a spot in IBM training at Kelly, and after he scored 99.5 on the final, he was made an instructor in computer programming and operating. But once again intelligence alone did not suffice for advancement. Sarabia never was promoted beyond a GS-12 and believed it was because of his affirmative action advocacy at Kelly, where "I did things that were not my purview, such as defending workers."

In telling his story to Ernie Cortes, Sarabia discovered that his life had been constrained not by his natural abilities, the basis upon which many Anglos would explain their city's racial assignments, but through the systematic withholding of resources. He was "agitated," in IAF terminology, and then he reinterpreted the chronic municipal disregard for his respectable but modest neighborhood.

> Where I lived it didn't flood, but just a block east of where I lived it flooded quite a bit. On my street we didn't have sidewalks, and so [after a big rain], there would be puddles on the driveway. So one time Ernie did a one-on-one with me there in the driveway, and he asked me, "Well, Mr. Sarabia, do you enjoy standing in water?" And I said, "Of course not. That's a stupid question." And he says, "Then why are you?" And sure enough, I'm standing in this puddle. And he says, "You're just used to it."

In his new consciousness, Sarabia began to see there was a problem; it wasn't nature's heavy rainfalls but city budgeting decisions that underwrote paving streets on the high ground to the north and then didn't build storm sewers to carry away the predictable run-off.

## Founding COPS (Communities Organized for Public Service)

As Sarabia met others in one-on-ones and then held larger house meetings on this issue, new relationships formed across the West Side Catholic parishes. The group built an agenda with other water-soaked neighbors and planned how to hold public officials accountable for solving flooding, which the group was redefining from private inconvenience to public problem. Within a year, eighteen West Side parishes had formed a confederation, Communities Organized for Public Service (COPS), to bring public attention to the physical requirements of their area.

In August 1974, after a torrential downpour flooded many homes on the West Side, COPS invited city manager Sam Granata to a meeting of concerned citizens. Sitting in groups with "placards indicating the location of community delegations," Sarabia remembers, the Mexican Americans presented themselves not as petitioners but as city residents entitled to answers. Speakers asked Granata when drainage channels would be built and booed when he offered the standard excuses about the city's lack of construction funds. A week later, COPS repeated its questions to the city council, and Mayor Charles Becker, an upstart business owner whose victory signaled the decline of GGL control, asked the city manager how many people the flooding affected. "The city manager says 'a hundred thousand,'" Sarabia recalls. "The mayor says, 'Well, how long have you known about this problem?' And the city manager says, 'About forty years.' And the mayor says, 'Why haven't you done anything about it?' And the city manager says, 'Because nobody's complaining.'" The response that blamed failure to improve drainage on the very people whose homes had flooded, Sarabia says, just incensed him further, and that was the moment he committed himself to being a leader in an organization that would speak up and eliminate Mexican American quiescence or apathy as an excuse for government inaction.

The city manager's response also shocked the mayor, who expected competent Anglo government services. When he charged the city manager to find the money to build a drainage channel that had been on the planning books since 1945, Anglo voices responded with concern. The *San Antonio Light* editorialized: "We admire Hizzoner's attention, and the work needed to be done, but we fear his reaction may open the door for numerous groups to petition the mayor. The Council needs to think out needs methodically" instead of responding to angry, well-organized groups.[30] COPS had broken the barrier to Mexican Americans' winning resources from city hall. Although the business community was splitting and the GGL fracturing, Anglo business leaders did not want this unprecedented level of public information and participation to become a regular practice.

With its first public victory in hand, COPS formally constituted itself at a founding convention in November 1974. Its presentation proclaimed its unmistakable Mexican American character, even as its name claimed the racially neutral status of citizenship, which Anglo groups had always assumed for themselves. The delegates adopted a set of bylaws that limited presidential terms to two years (and required that officers and voting delegates have civil service status or protection under a collective bargaining agreement to avoid intimidation from an employer) and elected Andy Sarabia as its first president. Archbishop Furey congratulated the new organization that had formed primarily from leaders in his West Side and South Side (understood as Mexican American) parishes, cheering them on with the slogan "Con COPS todo, sin COPS nada," affirming the use of Spanish in public meetings.[31]

COPS began building an organization that required relationship skills more than the belligerent charisma characteristic of Chicano movements. Women who had been secondary and supporting players to the macho men of the Chicano resistance became central in COPS fights centered on neighborhoods and homes, and the IAF emphasis on building social networks gave women's associations as much value as men's.[32] Women had to learn somewhat different lessons than men did: to see connections between their private home responsibilities and public decisions and to recognize how norms of feminine politeness were not useful in swaying power holders.

When Ernie Cortes contacted Beatrice Gallego at the suggestion of her parish priest for a conversation about the neighborhood, the young housewife and mother had been a PTA officer in her three children's public schools and active in St. James parish as costume maker for festivals, cook for church events, and leader of parish women.[33] She had gone through Tech High School's secretarial track and got her first job as a usefully bilingual receptionist at the Catholic chancery (where, in the early 1960s, only Anglo women got the prestigious secretarial jobs). She had wed Gilbert Gallego at the chancery, with many of the local Catholic hierarchy attending. In 1974 Beatrice Gallego was building a solid middle-class existence supported by the good paychecks her husband, a skilled carpenter, earned. She took care of her home and family and ignored politics, remembering her father's warnings about how the "powers that be" bought up the Mexican neighborhoods' votes in the 1940s and 1950s and gave nothing back beyond the Election Day bribery money. In the old GGL pattern of city governance, fading in 1974, the city council made decisions privately and then announced them at public sessions. Ordinary citizens did not participate, and the city's elite resisted efforts for citizens to become more than compliant subjects. The customary secrecy was largely invisible, because Anglo citizens felt the GGL represented them and so didn't make requests at council meetings or governmental offices. After Ernie Cortes engaged Gallego to work in a COPS campaign to get better water service at fairer rates, an issue that affected her household budget, she went with Cortes to the Public Works Department to ask for information. "The clerk said, 'Well, I can't give you that because that's internal, family affairs.' And Ernie looked at me and he looked at him and he says, 'You know that's public information.' And he said, 'No, No.' He got really nervous, but nobody had ever asked him. You know, we're completely out of their agenda," she assesses in retrospect.

Having obtained information about water rates, Gallego went to the council offices early one morning to sign up for the first public speaker's slot at that night's council session on proposed water rate increases. That evening, the mayor used his prerogative to call on the city bureaucrats to speak, using up all the time with their prepared statements and ignoring the citizen roster. By the end, Ernie Cortes recalls, Gallego was furious. The mayor's ignoring the rules violated what Cortes calls an "inherent ideology" of fairness and human respect that exists in the traditions of many communities, and it convinced Gallego and other COPS members that they would not be heard until they broke out of old norms of politeness and confronted politicians who used genteel manners to cut off discussion. The next time she appeared at the council, Gallego nerved herself to violate the norms of female propriety. "I wore pants," she recalls, "so they couldn't see my knees shaking when I spoke." Gallego wanted to present evidence that the GGL's proposed water rate increase would redistribute funds from inner-city neighborhoods' water bills to aid developers extending water lines to North Side, Anglo-owned housing developments. When the chair refused to hear COPS's statements, Gallego picked up an ashtray and gaveled it on a table, shouting, "You're out of order, Mr. Chairman, you're out of order" for refusing to hear citizen comments. The resulting media attention helped COPS win a good part of its point, and the water authority compromised; it halved the rate increase and also the contribution to the real estate developers.[34]

Behaving in unorthodox ways, COPS also pushed its presence into centers of Anglo economic power and revealed the system's basic Anglo exclusivity. In early spring 1975, COPS initiated a series of actions to move out of the political margins and build relationships with the city's business leaders. West Side COPS members "shopped in" at the venerable downtown Joske's department store, filling the aisles and trying on expensive clothes that a few years earlier would have been off limits to Mexican American customers. They mounted a "change in" at Frost Bank, standing in teller lines by the dozens to exchange bills for coins, and then rejoining the lines to change the coins back to currency, clogging bank operations and shutting out other customers. Tom Frost, family head of the privately owned bank, and the Chamber of Commerce finally agreed to meet COPS to discuss city budget issues.[35] The significant participation of women visibly expanded the idea of public leader beyond male or elite Anglo. Women learned, as Beatrice Gallego had, to do research, to speak to the media, and to be impolite when they were ignored. Within two years of COPS's founding, its representatives from the member parishes were mainly women.

These women visibly rejected Anglo benevolence and embodied IAF's basic principle of organizing, the iron rule: "Never ever do for others what they can do for themselves."[36] Under women's leadership, COPS challenged Anglo businessmen to see public expenses for developing people not as benevolent charity but as a necessary investment in the city's economy. Human development wasn't a soft interest or the private responsibility of individuals but a community's foundation for economic well-being, Beatrice Gallego argued. COPS pushed the city's Anglo economic leaders for a development plan focused on increasing worker skills, instead of continually assuming that the Mexican American population had limited intelligence and could attract only low-wage enterprises.[37]

## Racializing COPS

Just over a year after its founding, COPS won the 1975 "politico of the year" award from *San Antonio Light* columnist Don Politico, whose long profile of the group subtly emphasized its identity as Mexican American and alien. "Briefings before [public actions] are also conducted in Spanish. All the leaders are fluent in both languages, and all the members—whether Spanish or English-speaking—are well schooled on the issue at hand," Don Politico reported. The group had been taught by "Ernesto Cortes," described as a "shadowy figure" who had trained at the "Alinski [*sic*] school in Chicago." The report depicted Sarabia and Gallego as responsible, though perhaps gullible, local homeowners. And "the spiritual leader," Bishop Patrick Flores, the author reminded readers, had earlier allied himself with the Chicano revolution when he "invited such friends as José Angel Gutiérrez" (the Chicano reference most likely to disturb Anglos) to participate in his consecration ceremony.[38]

In 1975, Anglos feared that the Mexican American demographic majority would finally contest San Antonio's long-established Anglo dominance. As in many other Southern and Southwestern cities, at-large elections for city council had favored wealthier candidates able to run city-wide campaigns, which in San Antonio had kept council representation almost a North Side Anglo monopoly. In 1975, as the GGL's hold diminished, federal Voting Rights Act amendments extended Justice Department protections to majority Spanish-speaking districts in the Southwest and put at-large elections under scrutiny. The San Antonio City Council offered voters the option of instituting district elections, which would guarantee that Mexican American and African American neighborhoods would elect representatives from their areas. COPS threw its energies into bringing out Mexican American voters to ratify the new charter over Anglo opposition.[39]

In the unprecedented 1977 city council elections that followed, voters elected five Mexican American, one African American, and four Anglo council members, along with an Anglo mayor, Lila Cockrell, making the nonwhite representatives the city council majority. The powerful 1960s GGL mayor, Walter McAllister Jr., spoke for Anglos when he complained that "council districting was 'creating racism that didn't exist,'" as if Anglos had no racial interests.[40] McAllister's accusation did not just echo the longtime Anglo appeal to white racial fears. It also implied that the goals of a majority of citizens were an illegitimate intrusion of "private interests" into public affairs, with the "public interest" equated with Anglo business goals. "The racial division," concludes urban analyst Heywood Sanders, "was the city's *new* political reality," suggesting that an Anglo-Hispanic statistical division in voting was racial while Anglos' historic exclusion of nonwhites had not been.[41]

A subsequent referendum on a major COPS-backed infrastructure initiative turned into a contest over racial control of the city. In January 1978, the newly elected city council proposed a $98 million bond issue, much of it for drainage, approved by all the council members and the mayor. Although every council district was to get a cut, the council targeted 70 percent of the funds to the most urgent drainage projects, a majority in West Side COPS areas.[42] The council's unanimity shattered when the six nonwhite members voted to cut about $1 million in funds targeted for an inner-city highway loop; in response, the Anglo council members and Mayor Lila Cockrell vowed to kill the bond issue.

As COPS president Beatrice Gallego gave interviews to argue the case that the bond issue was essential to protect the lives of children, one or two of whom drowned in every big storm, the two Anglo Chambers of Commerce, the North Side and the San Antonio, came out against the bond issue. The city papers pounded out a drumbeat of headlines—"City Hall's War over Bond Issue Grows Hotter," "S.A. Bond Issue a 'Battle Royal,'" "Northside Says No to Bonds," "Gallego Blasts Cockrell," "Taxpayer League Opposed," "Factions Collide over Bond Necessity" in the *San Antonio Light*; and "City Hall Bond War Continues" in the *Express*. One headline announced the real contest: "Is Election over Bonds, or Who's Boss in S.A.?"[43] On Election Day, the *San Antonio Express*, the morning daily, editorialized "Do Your City a Favor—Vote No." The paper implied that Anglos could protect "their" city by voting against a Mexican American–initiated program. With an unprecedented turnout of over 100,000 voters, the Anglos won the "war."

The loss, Sr. Pearl Ceasar remembers, devastated many of the residents whose organizing had put their neighborhood's infrastructure needs onto the city's agenda.[44] She had been working on the West Side to get out the voters, and on election night,

we were having what was supposed to have been the victory party
in the basement of Immaculate Heart of Mary, and [this girl] came

and was just sobbing. . . . And she kept saying, 'Why do they hate us so much? Why do they hate us so much?' And I just could not answer that question. How do you tell a kid why people hate them? Because she understood that in San Antonio people were drowning because of the floodwaters that this bond was to alleviate. But the Anglo community had voted against it because they didn't want Hispanics running the city.

Sister Pearl recalls vowing then that she would do something so that she'd never again have to read headlines that converted an issue about saving lives into a battle over racial control of city politics.

### Recruiting Anglo Allies

Sr. Pearl Ceasar had arrived in San Antonio when she was eighteen years old to enter the Congregation of Divine Providence and to train as a teacher at the congregation's Our Lady of the Lake University. "The Lake" stood out as an educational beacon on the West Side and was the site of the mother house, the spiritual and administrative center of the nuns' order. The convent and the university offered liberation to a young white woman in the early 1960s. Sister Pearl observes:

I grew up in Louisiana in the 1940s and 1950s. That was before the women's movement, that was before women did anything different than get married, have children, and stay at home and raise their children. I wanted to do something more with my life than that. . . . In today's world, I probably would have got married, had children, and then worked outside of the home. But that option wasn't there.

In her Catholic schools, Sister Pearl saw a few women who did run things, "Catholic nuns, because in that world nuns taught, they were principals, they ran hospitals." The sisters escaped the domestic restrictions for white Louisiana women, even a middle-class girl descended from Syrian Catholic immigrants such as Sister Pearl.

Trained to be a Catholic schoolteacher and without a secular teaching certificate, Sister Pearl went to work in Louisiana in an all-black school where nuns were aiding the poorly funded public schools. Even with some help, the unprepared children continued to fail, while their parents saw no way to improve the situation. After two years, Sister Pearl moved into

Catholic schools that were officially integrated but were being inundated by white students fleeing the newly desegregated public schools. She protested to the head of her order, Sr. Elizabeth McCullough, that she would not devote herself to abetting a new version of segregation. Backed by the Congregation of Divine Providence, Sister Pearl left Louisiana, took a master's degree in social work at the Lake, and in the early 1970s worked as a lobbyist for a women's religious network in Washington, D.C. During her years of teaching, social work, counseling, and legislative lobbying, she observed that these programs only patched up people injured by powerful structures. She had learned that benevolence didn't bring change, but, she recalls, "I didn't know how to make change."

When Sister Pearl returned from her lobbying job in Washington in 1976, she saw a possibility in COPS's organizing in parishes near the Lake and told her order's counselor that she wanted to work with the group. "They blessed it. Ten years before, that would not have happened. The whole shift in Vatican II, the shift in our order, opened up that opportunity for me." Sister Pearl and three other nuns were hired by four of the West Side parishes to work with the IAF organizer—to talk about issues with parishioners, to identify leaders, and to encourage them to plan and to advocate for a fairer share of public resources. The 1978 bond campaign clarified that Anglo leaders were not graciously going to welcome a mobilized West Side into city politics.

During and after the hostilities and disappointments that followed the 1978 election, even the Anglo ministers who had supported Ernie Cortes in COPS's early years couldn't convince their Anglo congregations to collaborate with COPS on urgent city needs. When a group gathered to explore reasons why North Side residents might want to ally with COPS to improve public services, a local newspaper columnist reported the formation of "a North Side COPS" and scared away pastors whose Anglo congregations did not want to be connected with a group that had been pegged as Mexican and "divisive."[45]

Anglo political leaders had relentlessly pushed a view that business development was the only legitimate public interest and had managed to persuade thousands of Anglo voters to see questions about the scope of public services as conflicts between Anglo self-reliance and selfish Mexican American minority interests. By 1978 the IAF had moved into some other Texas cities and used what it called "broad-based organizing," ignoring historical racial distinctions to bring together a variety of citizens with shared interests in improving public services. Without naming race, the

IAF self-consciously practiced racial inclusion and defined issues in reso-
lutely nonracial terms. In San Antonio, however, where the organization
had begun with a group that could be racialized in opposition to Anglos
(and African Americans), the processes by which Anglos could come to
see themselves as allies to a racial other help reveal the mental shifts white
Americans made in order to find shared interests with minority groups.
How could middle-class Anglo San Antonians conceive of themselves and
of COPS in ways that allowed them to share political efforts and give up a
central prerogative of racialized Anglo identity: the unself-conscious, benevolent direction of public affairs on behalf of inferiors?

One answer is that many of the Anglos who responded were newcomers who had not been bred in San Antonio's racial protocols, among them
Rev. Homer Bain. When IAF's Ed Chambers came to San Antonio to investigate how to break through the North Side's aloofness, he became re-
acquainted with Bain, a white Floridian. Bain had studied at Union Theological Seminary in New York City and, after a brief Florida pastorate,
immigrated in the early 1960s to Chicago to take a PhD in theology and
counseling at the University of Chicago Divinity School.[46] He had lived
and worked as an assistant pastor in a neighborhood on the border of Chicago and Oak Park. He first met IAF organizers when black families began to move into the area, setting off blockbusting and panic selling. Bain
found IAF allies to dissuade his congregation from a traditional Chicago
solution to integration: bombing out the black families. Bain had moved
to San Antonio in 1969 to head a counseling program at the Ecumenical
Center for Religion and Health founded alongside the new UT Medical
Center but had remained in contact with the Chicago IAF. Now Chambers
persuaded Bain, one of the few Protestant clergy independent of a congregational paycheck, to attend IAF training.

Homer Bain and a group of other Protestant ministers, quietly backed
by Archbishop Furey, who judged that Protestants had to take the lead
with North Side Anglos, began to raise money to hire an organizer. After two years, Bain says, when the organizing group hadn't raised enough
to meet IAF requirements, Ed Chambers conceded that they had raised
enough "for someone in parish development—not an organizer and not
trained, but perhaps able to do leadership training." Bain pauses before
delivering the punch line: "And that was Pearl Ceasar." Sister Pearl was
ready. Since 1978, she had gathered her strength and worked in a Houston
ecumenical center, fortuitously learning about Protestants. "I had never
stepped foot in a Protestant church [before]. . . . I had been brought up at

a time when if a Catholic married a non-Catholic, you could not go to the wedding. . . . You know, as God would have it, [the ecumenical experience] really prepared me for the work in San Antonio, because when I went to San Antonio I understood the polity of the different Protestant churches." Paid by Homer Bain's committee, Sister Pearl began to visit the middle-class Anglo North Side Protestant churches to find leaders who could be inspired by an enlarged vision of public interests that included them and West Side citizens, too.

Sister Pearl used the IAF techniques that had energized COPS leaders. She held hundreds of one-on-ones and  house meetings with men's and women's groups and Sunday school classes to agitate and to reorient Anglos on the North Side. She prodded older Anglos to discover their interests in getting assistance for their aging 1950s and 1960s neighborhoods just inside and outside the I-410 Loop, which were being bypassed by northward-moving residential and commercial developments as they became more racially diverse and nonwhite. Like the West Side Mexican Americans, the near–North Side Anglos needed infrastructure work to repair old streets, drainage, and sidewalks. Sister Pearl suggested that they, too, could identify public needs and apply for community development grants to maintain the areas in which they had invested their lives.[47]

Relying on a public program required these Anglos to make a mental shift, but one somewhat different from what COPS's leaders had experienced. West Side Mexican Americans had moved from a view that current arrangements were natural to an understanding that the city's system of decision making was responsible for flooding problems, underfunded public schools, and underrepresented neighborhoods. Additionally, North Side Anglos had assumed an identity of interests with Anglo developers and taken for granted the provision of adequate city services—not as a public function argued over in council meetings but almost as a private good purchased along with a home. Equating good services with Anglo housing, North Side homeowners expected to phone a council member simply to request street repair, not as an exertion of citizen power but as a matter of course.

In conversation with Sister Pearl, some residents began to see they had taken for granted that the city would always serve them, even when the middle class had little voice. Big churches just outside the I-410 beltway, such as Colonial Hills United Methodist and San Pedro Presbyterian, Sister Pearl remembers, "were wanting more power in the city, and not having the city make decisions without them." When a large developer proposed to build a shopping mall over the aquifer, the naturally occurring underground reservoir just north of the city, it catalyzed many middle-class voters to reconsider their complacency. Anglo professionals, many of whom worked in the Aquifer Protection Association led by former League of Women Voters president Fay Sinkin, defended the aquifer against an Anglo business community that pushed unregulated development. COPS worked as an ally in the public battle. The recognition that they had little influence in city decisions led a number of congregations to respond to Sister Pearl's vision of an active citizenry. By 1982 she had enlisted almost twenty North Side congregations to hold a founding convention, to constitute itself the Metropolitan Congregational Alliance (shortened to Metro Alliance in the late 1980s), and to build a relationship with COPS.[48]

# Anglo Interracial Consciousness and the Metro Alliance

Although many Anglos learned one lesson similar to those the COPS membership learned—that the concept of systems explained more than did the concept of nature—Anglos who affiliated with COPS/IAF gained another set of insights from the new connection with Mexican Americans. Inhabiting a different racial location, middle-class Anglos historically had been able to assume as their due better education, jobs, and neighborhoods and a racial connection with the city's leadership. Through listening to Mexican Americans recount their life circumstances and from working with Mexican Americans, some Anglo men and women began to understand that they had built their faith in American fairness and the efficacy of their professional skills on a narrow set of experiences. The society had guaranteed opportunities to them, but not to many others who were as worthy. The realization that their actions, even if unwitting, helped sustain a system of inequality drew many into Metro Alliance.

Some Anglos, like Jane Tuck, came into Metro as a commitment to one more worthy cause. Raised in a comfortable Philadelphia household and trained as a teacher, Tuck earned a college degree in special education and then, after her marriage, volunteered in neighborhood organizations while she raised her three children. She moved into a comfortable North Side home when her air force officer husband was posted to San Antonio in 1971. Disheartened by the Vietnam War's coarsening of their beloved military, Jane and her husband found a congenial community in the

Unitarian-Universalist congregation. Jane focused her educational efforts on the free speech work of the American Civil Liberties Union and the nuclear disarmament campaign of Women for Peace. In 1979, Tuck was recruited to the North Side IAF organizing committee by Presbyterian minister Rev. Bill Lytle, who knew her from shared work with the peace group, Fellowship of Reconciliation. She helped bring the Unitarian-Universalists into Metro as one of its first member congregations.[49]

Despite her constant work for peace and for free speech, such as her son's right to wear long hair to the local high school, Tuck hadn't at first seen a connection between herself and the residential, racial, and religious identities attached to COPS. She remembers that "you couldn't help but be aware of COPS, but it was located just on the West Side of town and strictly Catholic, and since I was not in either of those positions, I had nothing at all to do with it."

For Jane, allying with COPS meant discovering some of the same lessons COPS members had learned: how feminine decorum could disable a woman's ability to assess and exert her civic power. Anglo women had to overcome their racialized gender image as polite, beneficent models of propriety long used to justify white superiority and to represent white charity. "The feeling in Metro Alliance was that that kind of aggressive behavior"—such as staging a confrontation with the council—"is not our nature. We're more rational," Tuck said, her implication being, more rational than Mexican American women. Tuck came to see that COPS staged political actions not out of a flamboyant Mexican American nature, but because the tactic worked to get issues on the agenda. We saw "that unless you are a bit aggressive, you're not going to accomplish very much." Anglo women recognized the limits of one mark of their whiteness—polite gentility—as they realized it was in conflict with other ethical concerns—for Jane, especially, the cause of peace.

San Antonio's chapter of the League of Women Voters (LWV) had long embodied Anglo women's decorum and reason carried into civic action. Though officially integrated during the 1950s, the League had few African American or Mexican American members.[50] In the mid-1960s, Texas's LWV volunteers wrote pamphlets, testified against poll taxes, and ran registration campaigns to sign up previously excluded African Americans; after the 1975 Voting Rights Act amendments, the League women staffed shopping mall tables to register previously discouraged Mexican American voters.

Diligent and capable Rowena Rodgers, a San Antonio wife and mother of four, had been the League's state election law chair and a leading volunteer in San Antonio voter registration. It had taken Rodgers a while to understand the history of Mexican American racializing in South Texas. She and her husband were surprised at the city's residential segregation when they moved to San Antonio in 1952 from Austin, where they had met at the University of Texas. When they wanted to buy a house on the near North Side, Rodgers said, the real estate agent instructed them in the city's racial etiquette. " 'You know, we're being very careful not to sell to Mexican Americans,' the agent said. And I said, 'Why?' He said, 'We just want to maintain the neighborhood.' That was one of my first brushes with discriminatory actions here in San Antonio in regard to the Mexican Americans," Rodgers remembers.[51]

Although Rodgers had grown up in Texas, her father, a dairy farmer, had moved from Illinois after World War I and "didn't fit the stereotype Southern philosophy [of white superiority]." Her husband had grown up in the Church of the Brethren faith in Kansas and shared her egalitarian views. When the family looked for a larger house in the early 1970s, the agents tried to move them out of their old neighborhood, where Mexican American families had now moved in. The real estate people "really did not encourage us to buy a house within the San Antonio School District; . . . they were always recommending Northeast School District" further out, where Mexican American families hadn't yet moved. When faced with living out segregation or not, the Rodgers family stayed in the San Antonio ISD, where their kids attended racially mixed public schools.

Even though Rodgers chose a desegregated residence and pushed inclusive voting, COPS's activities led to a revelation for her: Citizen engagement required more than formal laws that equalized voter access or get-out-the vote drives, the League's politically neutral approaches. As an Election Day poll watcher, Rodgers had observed COPS's power to engage citizens to come out to vote. She began to realize that voting was a formalistic ritual unless voters had helped set the voting agenda so that it reflected their thoughts and interests. When the idea of forming Metro as a COPS ally was presented at her Universalist-Unitarian church, Rodgers shifted her energies and today proudly asserts, "I've been a part of [Metro] for most of its life." Taking a new kind of risk for a white woman, she recognized that public decisions required organization and power and not just enforcing seemingly impartial rules of order.

The ideal of the rational white intellect as above politics and able to present measured, polite recommendations to power holders had defined professional life for Marilyn Stavinoha, another Unitarian-Universalist supporter of Metro. Stavinoha and her husband had moved to San Antonio and bought a large, tree-shaded lot just outside the I-410 Loop when he joined the new UT medical faculty in 1969.[52] With BA and MA degrees in child development and a stint running the Head Start program on a Sioux reservation in South Dakota, Stavinoha had strong professional credentials and a desire to continue using her skills while she raised her four children. In the 1970s, she advocated for new state programs for early childhood education and taught in a continuing education program to get teachers certified to teach in newly funded kindergartens. As the League of Women Voters' juvenile justice expert, she appealed to the county commissioners court for public funds for food for the county lockup, where jailers were making personal contributions to buy food for hungry kids brought in as vagrants or troublemakers. As a child development expert, she testified at the regional council of governments on the need for funding early childhood education, where she argued that children should not be expected to pull themselves up "by their bootie-straps. . . . You should at least be able to grow up and get in man-sized boots before you have to pull yourself up." Stavinoha had trusted her expert testimony to persuade public officials to treat children and young people more humanely, displaying her professional expertise in ways that fit the conventional idea that men in charge responded to well-informed, well-behaved women with an interest in children.

Stavinoha saw herself as fulfilling the moral injunctions she had internalized as a college student. As a white child in Oklahoma and the daughter of a man who defended her small town's ordinance prohibiting a black person from being in town after dark, Stavinoha had loved her childhood Methodist church. When she left for the larger world of the recently desegregated University of Oklahoma, she found a niche in the campus Methodist student fellowship. From its informal curriculum, she came to see "social justice as an obligation, not 'you *might* do this. You *might* consider voting, you *might* consider thinking people are equal.'" You *must* improve the world, she learned. She had followed this imperative in her advocacy for children in Head Start and through the League and now wondered about her professional efficacy.

As a Metro member, Stavinoha attended an IAF training session for leaders. Ernie Cortes challenged her assurance in her expert influence. "Ernie was talking about how this is *not* a civic organization. And I realized that most of the things I'd been doing, I had been doing as either service or civic."[53] Like Sister Pearl a few years earlier, Marilyn felt that her actions had been ameliorative but had not challenged the distribution of power; her considerable intelligence hadn't been able to change the basic system that denied kids necessary resources. Marilyn resigned from the League and devoted herself to Metro/COPS to enlist citizens to push for more funding for the public schools. Instead of relying on her expertise to win agreement or programs, she used it to inform and to inspire others to mobilize to exert pressure on public officials.

White women in Metro traded the polite behavior and benevolence expected of Anglo women for assertiveness and empathy with hardship. These middle-class Metro Alliance women, whose influence came from higher education, college degrees, and well-honed social skills, gained a new respect for the obstacles working-class Mexican Americans had to surmount. "[Mexican American women] tell these stories about how they wanted to go to school, but they had to stay home and work to take care of younger brothers and sisters. So they've had difficult lives. . . . I certainly developed a deeper appreciation of their struggle," Jane Tuck recalls. The longing for formal education resonated with women who took pride in their professional skills, and the white women could feel regret for a loss they had not personally faced.

White men who joined Metro faced a racialized gender imperative different from white women's. They were expected to hold power as a result of their competent direction of national strength, public security, and economic development, but they were also responsible for developing and maintaining opportunities for every citizen. Having gained positions of leadership, the men who joined Metro Alliance were distressed by failures of fairness, which challenged their integrity as the people supposed to be in charge.

Among these was David Semrad, who came into Metro with Colonial Hills United Methodist Church, one of the largest churches at the 1982 founding meeting. Semrad's family had joined the church when he moved to San Antonio in 1976 to direct the Methodist campus ministry at San Antonio College, the city's heavily enrolled community college.[54] After an Oklahoma farm childhood, David discovered intellectual life at Oklahoma State University and participated in vibrant civil rights debates when he went for training at Perkins Theological Seminary in the late 1960s. He chose San Antonio as a more diverse city for raising his children than the all-white college in an all-white Kansas town where he had accepted a chaplaincy after graduating from seminary.

Semrad realized that he needed the help of the Rio Grande Conference of Spanish-Speaking Methodist churches to help him attract students from San Antonio College's predominantly Mexican American student population. In the past, the financially modest churches of the Rio Grande Conference had been ignored, because money for the campus ministry had always come from the wealthier Southwest Conference of English-Speaking churches. Semrad had to persuade the Anglo conference to see the value of the human contribution of the Mexican American churches and to reassure the Rio Grande Conference that it would have equal authority with the Anglo financial backers.

Semrad optimistically began a Bible study class, "and when I asked some of my students to read the scriptures, they couldn't read. And they were college students. And it was embarrassing to them. It was embarrassing to me. I felt bad about it." David felt personally insulted, he remembers, because the young people's failure showed that many adults were not taking responsibility for the "Methodist value of seeing that there's access to college for every kid," that good education is a "birthright." Who had failed these young people? How had the responsible people, white men who looked like David Semrad, failed in their duties?

Self-righteously outraged and determined to rectify the educational inequity, Semrad announced to Homer Bain, a fellow congregant at Colonial Hills, that he was going to run for public office to rally voters and cure the public school deficiencies. Fortunately, David now recalls, Homer "saved me. 'I have a better idea,' Homer said, and he introduced me to Metro." Focusing on organizing instead of politicking required Semrad to shift away from an individualistic, middle-class ideal of male heroism to the less valiant concept of collaboration and community organizing, of persuading other people to come along with him instead of stepping forward to lead them into the fray. David became the cochair of a COPS-Metro alliance to raise scholarship funds from the business community. The program did not end funding disparities among the city's fourteen school districts, but it did result in the city's committing funds to assist hard-working students whose parents could not pay their college costs.

The Anglo middle-class men and women who joined Metro formulated new ways to live as white women and men in sympathy and respectful collaboration with Mexican Americans. An important aspect of their revised white identity was a positive view of social connection at odds with the prevailing Anglo distrust of public programs. The Protestant Anglos in Metro questioned the view that individualistic self-reliance was an adequate ethic and found merit in some ideas more identified with Roman Catholicism—that social institutions like schools and walkable streets were essential elements of community health. The Anglos who adopted a more expansive discourse of public responsibility helped shift the political discourse so that low taxes and minimal city services no longer equated with whiteness. As Charlie Cottrell says of his own early work with the Mexican American organizers from St. Mary's, they were "people speaking about cardinal, fundamental religious and democratic values. . . . It's not a question of ethnic identity so much as it is a kind of simple justice, of what's fair." At last, some Anglos welcomed Mexican American political participation that raised issues essential to good city governance.

## Democracy as Civil Engagement

In the early 1980s the city's voters approved bond issues and adopted patterns of public spending that included "older minority neighborhoods" along with "newer, middle-income areas" and business development. A city bond issue that passed in 1980 included some of the West Side projects rejected in the 1978 vote. A citywide infrastructure plan set spending goals, and in 1983 citizens approved the first stage of a five-stage improvement plan. San Antonio planning historian Heywood T. Sanders argues that COPS pushed the city to "sustain a neighborhood-oriented investment agenda, [but was not able] to stop or reshape the economic development agenda of the local business community."[55] Sanders's conclusion, while a reasonable reading of city budget data, misses a less tangible political shift made possible by Metro Alliance's collaboration with COPS.

The ideal of human development as a city goal became the basis for much COPS/Metro work in the 1980s and shifted political discussions. Marilyn Stavinoha reflects on the contrast between these new values and the old ways of doing business: Before, the city's politicians "would be talking about building this or dredging that or changing this, but never about the people, about developing the human capital of San Antonio." This changed with Mayor Henry Cisneros, who became the city's head cheerleader and planner in four terms, 1981–1989. Although Cisneros had entered politics on the GGL's at-large slate in 1975 and spoke the language of the city's business developers, by 1984 his rhetoric came much closer to that of COPS/Metro; he argued that the most urgent infrastructure for business in the technology age was "quality education at all levels."[56] The mayor took credit for instituting an engineering degree program at the San Antonio branch of the University of Texas in 1980, magnet high schools of technology and health careers, a library foundation, and new programs for the University of Texas Medical Center.[57] Without COPS/Metro's constant assertion of, and publicity for, a new vision of development, it is hard to imagine how a Mexican American mayor could have sold ideas of child nurture and educational opportunities to the city's business leaders and Anglo voters.

COPS/Metro then argued that it was a public responsibility to aid families to overcome barriers that were invisible to most middle-class Anglo households, like low family income and a need for teenage children to take jobs to help support their families. The allies proposed a San Antonio Educational Partnership, which the Chamber of Commerce and local education institutions approved in August 1988. The group pledged city and private business funds to support scholarships for students who maintained a B average and 95 percent attendance rate in high school. If the young people fulfilled their academic responsibilities, then the city and its business leaders would pay out money toward their advanced education.

One of the Metro leaders who advocated for a San Antonio Educational Partnership was Swen Borg, a native Texan Anglo who had gone from a farm childhood to the University of Texas and then a successful career with a large Midwestern manufacturer.[58] When he returned to Texas in the mid-1980s and joined Colonial Hills United Methodist Church, Borg assessed the Educational Partnership through the lens of his longtime employer, Owens-Illinois, a company that viewed service to the community as congruent with sound business principles. The problem was not with the students, but with the possibilities that the adult-run economic environment presented to them, Borg believed. Financial aid was essential to change the prospects of young people "from the low economic end of town where 80 to 85 percent of the families were low income, and kids didn't have any incentive to finish high school [because] they weren't going to go to college anyway," Borg recalls. Without hope of good training and a better job at the end, why would students do the hard work necessary to succeed in school?

Metro/COPS convinced the city's political and business leaders to "move away from the low-wage concept San Antonio has been tied to," Borg explains, the economy that Anglos had built on the assumption of a large immobile Mexican American working class, and toward the recognition that "if you don't make these opportunities available, then your city is not going to progress. It's not going to maintain the pace it needs to maintain in the future. . . . You have to look at the vision that whatever raises the economic standard of the community is good for everybody." Working in collaboration with COPS, the Metro Alliance Anglos moved away from the city's history of Anglo racial dominance and its assumptions that Anglo interests were different from minority interests and needed to be defended against Mexican Americans.

COPS had created an effective neighborhood training ground for Mexican Americans to advocate a different agenda for the city and to organize as a community to negotiate with Anglo power holders. When COPS celebrated its tenth anniversary in 1983, its first president, Andy Sarabia, summarized how he saw the past decade:

> Ten years ago, the city leaders said, "Leave them alone. They're Mexicans. They can't organize." Today we have power, we have our culture, we have our faith, we have our communities, we have our dignity, and we're still Mexicans. They feared the successful revolution we started that changed San Antonio from a government of the few by the few to a government of the people, by the people, and for the people.[59]

COPS had brought into the city's political discussions the Mexican American community and its political values of a person's right to participate in the central elements of existence—family, workplace, neighborhood, city—and of society's duty to enable that participation.

By the early 1980s some Anglos had responded positively to the integrity of these Mexican American citizens and the community history, values, and issues they brought to the political arena. While Anglos remained firmly grounded in their own histories, they learned that achieving the values they held dear required a willingness to listen, to talk, and to collaborate. They gave up the old Anglo stance of distance and dominance for new relationships, learning a new form of politics, Homer Bain concludes, that "is not one group overpowering another by either logic or force; it's hearing others' stories and finding that common experience." To Anglos who had historically held the power in San Antonio based on residential, economic, and political distance from the Mexican American community, Metro offered the chance to engage in the democratic, egalitarian, productive tension of building relationships and sharing governance.

# Conclusion

Democracy must be learned anew in each generation.
—*Gordon Allport on Kurt Lewin, 1948*

Properly understood, democracy is a set of *practices*. It
requires skills that enable people to engage one another
about their experiences, their hopes, their dreams,
and what they expect from their government.
—*Ernesto Cortes Jr., 2006*

## Inspiration

During the civil rights movement African Americans, Mexican Americans, American Indians, various communities of Asian Americans, and other groups racialized as nonwhite held up an image of the United States at odds with the one most white Americans had of themselves and of their nation. These peoples of color used historic U.S. rhetoric to advocate that principles of liberty and equality extend to all citizens, not only to white ones. They elaborated these principles with values from their own minority communities and asserted that a genuinely democratic nation nurtured the well-being of all its citizens and enabled them to argue and make decisions fairly.[1]

White Americans, who held a near monopoly of the nation's benefits and its governance, had to decide how to respond. Would they resist the diminution of their power and confidently hold onto their cultural, economic, residential, educational, and political advantage? Would they make a few palliative adjustments and minimize any loss of privilege? Would they parcel out a few more resources, then walk away from any further discussion? Many, historians tell us, did react in only these limited ways.

But some white Americans, as these interracial stories illustrate, felt inspired by the civil rights movement to risk living in new relationships that had few precedents. They put themselves into conversations, neighborhoods, and alliances that meant their lives would diverge from those they had expected. Taking these risks in turn added energy to the civil rights movement to confront the dominance and inequalities of gendered/racialized difference.

The white Americans I have followed in this book chose to associate with people who had been off-limits, to live in areas of cities that had been defamed, and to collaborate with fellow citizens who had been patronized and feared. The nonwhite participants were aware of the delusions of some white do-gooders who expected to overcome racism by, as some of the mid-1970s NCCJ campers put it, "being willing to be [the] friend" of a black person. But for the most part these white innovators, in tandem with equally hopeful and skilled African American, Mexican American, and Asian American allies, built new frameworks of camp, neighborhood, and political alliance that authorized and enabled African American and Mexican American, Chinese American and Filipino American to rebut white denials of privilege and to encourage genuine listening and affirmation. These white Americans had no assurance of the outcomes; they were simply unwilling to continue the unjust arrangements the civil rights movement had exposed. That they were able to act on their visions was possible only because they found associates in communities of color who were equally daring and committed to building new relationships.

As historian and author, the hardest thing for me to overcome has been my fear that colleagues and critical readers will dismiss these stories as feel-good and naive. "Relationship" is a suspect term that historians and social scientists have ridiculed as an example of the therapeutic turn in U.S. culture that, since the early twentieth century, has replaced social critique and self-examination with a rather painless, if highly emotional, readjustment of individual psyches. The therapeutic implies a self-delusory shift in feeling without any change in the social realities of privilege and disadvantage. The therapeutic "I" doesn't have to take responsibility for much more than feelings—no need to understand history, politics, income distribution, or the quality of neighborhood schools. In this critique, feeling does not inspire reflection and thought.

One purpose of this book has been to retrieve relationship building as essential to democratic life and to show that such a goal was not invariably escapist or easy. Making a genuinely new relationship required that people meet as equals and figure out together the terms of their playing, living, and working together. New relationships allowed for speaking and listening, sadness and guilt, anger and comfort, disagreement and questioning. But the test of a new relationship was whether it resulted in changed behavior—not white self-flagellation, but white determination to reduce dominance and convey respect.

In building these interracial sites, most of the white people who participated did not know what they would learn or how their lives would change. Challenged and buoyed by the civil rights movement, they were willing to enter new environments and to have new conversations. Inspired by religious principles, humanist ideals, New Deal histories, 1960s youth rebellion and hopefulness, labor union unity, and commitment to fundamental U.S. values of democratic governance and equal human worth, some white Americans came together with brother and sister citizens of color in delimited places to see what they could do together.

## Intentionality

Living as equals took learning. In a country and culture with entrenched institutions and compelling cultural images that constructed gendered/racialized citizens and rationalized inequality, free spaces had to be planned. The camp, neighborhood, and community organization defined spaces to try out new behaviors, equalized power within these spaces, and taught techniques to break out of old habits. These methods have become commonplace in recent years, especially in peace work in Northern Ireland and in Israel/Palestine. (These may seem extreme comparisons to the United States, but watching a few episodes of *Eyes on the Prize* will remind readers that parts of this country descended into public warfare on many occasions in the civil rights era.)[2]

For example, the Children's Friendship Project for Northern Ireland ran teen camps at De Sales University in the United States for a number of years to bring together Irish Protestant and Catholic young people.[3] The best-known teen camp, the well-documented Seeds of Peace three-week summer camp for Israelis and Arabs (of whom 50 percent are Palestinians), has run since 1993. Its first-year class had only boys, suggesting how much trickier co-ed associations are, but since 1994, the camp has recruited 50 percent boys and 50 percent girls. Though their governments choose these campers and their presence has quasi-official authorization, the human relations practices echo those in NCCJ camps. The directors guarantee a neutral safe space and model approval of the "national identity" of each camper, some of whom return a second year as leaders. The young people are taught how to listen, to be candid in their responses, to speak of their pain, to acknowledge emotions, and to "make one friend" to break stereotypes. When the young people " 'realize that someone is willing to listen to them,' " one leader says, "the youngsters are able to begin making a transition from demanding to be heard to hearing what the other side has to say."[4] As with the earlier NCCJ camp staff, Seeds of Peace leaders assume that these young people will return home, teach what they've learned to their classmates and families, and challenge the ongoing definition of Israeli as enemy to Arab and vice-versa. The planners believe "it will take several generations for populations reared in fear, mistrust, and hatred to begin to trust one another," a reminder to Americans of the hard process only begun during the civil rights movement.[5]

Fewer attempts have been made to build intertribal neighborhoods. One recent example is also from the Middle East, where the Presbyterian Church USA gives support to a village of twenty-six Israeli Jewish families and twenty-six Israeli Palestinian families. In the Oasis of Peace, the children learn both Hebrew and Arabic; parents and children participate in workshops to learn how to manage conflict; and the community maintains a spiritual retreat center.[6]

These endeavors work from the premise that most people learn social divisions—of race or language, religion or immigration status, and so forth—and do not learn to see each other with kindness, respect, and caring. In the United States, even young children learn the nation's predominant public values of individualism and competitiveness, with benevolence the primary form of authorized caring. The skills of democratic self-assertion, listening, empathy, and negotiation are so rare that a group of prominent Harvard Business School professors recently released a best-selling book about how to learn them and how to hold "difficult conversations."[7]

At the NCCJ camps, in Neighbors Inc., and in the COPS/Metro Alliance, planners defined physical or metaphorical spaces that were inclusive, respectful of each person, and hopeful. Camp directors in the 1950s and early 1960s notably treated every gendered/racialized body as if it had the same value, giving up the normative white body and associated gender roles. In the late 1960s and early 1970s, camp leaders responded to racial power movements by more explicitly welcoming and affirming the array of histories and viewpoints the campers expressed. Neighbors Inc. used newsletters, monthly socials, public celebrations, and civic activism to learn about different heritages, practice friendship, and protect a heterogeneous neighborhood. IAF organizers treated each person's life story, first in COPS and then in Metro Alliance, as integral to the group's developing political capacities.

## An Inventory

A second purpose of this book is to break out of the fruitless argument over whether the United States is less racist now than in the past (in some ways it is, in other ways it isn't; it's different) and to ask more constructive questions.[8] The interracial sites where white and nonwhite Americans encountered each other may lead us to greater scrutiny of three particular systems of making race and inequality: white superiority and social distance; residential separation; and noninclusive governance.

First, regarding white superiority, one place to look at differential estimations of intelligence is public funding for education, which has been a heated political topic since the tax revolts of the late 1970s. Discussions around the national No Child Left Behind (NCLB) legislation of 2001 reveal both egalitarian and discriminatory actions. NCLB's requirement that schools monitor student progress according to racial grouping and special education needs places responsibility on school authorities to make certain that every child succeeds, a huge change from the expectations of the legally segregated school systems of the 1950s. Yet, annual NCLB reports reveal ongoing inequalities in performance that reinforce images of white students' (and groups of Asian students') intellectual superiority. Without placing the results in context—information about family income, school budgets, and available school resources of space, books, and equipment—the data perpetuate the cultural impression that white students are more capable than African American, Latino, and Native American children and that high dropout rates among children of color are not a public crisis. NCLB commentary also ignores the historical tax revolt, which could be characterized as a white response to desegregation that reduced public funding for education at precisely the historical moment when children of color began to fill a substantial number of seats in school classrooms.[9]

Second, the persistence of residential segregation, which has abated only modestly since its high point in 1970, explains ongoing de facto school segregation.[10] The suburban flight of the 1950s was succeeded by flight to sprawling exurbs or to exclusive enclaves protected, in our era, by gates and guards instead of real estate agents and mortgage brokers.[11] The symbiosis of racially segregated housing and schools remains so complete that the state of Texas was able to solve its political need to recruit African American and Mexican American students to the state's flagship university campuses by adopting a top-ten-percent program. Admitting the top ten percent of every one of the state's high schools automatically brought substantial numbers of African Americans and Mexican Americans to campus from their primarily monoracial high schools. The new policy also, as Lani Guinier and Gerald Torres remind us, revealed the widespread consequences of attaching good educations to privileged white neighborhoods when the new admissions criterion enrolled numbers of rural white youngsters who had been disqualified by their inferior preparation in poor rural school districts.[12]

Third, in terms of levels of engagement in public decision making, the past two presidential elections have brought attention to voting procedures and voter qualifications that reduce turnout. While I agree with the IAF analysis that voting is a feeble proxy for democratic participation, recent studies reveal a need to attend to the racial effects of our current policies. Paradoxically, in the post–Voting Rights Act decades of the 1980s and 1990s, voting rates dropped to "one of the lowest turnout rates among the world's democracies."[13]

Though those who bemoan low black and Latino turnout invoke voter intimidation, while others point to apathy to explain voters' choice not to participate, two other systems are at work to reduce, disproportionately, the voter interest of nonwhite citizens. The automatic (and sometimes permanent) disenfranchisement of felons leads to a particularly horrible symbiosis of high incarceration rates for black and Latino males and low turnout rates in their home communities.[14] The shrinking of a public agenda for government action and the knee-jerk hostility to taxes for public services disqualify many programs that poorer neighborhoods—again disproportionately African American and Latino—have interests in.[15] In both systems, white voters and citizens could join coalitions to change these racialized practices.

# Inheritance

The three sites that make up this book continued to be magnets for inter-racial action, though diminished in some cases from their civil rights hey-day. The National Conference of Christians and Jews retained its acronym, NCCJ, but changed its name to the National Conference for Community and Justice in the late 1990s. It remained an active human relations group, having expanded its purview to include concern for Hindus, Buddhists, and Muslims in the United States and for hostility to gay men and lesbi-ans, until 2006. Local groups are picking up the pieces of the now-defunct and much-missed NCCJ, and the Southern California version has recon-stituted as the California Conference for Equality and Justice.[16] Although the Los Angeles Brotherhood camp ended in the early 2000s, the South-ern California regional office continued to run high school programs until 2006 called Building Bridges and On-Campus Dialogues, "where diverse students address human relations issues around race and culture and how they impact our school communities."[17]

The official organization of Neighbors Inc. dwindled away in the early 2000s, but the neighborhood remains one of the few stable interracial areas of the nation's capital. Shepherd Park is even more upper middle class than in the 1960s and early 1970s, and Takoma Park, D.C., has many new condominiums around the subway station, with house prices rising due to intense economic development in nearby Silver Spring, Maryland. Georgetown University law professor Sheryll Cashin describes buying a house on one of Shepherd Park's quiet, leafy streets in the belief that the neighborhood represented a "true melding of the races," only to discover the census breakdown was 72 percent black and 21 percent white, with vir-tually no Latinos. She views the black preponderance as a revelation about the reluctance of most white Americans to live in places where they are not the clear majority and speculates that "a lot more integration between the races would occur if whites experienced being outnumbered more fre-quently and were therefore forced to adjust to and learn about people who may or may not be different from them."[18] A few white families in the old NI area still take that dare.

Some white families who live in Shepherd Park and Takoma Park moved in as part of the original interracialism of the 1950s and 1960s. Joining them are young families, many of them Jewish and attracted to Tifereth Israel or to its revitalized neighbor, the Orthodox synagogue, Ohev Shalom. Many of these young parents want to raise children in an interracial environment, which Shepherd Park and Takoma Park enable. The younger families have generally higher incomes than their parents' generation had, but they face the same dilemmas about the poor quality of the area's public schools. For many, including Tifereth Israel's current rabbi, the solution has been to send their children to Jewish parochial schools. Others have wavered between joining with black, middle-class neighbors to sustain Shepherd Park Elementary and paying for nonparochial private schools—the same choices that faced the 1960s and 1970s NI households. So the cycle continues as the middle-class parents, in black families and in white, take their children out of the neighborhood school.[19] White families continue to see the area as a place for comfortable interracial residence, but the schools, an important basis of interracial connection, remain almost completely black.

COPS/Metro Alliance continues as one of many statewide affiliates of the Texas IAF. The group challenges Texas's history of maintaining paltry expenditures for public services (what one white resident calls the "thank God for Mississippi" mentality—knowing that so long as Mississippi exists, Texas will come out ahead of at least one other state in its standards of citizen deprivation). The IAF's two-page agenda for politicians seeking votes in the fall 2006 elections began: "The Network of Texas IAF Organizations supports a strong public sector. . . . We believe that the public sector is necessary to have a strong and vibrant economy and promote the development of Texas families."[20] The agenda includes specific proposals for public obligation and spending in education (Texas ranks forty-eighth in SAT scores and fiftieth in graduation rates), health care, immigration reform, affordable housing and residential infrastructure, workforce development, and tax reform.

The IAF agenda nowhere mentions race, religion, or language but puts its supporters on the side of public concern that sees as problems the systems that have helped sustain white privilege and racialize Mexican American and African American citizens of Texas. At state IAF conventions, Anglos, African Americans, and Mexican Americans gather, signaled by informally bilingual proceedings (where someone is always around to translate to Spanish-only or English-only delegates) and by black church choirs and Roman Catholic, Jewish, and Protestant prayer leaders, all invoking the religious necessity to seek a public good. In San Antonio, the multiracial, multireligious, multicultural gatherings embody a vision of the city seen in no other venue, except perhaps the public celebrations of the San Antonio Spurs basketball team.

# Choices

The final purpose of this book is to remind readers that people make history. Our choices matter. Especially in a nation pledged to democratic government, our choices and actions matter. In view of the horrors of World War II, his understanding of the effects of social forces on individuals, and his hopes for a tolerant and democratic postwar world, Kurt Lewin believed that one generation could not do the work for all time. Each generation, indeed each person, had to learn to live democratically. Societies needed social groups that provided the necessary experiences for each citizen to become a democratic human being, and humans also had to create these anew.

A primary hindrance to democratic learning in the postwar United States was the undiminished idea, with its panoply of supporting institutions and images, that race divided humans into categories of those who dominated and those who acquiesced. How could white Americans give up their historical racial dominance and its pleasant feelings of superiority? How could white Americans risk connecting with peoples depicted as problems? How could white Americans accept views of the nation that moved them out of its center? And how could they give up white control of public debate and admit the legitimacy of other voices? How, as political theorist Danielle S. Allen asks, could white Americans even learn to "accommodate frankness about difference?"[21]

To build a less racialized and more equitable country is not the work of finding and adopting the correct political agenda. What this book suggests is that change has happened when people risked developing relationships across racialized boundaries and deconstructing inequality. Such relationships were not the easy backslapping or polite greeting of casual acquaintances; they were not personal in the sense of liking someone separately from their history, family, and neighborhood. Instead, genuine relationships required the same kind of work as friendships.

The new relationships had the quality of what Danielle S. Allen names "political friendship," which "consists finally of trying to be *like* friends," when friendship is understood "as not an emotion but a practice."[22] Expectations among friends include taking turns, making and recognizing each other's sacrifices, reciprocating in carrying burdens, and coming to trust that these are the functioning rules of the relationship. Like personal friendship, building political friendship is time consuming and risky. But, like a strong personal friendship, political friendship expands our knowledge of the world, opens up new insights and emotions, increases our responsibility to others and theirs to us, and moves the world toward what Metro Alliance member Homer Bain calls "the realm of God."

Generations of theologians have reminded us that "love," or "political friendship," is hard work. Even though they were supported and challenged by the large-hearted spirit of the civil rights movement, camp directors and campers, neighborhood defenders, and political advocates for Mexican American participation quickly learned that treating one's neighbor as an equal was a public expression often not supported by schoolmates and parents, by housing markets and public officials, or by community leaders and business developers. For white Americans, stepping out of one's privileged group and role endangered ongoing and prevalent systems that discouraged crossracial affection and care, valued the commodity nature of public schools, and provoked and manipulated racial distrust for electoral victories.

The challenges of learning democracy and living as equals in our own time have not diminished. With rising fears about global terror, economic competition, and environmental degradation, the challenges may even have increased. Who, holding the ordinary privileges of white Americans or of U.S. citizenship generally, would risk losing this advantage? Yet, these stories show the promise that we all are capable of courageous connections, of moving outside comfortable spaces filled with familiar and presumably similar people and of doing the hard intellectual work of analyzing and confronting divisive and destructive systems.[23] This book offers an enticement, I hope, to readers of whatever racial identification and categorization to reject building barriers and to pursue relationships that nurture all young people, extend neighborliness, and expand political friendships. It's our choice.

# Notes

## Introduction

1. The convention of not capitalizing "black" and "white" implies that these are descriptive terms, which poses a problem for a scholar of race. Even as I write to demonstrate how "race" is constructed and deconstructed by human action, the uncapitalized use of racial categories implies that these are biologically based and manifested in incommensurable groups: a black race, a white race, Hispanics who are either white or not white. Scholars of race use both conventions—capitalizing or not. Because the practice of capitalizing has been less common among historians, I will not capitalize these terms in this book. Occasionally I juxtapose "white" versus "nonwhite" to indicate the historical view that "white" people constituted a demographic majority, a dominant cultural expression, or both, which viewed those designated "nonwhite" as unable to constitute the normative "American."

2. After a jury found O. J. Simpson not guilty of murder in a criminal trial in October 1995, a Gallup poll recorded responses in the same racial terms as the trial's reporting: 78 percent of blacks and only 42 percent of whites agreed with the verdict. After a civil trial that found O. J. Simpson responsible, 26 percent of blacks and 74 percent of whites supported the verdict. This manner of reporting intensified notions of racial difference, even as the poll numbers revealed that 42 percent of whites aligned with blacks in the first instance and that 26 percent of blacks adopted the same position as whites in the second. The figures are from Gallup Poll News Service, 7 February 1997, cited in Howard Schuman, Charlotte Steeh, Lawrence D. Bobo, and Maria Krysan, *Racial Attitudes in America: Trends and Interpretations*, rev. ed. (Cambridge: Harvard University Press, 1998), 362, n1.

3. Examples include Numan V. Bartley, *The Rise of Massive Resistance: Race and Politics in the South in the 1950s* (Baton Rouge: Louisiana State University Press, 1969); Ronald P. Formisano, *Boston against Busing: Race, Class, and Ethnicity in the 1960s and 1970s* (Chapel Hill: University of North Carolina Press, 1991); and Thomas Sugrue, *Origins of the Urban Crisis: Race and Inequality in Postwar Detroit* (Princeton: Princeton University Press, 1996).

4. Examples include Mary King, *Freedom Song: A Personal Story of the 1960s Civil*

*Rights Movement* (New York: Morrow, 1987); Constance Curry, Joan C. Browning, Dorothy Dawson Burlage, Penny Patch, Theresa Del Pozzo, Sue Thrasher, Elaine DeLott Baker, Emmie Schrader Adams, and Casey Hayden, *Deep in Our Hearts: Nine White Women in the Freedom Movement* (Athens: University of Georgia Press, 2000).

5. Jason Sokol, *There Goes My Everything: White Southerners in the Age of Civil Rights, 1945–1975* (New York: Knopf, 2006). Sokol describes the "everyday revolution" in racial behaviors that some white Southerners experienced as liberation and others preferred to forget (356, 326).

6. Kevin M. Kruse, in *White Flight: Atlanta and the Making of Modern Conservatism* (Princeton: Princeton University Press, 2005), describes the rise of white suburban conservatism as the product of ideas developed in response to urban desegregation. Matthew D. Lassiter, in *The Silent Majority: Suburban Politics in the Sunbelt South* (Princeton: Princeton University Press, 2006), argues that nationwide a 1970s white, suburban silent majority protected "private property values, individual taxpayer rights, children's educational privileges, family residential security, and white innocence" as political stances having no origin in, or bearing on, racial segregation and inequality (304).

7. Matthew Frye Jacobson, *Roots Too: White Ethnic Revival in Post-Civil Rights America* (Cambridge: Harvard University Press, 2006), makes the case generally for white ethnics replacing suspect WASPs culturally as the normative white American by the mid-1970s. Of many texts Jacobson analyzes, Norman Podhoretz's "My Negro Problem—and Ours," published in 1963 in *Commentary,* made clear that the early twentieth-century European immigrant had no share "in the exploitation of the Negro" and therefore no need to change in response to civil rights. See esp. 187–97; 195, quoting Podhoretz.

8. Tracy Elaine K'Meyer, *Interracialism and Christian Community in the Postwar South: The Story of Koinonia Farm* (Charlottesville: University of Virginia Press, 1997), makes a significant distinction between "integration" and "interracialism" based on the ideals of the radical white Christians who organized Koinonia Farm in Georgia. Its leaders saw "integration" as "a coercive political and legal process. . . . Instead, they believed they were fostering interracial relationships within a community based on spiritual and material sharing" (102). My interracial sites never reached the level of spiritual self-consciousness or material sharing of Koinonia, but their basic hope of human connection was similar.

9. Paul L. Wachtel, *Race in the Mind of America: Breaking the Vicious Cycle between Blacks and Whites* (New York: Routledge, 1999), 37.

10. Peggy McIntosh, "White Privilege and Male Privilege: A Personal Account of Coming to See Correspondences through Work in Women's Studies," in *Race, Class, and Gender. An Anthology,* ed. Margaret L. Andersen and Patricia Hill Collins (Belmont, Calif.: Wadsworth, 1995), 76.

11. Nikhil Pal Singh offers a passionate and stringent argument for a much-

extended civil rights chronology in *Black Is a Country: Race and the Unfinished Struggle for Democracy* (Cambridge: Harvard University Press, 2004).

12. Kenneth Jackson, *Crabgrass Frontier: The Suburbanization of the United States* (New York: Oxford University Press, 1985), and George Lipsitz, "The Possessive Investment in Whiteness: Racialized Social Democracy and the 'White' Problem in American Studies," *American Quarterly* 47 (September 1995), lay out the public policies, economic consequences, and cultural rationales for planning the postwar suburban building boom that segregated the nation spatially at the very moment it was desegregating legally.

13. John A. Booth and David R. Johnson, "Community Progress and Power in San Antonio," in *The Politics of San Antonio: Community, Progress, and Power*, ed. David R. Johnson, John A. Booth, and Richard Harris (Lincoln: University of Nebraska Press, 1983). For the statewide context of Anglo-Mexican segregation, see David Montejano, *Anglos and Mexicans in the Making of Texas, 1836–1986* (Austin: University of Texas Press, 1987).

14. Richard A. Garcia, in *Rise of the Mexican American Middle Class, San Antonio, 1929–1941* (College Station: Texas A & M Press, 1991). Rodolfo Rosales describes, in *The Illusion of Inclusion: The Untold Political Story of San Antonio* (Austin: University of Texas Press, 2000), a failed struggle of middle-class Chicanos to gain political power. Rosales shows how the middle-class politicos were able to move out of barrio poverty and become acceptable only when they acted like middle-class Anglos; when they advocated the interests of working-class and poor Chicanos, Anglos voted them out of office (138).

15. COPS has received much attention from scholars of democracy and community power building, who typically do not analyze it in the context of race or examine the antiracializing consequences of its alliance with Metro. For a good account that puts the San Antonio organization in a statewide context of organizing Mexican Americans, African Americans, and Anglos, see Mark R. Warren, *Dry Bones Rattling: Community Building to Revitalize American Democracy* (Princeton: Princeton University Press, 2001). Although Warren recognizes that persistent racializing and racial competition inhibit community organizing and citywide alliances, he does not explore how COPS and Metro overcame the old racializing ideas (26–27).

16. Peter Stearns and Jan Lewis have recently advocated what they call "emotionology," the historical study of the culture and standards for feeling and emotional expression held at particular historical moments. See their introduction to *An Emotional History of the United States*, ed. Peter N. Stearns and Jan Lewis (New York: New York University Press, 1998). Emotional states—whom I can like, whom I can order around, whom I can speak back to, whom I feel is a peer and equal—were central to the national change required by civil rights, and oral history interviews provide insight into this understudied aspect of the era.

17. Ruth Frankenberg, *White Women, Race Matters: The Social Construction of Whiteness* (Minneapolis: University of Minnesota Press, 1993), 20.

18. Ashley Montagu, *Man's Most Dangerous Myth: The Fallacy of Race,* 6th ed. (Walnut Creek, Calif.: AltaMira Press, 1997), 57–62. Montagu cites both an eighteenth-century origin and a fifteenth-century Portuguese text and concludes that it was "only among peoples who kept slaves that the hereditary or biological conception of race differences developed" (60). Montagu's famous text preceded his authorship of the 1950 UNESCO statement on race, which was characterized as showing that "race was less a biological fact than a social myth." For a recent review of the topic, see the Social Science Research Council's Web forum "Is Race 'Real'?" at *http://raceandgenomics.ssrc. org/* (accessed May 18, 2007).

19. K. Anthony Appiah and Amy Gutmann, *Color Conscious: The Political Morality of Race* (Princeton: Princeton University Press, 1996), 54.

20. Stuart Hall, "Reflections on 'Race, Articulation, and Societies Structured in Dominance,'" in *Race Critical Theories,* ed. Philomena Essed and David Theo Goldberg (Malden, Mass. : Blackwell, 2002), 453.

21. Judith Butler, *Bodies That Matter: On the Discursive Limits of Sex* (New York: Routledge, 1993), 247, n15.

22. Gayle Rubin, in "The Traffic in Women: Notes on the 'Political Economy' of Sex," in *Toward an Anthropology of Women,* ed. Rayna R. Reiter (New York: Monthly Review Press, 1975), argued that social roles of "gender" were elaborated on the physical basis of "sex," meaning genitalia, and that the two should not be confused. The behaviors women had been constrained to perform were not marks of innate female nature and could not be used to justify cultural norms of incommensurable genders. Simone de Beauvoir had made a similar, though differently argued, point in the classic *The Second Sex* (1952), opening the book with the then-shocking statement: "Woman is made, not born."

23. The earliest analysis of the intersection of race, gender, class, and sexual social constructions is the Combahee River Collective's "A Black Feminist Statement," in *Capitalist Patriarchy and the Case for Socialist Feminism,* ed. Zillah R. Eisenstein (New York: Monthly Review Press, 1979). The most widely popularized statements came in the anthology *This Bridge Called My Back,* ed. Gloria Anzaldúa and Cherríe Moraga (New York: Kitchen Table/Women of Color Press, 1983). Of popular culture in the late 1940s, Judith E. Smith, in *Visions of Belonging: Family Stories, Popular Culture, and Postwar Democracy, 1940–1960* (New York: Columbia University Press, 2004), writes: "Because racialist boundaries had previously relied on strictly enforced gender and sexual norms, reimagining any of these opened up the others to instability" (138).

24. Mae M. Ngai, *Impossible Subjects: Illegal Aliens and the Making of Modern America* (Princeton: Princeton University Press, 2004), 131; see generally "The Creation of the Mexican Agricultural Proletariat in the United States," 129–68. Ngai also argues that treating Mexicans and Asians as "noncitizens" was more palatable than declaring them "nonpersons" in a racialized fashion, even though citizenship regulation had the same exclusionary function; see epigraph and 1–9.

25. For a representative set of essays, see Birgit Brander Rasmussen, Irene J. Nexica, Eric Klinenberg, and Matt Wray, *Making and Unmaking of Whiteness* (Durham: Duke University Press, 2001); David Roediger, a prominent U.S. historian in this field, has written *Towards the Abolition of Whiteness* (London:Verso, 1994). For a historian's sympathetic critique, see Peter Kolchin, "Whiteness Studies: The New History of Race in America," *Journal of American History* 89 (June 2002).

26. Noel Ignatiev and John Garvey, eds., *Race Traitor* (New York: Routledge, 1996), is the leading statement for conceiving the task as the *abolition* of whiteness.

27. Thomas C. Holt, "Marking: Race, Race-Making, and the Writing of History," *American Historical Review* 100 (February 1995): 7.

28. Lassiter, *The Silent Majority*, 322–23.

29. Debian Marty, "White Antiracist Rhetoric as Apologia: Wendell Berry's *The Hidden Wound*," in *Whiteness: The Communication of Social Identity*, ed. Thomas K. Nakayama and Judith N. Martin (Thousand Oaks, Calif.: Sage Publications, 1999), 66.

30. Social theorist Avery Gordon is attempting to reclaim the promises of "utopia." See two essays, "Some Thoughts on the Utopian" and "Something More Powerful Than Skepticism," in *Keeping Good Time: Reflections on Knowledge, Power, and People* (Boulder: Paradigm, 2004), 187. The first essay critiques the cynicism and detachment engendered by analyses of oppression, with an appreciation of Herbert Marcuse's idea that humans have an "instinct for freedom," which is for self-expression within human community. The second rethinks the political vision of writer Toni Cade Bambara, who came out of both local African American and socialist intellectual traditions to write books and movie scripts. Bambara, Gordon argues, tells each person it is better to "be right here than out there" (200) and to work together in communities "to develop a practice of being unavailable for servitude" (204), which I interpret in this book as giving up racializing actions that inflict social separation and a lack of care for sister and brother human beings.

31. Kurt Lewin, *Resolving Social Conflicts* (New York: Harper and Row, 1948), was the founding text, and the journal *Human Relations* began publication in 1948. The National Training Institute, which Lewin helped plan, held its first meeting in summer 1949, a few months after his death.

32. Although the author is personally dismayed that only prophetic religion had the motivating force to turn Americans against segregation, and although he concentrates on black activists, David L. Chappell's *A Stone of Hope: Prophetic Religion and the Death of Jim Crow* (Chapel Hill: University of North Carolina Press, 2004) is the most recent book to argue that the liberal faith in reason and inevitable human progress lacked the emotional power to move activists to the risks necessary to overthrow segregation. Prophetic religion named segregation a sin and aroused people to fight it (3–4). Charles Marsh, in *The Beloved Community: How Faith Shapes Social Justice from the Civil Rights Movement to Today* (New York: Basic Books, 2005), not only recounts familiar stories of civil rights but also rebuts the exclusively secular nature of

early twentieth-century labor organizing and links the work of church people in the labor movement with the desire to create the same kind of "beloved community" they pursued in civil rights work (5, 135–36).

33. John T. McGreevy, *Parish Boundaries: The Catholic Encounter with Race in the Twentieth-Century Urban North* (Chicago: University of Chicago Press, 1996).

34. James. F. Findlay Jr. shows in *Church People in the Struggle: The National Council of Churches and the Black Freedom Movement, 1950–1970* (New York: Oxford University Press, 1993) the disconnect between the "elitist effort initiated largely by ministers and church bureaucrats" (223) and the disinterest in and animosity to racial change of white congregations. As a scholar in the era, Kyle Haselden, put it in *The Racial Problem in Christian Perspective* (New York: Harper and Brothers, 1959): "There is little evidence that the local white churches are as yet taking seriously the resolutions and pronouncements of their respective official bodies" (33). Sara M. Evans, ed., *Journeys That Opened Up the World: Women, Student Christian Movements, and Social Justice, 1955–1975* (New Brunswick, N.J.: Rutgers University Press, 2003), is an autobiographical collection that shows the influence of campus-based Christian organizations on individual women who joined the civil rights movement.

35. Among the nine autobiographers in Curry et al., *Deep in Our Hearts*, six came out of Protestant congregations—Presbyterian, Methodist, and Swedenborgian—and one from a Jewish faith background. Only two did not mention influences of youthful religious training. Many other autobiographical accounts of white civil rights activists fit this pattern.

36. Marsh, *The Beloved Community*, 49–50.

37. John T. McGreevy, *Catholicism and American Freedom: A History* (New York: Norton, 2003), 200.

38. See McGreevy, *Catholicism*, 204–11, on growing Catholic liberalism and recognition of racism as a spiritual and political problem.

39. Michael Warner, *Changing Witness: Catholic Bishops and Public Policy, 1917–1994* (Washington, D.C.: Ethics and Public Policy Center, 1995), 59.

40. Peter Steinfels organizes *A People Adrift: The Crisis of the Roman Catholic Church in America* (New York: Simon and Schuster, 2003) around arguments between liberals and conservatives over the meaning and legacy of Vatican II, with liberals emphasizing messages of justice, democracy, and consultation and conservatives stressing the pope's continued authority to govern the faithful.

41. Paul Buhle and Robin D. C. Kelley, "Allies of a Different Sort: Jews and Blacks in the American Left," in *Struggles in the Promised Land: Toward a History of Black-Jewish Relations in the United States,* ed. Jack Salzman and Cornel West (New York: Oxford University Press, 1997), provides a useful synopsis of this history.

42. Jonathan D. Sarna, *American Judaism: A History* (New Haven: Yale University Press, 2004), 310–11.

43. Abraham Heschel, *God in Search of Man* (New York: Harper Torchbooks, 1955).

44. James J. Farrell, *The Spirit of the Sixties: Making Postwar Radicalism* (New

York: Routledge, 1997), 6. Without citing Farrell's book, David Chappell, in *A Stone of Hope*, is adamant that Martin Luther King Jr. did not fall under the influence of "personalism" at Boston University. Chappell depicts personalism as "central to liberal ideas of man and Jesus," overly optimistic and assured of the unfolding of human progress (53).

45. Marsh, *Beloved Community*, 4.

46. This reading of Paul Tillich comes from COPS organizer Ernie Cortes's paraphrasing of Tillich's analysis in *Love, Power, and Justice: Ontological Analyses and Ethical Applications* (1954), quoted in Mary Beth Rogers, *Cold Anger: A Story of Faith and Power Politics* (Denton: University of North Texas Press, 1990), 46.

47. Fannie Lou Hamer, "The Special Plight and the Role of Black Women," a speech excerpted as "It's in Your Hands," in *Black Women in White America: A Documentary History*, ed. Gerda Lerner (New York: Vintage Books, 1973), 613–14.

## Chapter 1

1. Gail Kern Paster, interviewed by author, Washington, D.C., 28 October 1995. All succeeding quotations are from this interview. The witnesses whose memories enliven this and the next chapter include camp directors, counselors, and campers from the New York City camps, which operated from the mid-1950s until the late 1960s; the Newark, N.J., camps, which ran from 1960 to 1965; and the Los Angeles camps, which started in 1950 and continued until 2006. Interviewees include two retired NCCJ officials (both white Christian men), five camp directors and staff (three white Christian women and two black Christian men), and seventeen campers (four white Christian women; two white Christian men; three white Jewish women; two black Christian women and two black Christian men; and one Filipino, one Chicano, one Korean American, and one Chinese American woman, all four raised as Christians). Four attended the New York City and New Jersey camps between 1957 and 1965. Twelve attended the Los Angeles camps between 1965 and 1975. I located camp leaders and campers through a snowball process beginning with two campers, who gave me names of acquaintances and friends. I obtained names and phone numbers of former staff people from former campers and from NCCJ offices in New York City and in Los Angeles. Some of the camper names are pseudonyms. Camp and NCCJ officials are identified by their actual names.

2. In "Culture/Wars: Recoding Empire in an Age of Democracy," *American Quarterly* 50 (1998), historian Nikhil Pal Singh sees the primary debate over postwar U.S. racial policies as between a "radical" commitment to democratic processes to include all Americans and a "liberal" belief in the preeminent need for unity to confront the threat of the Soviet Union, even it this meant public quiescence about racial segregation. Historians of U.S. cultural pluralism agree that when racial tolerance arrived on the postwar national agenda—after almost a decade of action by African American civil rights groups—the issue was construed as one of white Americans

allowing black Americans to enjoy the same legal protections and government assistance white Americans, including European immigrants, had gained. In *American Crucible: Race and Nation in the Twentieth Century* (Princeton: Princeton University Press, 2001), esp. chap. 5, Gary Gerstle argues that the acceptance of nonwhite Americans as fully entitled to citizenship had not occurred during the war. The crises of wartime race riots and the imperative to maintain prestige in a decolonizing world, however, pushed political and intellectual leaders to advocate extending tolerance to nonwhite citizens. In Gerstle's view the appeals to universal brotherhood were essentially assimilationist (274). Philip Gleason, in *Speaking of Diversity: Language and Ethnicity in Twentieth-Century America* (Baltimore: Johns Hopkins University Press, 1992), argues that " 'cultural pluralism' seemed to celebrate differences between groups, [but] actually rested on the assumptions that basic consensus made Americans one people in essentials, that the differences between groups were relatively superficial, and that toleration of those differences was required by the value system on which consensus was grounded" (60). David A. Hollinger adds, in *Postethnic America: Beyond Multiculturalism* (New York: Basic Books, 1995), that "antiblack racism" had not interested cultural pluralists of the 1920s and argues that the 1950s emphasis on integration gave "little incentive to embrace the pluralist emphasis on the autonomy and durability of ethno-racial groups" (98). Multiculturalism, as a 1990s version of cultural pluralism, elicited similar debates and criticism, both for treating the cultural expressions of nonwhites as exotic spice for an essentially homogeneous United States and for threatening the unity of a nation founded on a universal principle of tolerance, with recognition that Anglo-Saxon European values constituted the national core. See Lisa Lowe, "Imagining Los Angeles in the Production of Multiculturalism," in *Immigrant Acts* (Durham: Duke University Press, 1996), for the first position, and Arthur Schlesinger Jr., *Disuniting of America* (New York: Norton, 1992), for the second.

3. James E. Pitt, *Adventures in Brotherhood* (New York: Farrar, Straus, 1955), is an authorized history of the organization from its founding until the date of publication. Biography of Everett Clinchy, in NCCJ Records, Social Welfare History Archives, University of Minnesota (hereafter NCCJ, SWHA). "Meeting of the NCRAC Committee on Interfaith Activities with NCCJ, September 22, 1948," NCCJ, SWHA, Box 7. In the multicultural late 1990s, the NCCJ kept its initials and continued as a human relations group under the name National Conference for Community and Justice, reflecting another historical change in immigration and a need to include Muslims, Hindus, and Buddhists among other faiths.

4. Andrew Schulze, *Fire from the Throne: Race Relations in the Church* (St. Louis: Concordia, 1968), 166–68. Schulze writes as a Lutheran, but the history covers other mainline churches.

5. "Meeting of National Community Relations Advisory Council [a coalition of Jewish civic and religious entities], Committee on Interfaith Activities with the NCCJ, September 22, 1948," NCCJ, SWHA, Box 7.

6. John P. Dean and Alex Rosen, *A Manual of Intergroup Relations* (Chicago: University of Chicago Press, 1955), ix.

7. Algernon D. Black, in *The Young Citizens: The Story of the Encampment for Democracy* (New York: Ungar, 1962), recounts the history and practices of the Encampment for Democracy program sponsored by the Ethical Culture Society. He argues that "churches and young-serving agencies and political organizations had used camps for recreational purposes and for the education of their young for their own particular purposes" (23), but postwar camps could serve to shape youth to a larger, all-encompassing understanding of the need to accord respect and to find common purposes across groups treated, on the principles of "democracy," as equally valuable. The encampments inspired some of the early planning for NCCJ camps, especially for Stewart Cole's design of the Los Angeles camps.

8. Prof. J. Milton Yinger, "Report on the National Program Commissions of the National Conference of Christians and Jews Inc., July 1958," NCCJ, SWHA, Box 7.

9. A. F. Marrow, *The Practical Theorist* (New York: Basic Books, 1969), is the standard Lewin biography. Marvin R. Weisbord, *Productive Workplaces: Organizing and Managing for Dignity, Meaning, and Community* (San Francisco: Jossey-Bass, 1991), offers an accessible summary of Lewin's work, chaps. 3–4. Lewin partnered with Margaret Mead during World War II to enlist citizen support for measures such as food rationing, using techniques he had developed during the late 1930s as a professor at the University of Iowa. Moving to MIT and hired as a consultant by the American Jewish Congress after the war, Lewin collected data about housing integration to back up proposals for open-housing legislation. Christopher Newfield, *Ivy and Industry: Business and the Making of the American University, 1880–1980* (Durham: Duke University Press, 2003), puts Lewin in the tradition of "radical humanism," along with William James and John Dewey. By contrast with a defense of individual liberty as the measure of freedom, the radical humanist "saw that freedom is a feature not only of individual lives but of societies: the freedom that finally matters is mass freedom in which freedom requires its own extension to the entirety of the society in which it operates," Newfield writes (226). Gordon W. Allport stated Newfield's summary in a slightly different way in the foreword to *Resolving Social Conflicts: Selected Papers* [of Kurt Lewin] *on Group Dynamics*, ed. Gertrud Weiss Lewin (New York: Harper and Row, 1948): Lewin, like Dewey, argued "that democracy must be learned anew in each generation, and that it is a far more difficult form of social structure to attain and to maintain than is autocracy"(xi). How Lewin might have participated in 1950s and 1960s civil rights work is sadly unknown, because of his early death at age fifty-seven. Elisabeth Lasch-Quinn argues in *Race Experts: How Racial Etiquette, Sensitivity Training, and New Age Therapy Hijacked the Civil Rights Revolution* (New York: Norton, 2001) that "sensitivity training" subverted the civil rights movement because the method "popularize[d] the notion that everyday experiences and tensions between blacks

and whites could be explained in psychological terms and addressed with sensitivity training–like approaches" (76). The process of sensitivity training took attention away from the "moral dimension" of individual change, especially political action, she continues. Lasch-Quinn makes no distinction between sensitivity training and more demanding practices of group dynamics training, though part of her complaint is borne out by my participants. Some responded to interracial encounters with psychological defenses of denial and deflection, while others went through these to more genuine empathy and moral commitments to action.

10. Margaret M. Heaton, *Feelings Are Facts* (San Francisco Board of Education, 1951), was one substantial pamphlet NCCJ used to argue for greater human relations consciousness in public schools. NCCJ, SWHA, Box 38.

11. I am indebted to Rachel Luft's *Race Training: Antiracist Workshops in a Post-Civil Rights Era* (PhD, UC Santa Barbara, 2004), for her recovery of this understudied and important history.

12. Black, *Young Citizens*, 97.

13. Margaret Gillmore, interviewed by author, New York City, 29 March 1994. All succeeding quotations are from this interview.

14. Nancy Trask, interviewed by author, San Gabriel, Calif., 20 June 1994. All succeeding quotations are from this interview.

15. "Eleventh Annual Human Relations Workshop of the NCCJ Southern California Region, Idyllwild Pines, July 1–8, 1961," program, NCCJ Los Angeles Office files (hereafter NCCJLA). Copy in possession of author.

16. Walter Chambers, interviewed by author, Roslyn, Va., 4 May 1994. Except where noted, all succeeding quotations are from this interview.

17. Charles T. Clotfelter, *After Brown: The Rise and Retreat of School Desegregation* (Princeton: Princeton University Press, 2004), 3, citing Gordon Allport's *The Nature of Prejudice* (1954).

18. Jackson, *Crabgrass Frontier*, is the classic study of residential segregation as one consequence of suburbanization.

19. Stewart G. Cole and Mildred Wiese Cole, *Minorities and the American Promise: The Conflict of Principle and Practice* (New York: Harper and Brothers, 1954). Stewart Cole, founder of NCCJ's Los Angeles camp program, reported on a 1948 study by the Bureau of Applied Social Research about depictions of "white Protestant Anglo-Saxons and nonwhites in the mass media. . . . In general, the Bureau indicated that a 'constant repetition of racial stereotypes was exaggerating and perpetuating the false and mischievous notion that ours is a white, Protestant, Anglo-Saxon country in which all other racial stocks and religious groups are of lesser dignity'" (106). In *Black Is a Country*, esp. chap. 1, "Rethinking Race and Nation," Singh offers the central argument that white and European heritage have been equated with the nation throughout the twentieth century to the exclusion of the histories of Americans racialized as not white. Chappell describes both postwar liberals' assurance that education would suffice to

cure antiblack sentiments and their detachment from black protests against lynching and job discrimination in *A Stone of Hope*, chap. 2, "Recovering Optimists."

20. Mary Field Belenky, Lynne A. Bond, and Jacqueline S. Weinstock, *A Tradition That Has No Name: Nurturing the Development of People, Families, and Communities* (New York: Basic Books, 1997), 161–64. The authors argue that "both the civil rights movement and the women's movement flourished because public homeplaces devoted to bringing the excluded into voice sprang up in local communities all across the country" (15).

21. Jay Watson, "Uncovering the Body, Discovering Ideology: Segregation and Sexual Anxiety in Lillian Smith's *Killers of the Dream*," *American Quarterly* 49 (September 1997), 49.

22. "The Brotherhood Youth Institute: A Living Experiment in Human Relations," New Jersey Region, National Conference of Christians and Jews, 1965. NCCJ, SWHA, Box 11.

23. Nina Asher, interviewed by author, Culver City, Calif., 22 June 1994. All succeeding quotations are from this interview.

24. Jim Horton, interviewed by author, Washington, D.C., 24 May 1993. All succeeding quotations are from this interview.

25. "Peacemaker" [the Los Angeles camp newsletter], 1 September 1960. NCCJLA. Copy in possession of author.

26. Jacqui Norris, interviewed by author, Plainfield, N.J., 14 March 1994. All succeeding quotations are from this interview.

27. "The Brotherhood Youth Institute: A Living Experience in Human Relations, Research Report No. 1," NJJC, SWHA, Box 11.

28. "Programs," NCCJLA. Copies in possession of author.

29. Walter Chambers, "Memorandum to Adult Resource Persons, Job Sheet for Resource Persons," 17 August 1961. Walter Chambers personal archives. Copy in possession of author.

30. "The Brotherhood Youth Institute" (my italics).

31. Walter D. Chambers, "On Being a Statistic," typescript, n.d. Walter Chambers personal archives. Copy in possession of author. Two standard books on black representation in film—Donald Bogle, *Toms, Coons, Mulattoes, Mammies, and Bucks: An Interpretive History of Blacks in American Films* (New York: Continuum, 1994), chap. 6; and Thomas Cripps, *Making Movies Black: The Hollywood Message Movie from World War II to the Civil Rights Era* (New York: Oxford University Press, 1993), esp. chap. 7—note the "integrationist" emphasis of postwar film, in which black characters continued to function as servants, only mentally deranged whites exhibited racism, and assimilation to white cultural norms defined success for African Americans. In popular film, the presence of just one acceptable black character constituted successful "integration," according to Cripps (250).

32. Singh argues in *Black Is a Country* that liberal historians have "consistently

underestimated or devalued the autonomous dimensions of black political discourse" (57) of the sort represented by Walt Chambers and Jim Horton's parents.

33. Elizabeth Louie Chikuami, Los Angeles, Calif., interviewed by author by telephone, 30 April 1996. All succeeding quotations are from this interview.

34. Norman M. Bradburn, Seymour Sudman, and Galen L. Gockel, *Side by Side: Integrated Neighborhoods in America* (Chicago: Quadrangle Books, 1971), 121, citing a 1963 survey by the National Opinion Research Center.

35. Clabe Hangan, interviewed by author, Pasadena, Calif., 21 June 1994. All succeeding quotations are from this interview.

36. Bradburn et al., *Side by Side*, cites National Opinion Research Center data showing that only 36 percent of white Americans opposed laws against interracial marriage in 1963, a number that rose to only 37 percent by 1968 (121).

37. Jacquelyn Dowd Hall, in *Revolt against Chivalry: Jessie Daniel Ames and the Women's Campaign against Lynching*, rev. ed. (New York: Columbia University Press, 1993), recounts the classic statement that justified white male "protection" of white women from black men's sexual assaults as a means to sustain white economic and political dominance; see esp. 145–57.

38. Harry C. Triandis and Leigh M. Triandis, in "Some Studies of Social Distance," in *Racial Attitudes in America and Findings of Social Psychology*, ed. John C. Brigham and Theodore A. Weissbach (New York: Harper and Row, 1972), credit Emory Bogardus with conceptualizing "social distance" to explain immigrant reception during the 1920s; it was measured by the "degree to which individuals are willing to accept people who differ from themselves into their own social group" (97). The Triandises' own research showed that in the late 1950s, race had by far the greatest weight for determining social distance by comparison with occupation, religion, and nationality. See Harry C. Triandis and Leigh M. Triandis, "Race, Social Class, Religion, and Nationality as Determinants of Social Distance," *Journal of Abnormal Social Psychology* 61 (1960): 110–18.

39. Schulze, *Fire from the Throne*, 130–32.

40. Peggy Pascoe, "Miscegenation Law, Court Cases, and Ideologies of 'Race' in Twentieth-Century America," *Journal of American History* 83 (June 1996): 44–69, analyzes the twentieth-century elements of opposition to interracial marriage, including unwillingness to protect the economic and inheritance rights of nonwhite women and their children.

41. Joanne Meyerowitz, "Beyond the Feminine Mystique: A Reassessment of Postwar Mass Culture, 1946–1958," in *Not June Cleaver: Women and Gender in Postwar America, 1945–1960*, ed. Joanne Meyerowitz (Philadelphia: Temple University Press, 1994), 332.

42. Wini Breines, "The 'Other' Fifties: Beats and Bad Girls," in Meyerowitz, *Not June Cleaver*, 385. Frankenberg, in *White Women, Race Matters*, records that her white respondents who came of age in the 1960s saw white women in interracial

relationships as "cool," as opposed to an earlier generation who saw them as "inadequate or perverse" (88–89).

43. Susan J. Douglas, *Where the Girls Are: Growing Up Female with the Mass Media* (New York: Times Books, 1995), 119, and see esp. chaps. 5–7.

44. Pascoe, "Miscegenation Law," analyzes the 1967 Supreme Court decision in *Loving v. Virginia* that finally offered protection to nonwhite women by striking down state laws that prohibited marriage across racial lines.

45. Crilly Butler, Davis, Calif., interviewed by author by telephone, 21 April 1996. All succeeding quotations are from this interview.

46. Douglas McAdam, in *Freedom Summer* (New York: Oxford University Press, 1988), asserts that "for many volunteers interracial sex became the ultimate expression of the ideology [of Beloved Community]" and a tempting way to prove political credibility (93). Lynne Olson, in *Freedom's Daughter* (New York: Scribner, 2001), argues that sex was the most incendiary black-white issue of Mississippi Freedom Summer, 1964. White women volunteers enacted racial equality by working with black children, encouraging black citizens to register to vote, and having sex with black men; their behavior enflamed Southern white hostility and offended black women (305–11). The interracial expressions of the NCCJ camps were quite different from the interracial sex charged with harming the movement's reputation and morale in the summer of 1964. The campers were younger, supervised, and not having intercourse. Sex was not the pointed weapon or valuable anodyne to fend off fear and danger that it became for Freedom Summer workers, especially in the months after James Chaney, Michael Schwerner, and Andrew Goodman had been taken by police and, as emerged in August, brutally killed.

47. *Let There Be Peace on Earth,* lyrics and music by Sy Miller and Jill Jackson, 1955, connected peace and brotherhood: "Let there be peace on earth. . . . With God as our Father/Brothers all are we." *No Man Is an Island,* inspired by John Donne's sixteenth-century poem, was a song listed as "traditional" in collections, again with the brotherhood theme: "No man is an island/No man stands alone. . . . So I will defend/ Each man as my brother/Each man as my friend." The use of "man" to stand for all humanity was especially paradoxical in a camp with girls in the majority.

48. Robert Cantwell, *When We Were Good: The Folk Revival* (Cambridge: Harvard University Press, 1996), 34.

49. Cantwell, argues in chap. 8 of *When We Were Good*, "Happy Campers," that white baby boomers were raised on a folk music stripped of its political past as a music of working-class, racial. or regional protest and turned into a representation of a pluralist past and, ultimately, a music of generational rebellion that could easily be commodified and turned into apolitical rock.

50. *This Little Light of Mine*, a traditional song, gave each person responsibility for the world's well-being: "This little light of mine/I'm gonna let it shine."

51. Grace Palladino, *Teenagers: An American History* (New York: Basic Books, 1996), describes the rise of a teen consumer market in the years after World War II.

52. The Coasters' 1959 recording of Jerry Lieber and Mike Stoller's *Poison Ivy* told the story of a tempting girl: "Now you can look but you better not touch." In an interracial camp, the song might have been heard as a warning not to get involved with girls whose racial/religious differences could cause trouble as prickly as poison ivy with family and friends. But the girl was evidently irresistible—"Late at night while you're sleepin'/Poison Ivy comes a'creepin'/Around." *If I Had a Hammer*, lyrics and music by Lee Hays and Pete Seeger, 1949, announced principles of freedom and brotherhood in a less sexist lyric: "If I had a hammer . . . I'd hammer out love between my brothers and my sisters." The Beatles' *Yellow Submarine* (1966) depicted a slightly stoned, loopy world where "we all lived [together] in a yellow submarine."

53. Mary Hart (pseudonym), Philadelphia, interviewed by author by telephone, 28 May 1996.

54. *Report of the National Advisory Commission on Civil Disorders* (New York: Bantam, 1968), 366.

## Chapter 2

1. Julie Cohen, interviewed by author, Los Angeles, Calif., 21 June 1994 (my italics). All succeeding quotations are from this interview.

2. According to the *Report of the National Advisory Commission on Civil Disorders*: "In 1960 the average segregation index for 207 of the largest United States cities was 86.2. . . . To create an unsegregated population distribution, an average of over 86 percent of all Negroes would have to change their place of residence" (13). With research conducted in the mid-1960s, Bradburn et al. concluded in *Side by Side* that "19 percent of the population lived in integrated neighborhoods in the spring of 1967." But this hopeful conclusion masked the fact that many of these "integrated" neighborhoods, especially in new cities of the West, had very few black families (12).

3. Bruce J. Schulman, *The Seventies: The Great Shift in American Culture, Society, and Politics* (New York: Free Press, 2001), 64.

4. Manning Marable, in *Race, Reform, and Rebellion: The Second Reconstruction of Black America, 1945–1982* (Jackson: University Press of Mississippi, 1984), links the classic civil rights movement and the subsequent black power movement as two parts of an ongoing process to gain political recognition and economic improvement for African Americans. Historical accounts of racial power movements include: Rodolfo Acuna, *Occupied America: The Chicano Struggle toward Liberation*, 1st ed. (New York: Canfield Press, 1972); Stephen Cornell, *The Return of the Native: American Indian Political Resurgence* (New York: Oxford University Press, 1988); Joanne Nagel, *American Indian Ethnic Revival: Red Power and the Resurgence of Identity and Culture* (New York: Oxford University Press, 1996); William Wei, *The Asian American Movement* (Philadelphia: Temple University Press, 1993); and Yen Le Espiritu, *Asian American Panethnicity: Bridging Institutions and Identities* (Philadelphia: Temple

University Press, 1992). Espiritu traces the launch of a yellow power movement in 1968 to a UCLA conference on Asian Americans and the Vietnam War (32).

5. Anna Yeatman makes a case in "Feminism and Power," in *Reconstructing Political Theory: Feminist Perspectives*, ed. Mary Lyndon Shanley and Uma Narayan (University Park: Pennsylvania State University Press, 1995), that power cannot be redistributed more evenly so long as we assume "natural persons [as a basis for] the discourse of 'natural rights' " that underlay the creation of a state in which only well-to-do white men ostensibly hold the natural capacity to exercise power. Instead, she advocates an idea "that persons have to be positively constituted through the agency of the state in ways that are not prejudicial to some for reasons of their sex" and, I would add, of their race, class, religion, or nationality (154). I am not equating camp governance with the state, of course, but for the brief duration of this bounded experience, camp directors and counselors did set rules of equality that contrasted strikingly with the hierarchically ranked social value accorded boys and girls of different racial groupings outside the camp setting.

6. Angus Campbell, *White Attitudes toward Black People* (Ann Arbor: Institute for Social Research, University of Michigan, 1971), reported survey data gathered nationwide in 1958, 1964, and 1970 (156–57).

7. Bernice Van Steenbergen, interviewed by author, Long Beach, Calif., 16–17 June 1994. All succeeding quotations are from these interviews.

8. "Daily Schedule, Brotherhood—Anytown—June 16–23, 1968." Typescript, NCCJLA. Copy in author's possession.

9. Lynn Lillieston, "Teens Tell It as It Ought to Be," *Los Angeles Times*, hand dated August 1968. NCCJLA. Copy in author's possession.

10. "Brotherhood—Anytown Staff Responsibilities, September 2–9, 1969." Typescript. NCCJLA. Copy in author's possession.

11. Memo from Ken Rosen to Garth Hintz, Director, Community Affairs, KNXT, Los Angeles, 2 July 1969, re: Brotherhood Camp. NCCJLA. Copy in author's possession.

12. Schulman, in *The Seventies*, argues that the racial nationalist positions joined by "unmeltable white ethnics" in the early 1970s represented a "tribalization" of the United States and the loss of a universalist vision of shared values joining diverse groups into the "we" of the nation (76–77). Schulman ignores any efforts to build bridges between "tribes."

13. Teresa Miles, pseudonym, Los Angeles, interviewed by author by telephone, 22 September 1994.

14. Angela Davis became a heroine in black and radical circles for being hunted by the FBI, charged with supplying guns used in a deadly courthouse shootout that killed a judge and a member of the Black Panthers. Though acquitted by a California jury, she remained a fearsome revolutionary to conservative and many white circles for being a communist thinker and proponent of political activism. William L. Van Deburg, in *New Day in Babylon: The Black Power Movement and American Culture, 1965–1975*

(Chicago: University of Chicago Press, 1992), talks about the importance of adopting "soul style," including the Afro hair style that refused chemical processing and hot combing, as a statement of pride in the qualities of black hair and black people (201–2). Kobena Mercer, in *Welcome to the Jungle: New Positions in Black Cultural Studies* (New York: Routledge, 1994), chap. 4, posits the black power use of the Afro as "natural" hair to contest white standards of beauty and also to identify African American political struggles with African ones. But she argues that the Afro had little to do with traditional African hair styles, was quickly adopted by other groups, fit the 1960s rebellious embrace of long hair, and might appropriately be interpreted not simply as an oppositional gesture, but also as an inventive opening up of possibility; certainly Teresa Miles didn't experience the pleasures of her hair as only political.

15. Jai Hwa Lee Wong, Los Angeles, interviewed by author by telephone, 1 May 1996. All succeeding quotations are from this interview. Espiritu, in *Asian American Panethnicity*, states that the two groups usually identified with Asian American interests were Japanese and Chinese. Filipino immigrants from the 1920s and postwar and Korean immigrants of the 1950s and 1960s always had to push for inclusion of their issues, which were often about U.S. effects on their home countries. The Filipinos and Koreans may have been particularly sensitive to the effects of U.S. intervention in Vietnam.

16. Bob Jones, interviewed by author, Los Angeles, 15 April 1994. All succeeding quotations are from this interview.

17. Terry Odendahl, interviewed by author, Washington, D.C., 5 June 1993. All succeeding quotations are from this interview.

18. Fernando Huerta, Los Angeles, interviewed by author by telephone, 30 April 1996. All succeeding quotations are from this interview.

19. Myke Santos, interviewed by author, San Diego, Calif., 17 June 1994. All succeeding quotations are from this interview.

20. Dorothy Smith (pseudonym), Portland, Ore., interviewed by author by telephone, 25 March 1994. All succeeding quotations are from this interview.

21. Eric Macy, interviewed by author, San Diego, Calif., 4 April 1994. All succeeding quotations are from this interview.

22. Marjorie Baer, interviewed by author, San Francisco, Calif., 24 June 1994. All succeeding quotations are from this interview.

23. Malvina Reynolds composed *Little Boxes* (1963), and Pete Seeger brought the song into the center of the folk-song revival. The first stanza lays out the premise of the song's social criticism: "Little boxes on the hillside/Little boxes made of ticky tacky . . . Little boxes all the same."

24. "Youth Program Evaluation and Suggestions," 1970. Typescript, NCCJLA. Copy in author's possession.

25. Murray Friedman, *What Went Wrong: The Creation and Collapse of the Black-Jewish Alliance* (New York: Free Press, 1995), and Jonathan Kaufman, *Broken Alliance: The Turbulent Times between Blacks and Jews in America* (New York: Scribner, 1988),

represent the alliance-conflict account of a shift in black-Jewish relations between the 1930s and the 1970s. Robert G. Weisbord and Arthur Stein, in *Bittersweet Encounter: African Americans and American Jews* (Westport, Conn.: Negro Universities Press, 1970), made one of the earlier claims that many Jews had learned and succumbed to traditional white American racism.

26. Melani McAlister, *Epic Encounters: Culture, Media, and U.S. Interests in the Middle East since 1945,* 2nd. ed. (Berkeley: University of California Press, 2005), 110–15.

27. Jacobson, in *Roots Too* (216–26), recounts the mid-1970s debate about the Jewish relationship to civil rights.

28. Michael Novak's *The Rise of the Unmeltable Ethnics* (New York: Macmillan, 1973), attacked the idea that WASPS were the predominant Americans, along with the idea that there was a *homo Americanus,* avowing a single culture (xv). Poles, Irish, Jews, Italians, Swedes, Scots, or Chinese—"*each* group has come to a different America, and each brought with it a different history" (xx). Even as Novak seemingly opened up cultural pluralism by arguing for diversity among white Americans, he narrowed the responsibility for racism by arguing that *his* ancestors had no responsibility for Indian removal or black slavery (xx). Whatever benefits his ancestors received by being admitted to the privileges of white America, these did not entail any responsibility for the historical processes of building white power, Novak argued, in a position that would become a common white defense during the 1970s. Although I had figured out this point before reading *Roots Too,* Jacobson wittily observes there that when Novak asked, "'What share had [immigrants] . . . in the exploitation of the Negro?' [it] was not a serious inquiry, but a rhetorical device" (195).

29. A Jewish theological commitment to healing the world influenced some third-generation Jewish Americans, such as Michael Lerner, to accept the responsibility to stand against racism and poverty and even, on occasion, to demand that Israel not behave as aggressively as other nations. See Jacobson, *Roots Too,* 219–24.

30. See Jane Gerhard, *Desiring Revolution: Second-Wave Feminism and the Rewriting of American Sexual Thought, 1920–1982* (New York: Columbia University Press, 2001), 99–103. Gerhard notes that white women's push for sexual freedom—usually freedom from white men's cavalier consumption of their bodies—was different from black women's (and those of other women of color, presumably, though she does not discuss them).

31. Clotfelter, in *After Brown,* contends that interracial school contact increased after 1970, primarily because residential segregation of the growing suburbs in the South and West decreased. But he also summarizes studies that indicate a "white avoidance" of racially mixed schools and four forces that sustained de facto segregation: white residential avoidance of racially mixed schools (91); white attendance at private, less desegregated schools; school board zoning and tracking of white-predominant schools and classes; and reduced judicial support for desegregation measures (181–84). The most notable judicial discouragement to desegregation came

with the Supreme Court decisions in *Keyes v. School District No. 1, Denver* in 1973 and *Milliken v. Bradley* in 1974, which ruled out combining urban and suburban school districts to share resources and students previously segregated by law and now separated by residential district, a segregation caused by market forces over which the courts refused any control (27–33).

32. Michael Omi and Howard Winant, *Racial Formation in the United States: From the 1960s to the 1990s*, 2nd. ed. (New York: Routledge, 1994), 117.

33. Darryl Smith, Los Angeles, interviewed by author by telephone, 21 April 1996. All succeeding quotations are from this interview.

34. Robert Wuthnow, *The Restructuring of American Religion: Society and Faith since World War II* (Princeton: Princeton University Press, 1988), describes the divisions within Protestant churches in response to activism to support the civil rights movement and to oppose U.S. engagement in the Vietnam War. Those who "saw direct action as being more effective than good intentions, increasingly focused their attention away from personal salvation . . . toward engaging religious people directly in acts of love." Evangelicals opposed direct action and stressed "personal salvation, piety and morality, Bible study, and missionary efforts" (148–49). The latter abandoned Protestant churches led by activist ministers during the late 1960s and early 1970s.

35. *Coming of Age*, prod. by Dennis Hicks, dir. by Josh Hanig, Marco Productions,1982.

36. Danielle S. Allen, *Talking to Strangers: Anxieties of Citizenship since* Brown v. Board of Education (Chicago: University of Chicago Press, 2004), 16–17. "A focus on the wholeness of the citizenry, rather than on its oneness," Allen writes, "might allow for the development of forms of citizenship that focus on integration, not assimilation, and on the mutual exchanges and appropriations that have already occurred among different groups and that will always keep occurring" (20). Her description sounds much like a Brotherhood Camp encounter.

## Chapter 3

The source of the epigraph is Eunice and George Grier, *Discrimination in Housing: A Handbook of Fact* (New York: Anti-Defamation League of B'nai B'rith, 1960).

1. Janet Brown, interviewed by author, Washington, D.C., 3 May 2002. All succeeding quotations are from this interview and from one on 25 May 2000. This section of the book relies on the Neighbors Inc. archives held in the D.C. Public Library, Washingtoniana Division, Community Archives, Collection 110 (hereafter NIMSS) and on interviews with twenty-four people who lived in the area between 1957 and 1975, nearly all of them active in Neighbors Inc. Of these, three had been children during the era, and all now live in or near their old neighborhood. The racial, gender, and religious makeup of the group interviewed is: three African American women and one African American man who are Christian; six white women who are

Jewish and five who are Christian; and six white men who are Jewish and three who are Christian.

2. Sheryll Cashin, in *The Failure of Integration: How Race and Class Are Undermining the American Dream* (New York: Public Affairs, 2004), summarizes critiques of postwar integration: "The twentieth-century notion of integration . . . was one of melding blacks with whites; it was mainly premised upon opening doors to black participation. Black people were expected to be the integrators, indeed, the assimilators" (80). Cashin, a professor at Georgetown University Law School, coincidentally lives in Shepherd Park, D.C., where the Browns lived.

3. Mary L. Dudziak, in *Cold War Civil Rights: Race and the Image of American Democracy* (Princeton: Princeton University Press, 2000), 96, 99–100, argues that racial segregation was more troublesome in D.C. because the city was under national control and its practices could not be excused as the aberrant policy of local Southern authorities. Lipsitz, "The Possessive Investment in Whiteness," gives a capsule history of the forces arrayed against integrated housing in the postwar housing boom.

4. U.S. President's Committee on Civil Rights, *To Secure These Rights* (Washington, D.C.: U.S. Government Printing Office, 1947), 89, 168–69.

5. Raymond Wolters, *The Burden of Brown: Thirty Years of School Desegregation* (Knoxville: University of Tennessee Press, 1984), describes Washington's reputation as a "showcase of integration" because it did not follow the usual Southern pattern of white resistance in harassing black students and shutting down public schools.

6. Howard Gillette Jr., *Between Justice and Beauty: Race, Planning, and the Failure of Urban Policy in Washington, D.C.* (Baltimore: Johns Hopkins University Press, 1995), 153–57. Gillette's history of planning and infrastructure development in the nation's capital provides a bleak picture of opportunities missed because of strenuous efforts to maintain racial segregation.

7. Kathryn Schneider Smith, ed., *Washington at Home: An Illustrated History of Neighborhoods in the Nation's Capital* (Northridge, Calif: Windsor Publications, 1988), chap. 7.

8. Ibid., chaps. 14, 19. Takoma, D.C., residents adopted that name during the early 1960s to distinguish their neighborhood from Takoma Park, Maryland, a still-segregated neighboring area just across the border. During the 1980s, when Takoma Park, Maryland, became an attractive place to live, the D.C. side returned Park to its name and became Takoma Park, D.C. During the period of this study, however, it usually went by the name Takoma, D.C.

9. The leading postwar suburban housing developer, William Levitt, justified his segregation policy: "As a Jew I have no room in my mind or heart for racial prejudice, but . . . I have come to know that if we sell one house to a Negro family, then 90 to 95 percent of our white customers will not buy into the community. . . . As a company our position is simply this: we can solve a housing problem or we can try to solve a racial problem, but we cannot combine the two." Quoted in David Halberstam, *The Fifties* (New York: Villard Books, 1993), 141.

10. Douglas S. Massey and Nancy A. Denton describe housing segregation that defined the nation's landscape from the great home-building boom of the 1950s until the early 1990s as "apartheid" in *American Apartheid: Segregation and the Making of the Underclass* (Cambridge: Harvard University Press, 1993). Sociologists, political scientists, and geographers have debated the causes of persistent housing segregation and recently looked for its diminution in newly developing Sunbelt cities, where some reduction in residential racial isolation seems to be occurring. Without querying the historical shaping of such feelings, social scientists treat housing segregation as a natural consequence of each person's racial consciousness and desire not to be a minority in the home neighborhood. An early 1990s study found that 16 percent of whites said they would feel "uncomfortable" in a neighborhood more than 8 percent black; if the black percentage rose to 20 percent, then 40 percent of whites would not move there; and if the neighborhood was more than half black, then 71 percent of whites would not move there. In a mid-1990s study of four cities, the majority of white respondents preferred a white-segregated neighborhood, while the majority of black respondents would choose an integrated one. These studies are cited by Michael K. Brown, Martin Carnoy, Elliott Currie, Troy Duster, David B. Oppenheimer, Marjorie Schultz, and David Wellman, *Whitewashing Race: The Myth of a Color-Blind Society* (Berkeley: University of California Press, 2003), 40. Historians, by contrast, have documented the national housing policies that subsidized the building of white-segregated suburbs, dissuaded nonwhite families from seeking a home in the burgeoning suburbs, and discouraged the construction of interracial housing. Jackson, in *Crabgrass Frontier* (208–15), recounts the consequences of the Federal Housing Administration's loan-guarantee criteria of "relative economic stability" and "protection from adverse influences"—both used to disqualify heterogeneous neighborhoods—as making it cheaper for white families to move to the suburbs than to rent in cities. See also Lipsitz, "The Possessive Investment in Whiteness." The outcome, as sociologist Gary Orfield concludes in "Race and the Liberal Agenda: The Loss of the Integrationist Dream, 1965–1974," in *The Politics of Social Policy in the United States*, ed. Margaret Weir, Ann Shola Orloff, and Theda Skocpol (Princeton: Princeton University Press, 1988), was that after fifteen years of civil rights activism, "the 1960s would end with an increase in residential segregation in the metropolitan areas of the United States" (323).

11. Lizabeth Cohen, in *A Consumers' Republic: The Politics of Mass Consumption in Postwar America* (New York: Knopf, 2003), 131–51, describes the postwar creation of segregated gender roles, which carries into her discussion of the implicitly segregated suburbs. Elaine Tyler May's *Homeward Bound: American Families in the Cold War Era* (New York: Basic Books, 1988), is the classic account of the 1950s cultural imperative for women to protect their families from Cold War threats by caring for the home.

12. Lisa Duggan, in *The Twilight of Equality? Neoliberalism, Cultural Politics, and the Attack on Democracy* (Boston: Beacon Press, 2003), usefully points out the significance

of shifting decisions from "public" ones requiring debate to "private" ones closed off from political decisions, in chap. 1, "Downsizing Democracy."

13. Marvin Caplan, speech to the National Association of Housing and Redevelopment Officials, 7 January 1960, NIMSS, Box 5.

14. Stephen Grant Meyer, *As Long as They Don't Move Next Door: Segregation and Racial Conflict in American Neighborhoods* (Lanham, Md.: Rowman and Littlefield, 2000), 136, citing *Where Shall We Live? Report of the Commission on Race and Housing* (Berkeley: University of California Press, 1958). Meyer gives a basic history of open housing policies from 1900 to 1968 and, unless noted, I rely on his legislative history. I disagree, however, with Meyer's primary argument that governmental lending agencies such as the FHA and VA, banks, and real estate agents were not the primary forces in the failure of housing desegregation. He blames, instead, white homeowners and renters who consistently fought the entry of nonwhites into their neighborhoods and created great public disorder; governmental authorities were not willing to send in armed police or military units to enforce order when white homeowners bombed or threatened their new black neighbors. Certainly so long as a discriminatory housing market resulted in persistent segregation that defined any racially mixed neighborhood as deteriorating, white families would want to protect their property by keeping out nonwhites. Only a truly open housing market could change that calculation.

15. Alan Brinkley, *The End of Reform: New Deal Liberalism in Recession and War* (New York: Knopf, 1995), 259–60, makes the point that the "progressive" GI Bill legislation forecast a more conservative postwar politics and gained conservatives' approval only through restricting these benefits to veterans and limiting expectations of benefits for employment, housing, and education assistance to those entitled by military service; the bill foreclosed expectations of a more general expansion of social responsibility for these basic goods.

16. Nelson Lichtenstein's chapter, "Uneasy Partners," in *The Most Dangerous Man in Detroit: Walter Reuther and the Fate of American Labor* (New York: Basic Books, 1995), sums up the stance of official labor as exhibited by the leader of the United Auto Workers. Reuther believed in civil rights legislation but would undercut it if he needed to appease the Southern white Democratic votes that kept liberal Democrats in the White House.

17. Singh, in *Black Is a Country*, argues that "by accepting a vision predicated on the subordination of racial equality to national security imperatives, mainstream black leaders acquiesced to the state-sanctioned thinning of the field of robust and independent black public interaction" (168).

18. Cohen, *A Consumers' Republic*, 125.

19. Brinkley, *The End of Reform*, chaps. 4, 9.

20. Marvin Caplan, interviewed by author, Washington, D.C., 30 November 1998. All succeeding quotations, except when noted, are from this interview. Caplan, an organizer to the end, kindly talked with me on many other occasions before his untimely death in January 2000.

21. Marvin Caplan, *Farther Along: A Civil Rights Memoir* (Baton Rouge: Louisiana State University Press, 1999), part 2.

22. Cynthia Mills Richter, *Integrating the Suburban Dream: Shaker Heights, Ohio* (PhD diss., University of Minnesota, 1999), tells the history of Shaker Heights, Ohio, which formed its first committee to halt the transition of a section that bordered the city of Cleveland in 1957, the year before Neighbors Inc. was founded. The committee that worked to create an interracial Shaker Heights was, however, battling for integration of an independent suburb that had control over public decisions such as housing subsidies and public schools, which neighborhoods in a large city like Washington could only partly influence. Judith Saltman, in *A Fragile Movement; The Struggle for Neighborhood Stabilization* (Westport, Conn.: Greenwood Press, 1990), offers a sociological analysis of the groups that formed to sustain integrated neighborhoods in Indianapolis, Akron, Rochester, Milwaukee, and Hartford. Saltman's emphasis on these groups as "movement organizations" ties them to a moment of historical civil rights confrontation and minimizes the formation of alternative ideals of community, including alternative gender ideals.

23. *Neighbors, Inc.*, September 1960. The complete run of newsletters is in the NIMSS. Timothy N. Thurber, in *The Politics of Equality: Hubert H. Humphrey and the African American Freedom Struggle* (New York: Columbia University Press, 1999), points out that in the summer of 1960 Humphrey was emphasizing his civil rights credentials in preparation for a bid for the Democratic Party's presidential nomination (109). Marvin Caplan, *Farther Along*, 172, and interview.

24. *Neighbors, Inc.*, September 1959.

25. *Neighbors, Inc.*, August 1960.

26. *Neighbors, Inc.*, March 1961.

27. (Mrs.) Margery T. Ware to Mr. C. E. Childs, Jr., Director, D.C. Insuring Office, Federal Housing Administration, July 22, 1964, NIMSS, Box 11.

28. *Neighbors, Inc.*, January–February 1960.

29. *Neighbors, Inc.*, September 1959. Marvin Caplan, in *Farther Along*, credits the "creative anxiety" of his wife, Naomi, with producing the idea for the Housing Information Service, without which, she believed, the neighborhood would attract no white families. Richter, *Integrating the Suburban Dream*, offers some support to Caplan's prioritizing; in Shaker Heights the planners adopted a similar housing service to attract white buyers in 1961 (46–51).

30. "Neighborly Reception for Diplomats and Families," *Washington Post*, 15 May 1961.

31. "9 Homes to be Shown by 'Neighbors'," *Washington Post*, 26 May 1962.

32. Richter, *Integrating the Dream*, tells a slightly different story about the new narrative created to sell integration in Shaker Heights. This suburban community revised the "utopian narrative" of the suburb as a stable, successful, healthy alternative to the city into a "new, *inclusive* utopian vision" (52). Neighbors Inc.'s international and urban vision may represent an opportunistic response to the specific circumstances of

Washington's emergence as an international capital during the Cold War, just as Shaker Heights' vision drew on its historical status as a model suburb. Suleiman Osman, "The Decade of the Neighborhood," in *Rightward Bound: Making America Conservative in the 1970s*, ed. Bruce Schulman and Julian Zelizar (Cambridge: Harvard University Press, 2008), provides yet another story of postwar interracial housing. In Osman's select interracial Brooklyn neighborhoods, the participants looked like those in Neighbors Inc.—white-collar professionals—but he defines their motives as antimodernist, romantic, and oppositional to "modernist" urban planners, while Neighbors Inc.'s New Deal antecedents favored governmental action, other than that of the urban planners. These are reminders that postwar white interracialism functioned in different locations with different political and demographic frameworks. There is no single story.

33. Norman Brown and Janet Brown, interviewed by author, Washington, D.C., 25 May 2000. All succeeding quotations are from this interview and from one with Janet Brown, 3 May 2002.

34. Meyer, *As Long As They Don't Move*, 94.

35. Carol Rose, "Property Stories: *Shelley v. Kraemer*," in *Property Stories*, ed. Gerald Korngold and Andrew P. Morriss (New York: Foundation Press, 2004), 197. Rose makes a significant amendment to the idea that suburban property selling and buying was conceptualized as solely a private contract in her argument that the Court was aware that racially restrictive covenants were "poised to reach out into the whole new geography of suburbanizing, white middle class America" (191). With that threat to any prospect of reducing racial discrimination, the Court acted so that "American courts could not be used to fortify that culture [of racial discrimination]" (198).

36. Marianne Meijer, interviewed by author, Washington, D.C., 12 January 1999. All succeeding quotations are from this interview.

37. Paul Meijer, interviewed by author, Washington, D.C., 12 January 1999. All succeeding quotations are from this interview.

38. Ruth [Stack] Jordan, interviewed by author, Washington, D.C., 8 December 1999. All succeeding quotations are from this interview.

39. Rabbi Nathan Abramowitz, interviewed by author, Washington, D.C., 2 December 1998. All succeeding quotations are from this interview.

40. Karen Brodkin, in *How the Jews Became White Folks and What That Says about Race in America* (New Brunswick: Rutgers University Press, 1998), attributes the transformation of Jews from a questionable, excluded group into a fully white group to the FHA and VA decisions to categorize Jews as homogeneous members of white suburban neighborhoods. In moving to racially exclusive suburbs, she implies, Jews gained whiteness. Jonathan D. Sarna, *American Judaism: A History* (New Haven: Yale University Press, 2004), 282–88, describes the movement of Jews to the suburbs in the postwar era as a challenge to maintain Jewish community and a proof of "acceptance in the culture of the United States" (283).

41. Rabbi Marc Schneier, *Shared Dreams: Martin Luther King, Jr. and the Jewish Community* (Woodstock, Vt.: Jewish Lights Publishing, 1999), gives many examples

of how, despite (usually secularized) Jewish people's overrepresentation among white civil rights activists, most Jewish synagogues, especially those in Southern cities, did not join civil rights activities. These Jewish leaders chose to identify with Southern white society and to protect their precarious position as a religious minority doing business and living in a white- and Christian-dominant society. See esp. chap. 3, "The Updated Covenant," and chap. 5, "Montgomery: The Journey Begins." Seth Forman, in *Blacks in the Jewish Mind: A Crisis of Liberalism* (New York: New York University Press, 1998), chap. 2, "The Liberal Jew, the Southern Jew, and Desegregation in the South, 1945–1964," more sympathetically recounts the tensions of Southern Jews, who wanted to maintain their distinctive religious practices instead of subsuming their identity into that of American liberal, antisegregation advocates.

42. Mollie Berch, interviewed by author, Silver Spring, Md., 8 November 1999. All succeeding quotations are from this interview.

43. Barbara Atkinson, interviewed by author, Washington, D.C., 16 December 1999. All succeeding quotations are from this interview.

44. Joe Hairston, interviewed by author, Washington, D.C., 23 November 1998. All succeeding quotations are from this interview. Joe Hairston's battles for fair treatment within the segregated and officially desegregated U.S. Army, much more hostile and dangerous than those in Neighbors Inc., are recounted in Henry Wiencek, *The Hairstons: An American Family in Black and White* (New York: St. Martin's Press, 1999), 254–71.

45. Meyer, *As Long As They Don't Move*, 169–70. Richter, *Integrating the Suburban Dream*, argues that the gendered work division in the Shaker Heights integration group "reinforced a conservative construction of gender, with the men taking public leadership roles and the women performing the less visible, daily work" (42). The Neighbors Inc. families initially presented a public image of conservative gender roles, but the families had other principles that supported more liberal gender roles. The pro–New Deal, pro-union, international background of some families; the high concentration of second-generation Jewish immigrant families with employed wives; the family decisions to be urban and not suburban—all conjoined to create an interracial neighborhood more gender egalitarian than the one Richter discerns in Shaker Heights, Ohio.

46. Stephanie Coontz, *The Way We Never Were: American Families and the Nostalgia Trap* (New York: Basic Books, 1992), argues that it was middle-class, college-educated married women who "initiated the ideological revolution of the 1960s, including the demand for gender equality and the idea that work was an important component of life satisfaction for women" (163). For NI families, the prospect of paying college tuitions and the freedom from driving children around certainly gave wives and mothers incentives to work for pay and time available to do so.

47. *Neighbors Inc.*, May 1960.

48. "Statement to the U.S. Commission on Civil Rights, April 13, 1962, presented on behalf of Neighbors Inc. by Marvin Caplan, President," NIMSS, Box 3.

49. Meyer, *As Long As They Don't Move*, 169–70.

50. "Statement of Neighbors, Inc., at a hearing before the Board of Commissioners regarding a fair housing regulation on July 26, 1963," NIMSS, Box 11.

51. *Trends in Housing*, National Committee against Discrimination in Housing, November–December 1963, 2.

52. Not until 1982 did the Supreme Court rule that "testers" could bring a case to prove discrimination, even if their suit benefited others and not themselves directly. Meyer, *As Long As They Don't Move*, 215.

53. Wolters, *The Burden of Brown*, 16, charts white and black enrollments between 1951 and 1981,

54. "The 'American Democracy in Action' Program at Paul Junior High School," Appendix D of amicus brief in *Hobson v. Hansen* (1967), NIMSS, Box 5.

55. Margery Ware, "New Challenges—1965," 17 July 1965, NIMSS, Box 5. Barbara Hogan, "Come Realty Sharks or Frowning Friends, They Shall Not Be Moved: Neighbors, Inc.," *Potomac Magazine*, 11 August 1963.

56. Art and Book Fair Program, 1963, NIMSS, Box 1.

## Chapter 4

1. "Meeting of Housing Recruitment Committee," October 1964, NIMSS, Box 7. Richter, *Integrating the Suburban Dream*, finds in the Shaker Heights organization similar debates about white recruitment, exacerbated again by the difficulties aspiring black families had in buying into stable neighborhoods with good schools (85–88). Saltman, in *A Fragile Movement*, distinguishes between "steering" and what she calls "affirmative marketing," which "encourages people of the race least likely to consider moving to an area to do so" (402). Affirmative marketing, she argues, "expands housing choice" instead of restricting it. Saltman assumes that all markets are equally open, which was not the case during the late 1960s and early 1970s.

2. Dudziak, in *Cold War*, concludes that, by 1966, "Vietnam had replaced race as an important matter of international concern" (242). The State Department's worries about rebutting Communist charges of racial discrimination had been mitigated by the passage of national civil rights legislation, and, when world attention shifted, Washington's foreign policy establishment lost interest in the legislation's effectiveness.

3. The commissioners opened the *Report of the National Advisory Commission on Civil Disorders* with their "basic conclusion: Our nation is moving toward two societies, one black, one white—separate and unequal" (1).

4. Neighbors Inc. ad, n.d., and letter to Mr. Harold Howe, 29 December 1965, NIMSS, Box 1, Box 7.

5. Minutes, Recruitment Committee to Promote Move-Ins, 5 January 1965, NIMSS, Box 7.

6. Maurice Isserman and Michael Kazin, *America Divided: The Civil War of the 1960s* (New York: Oxford University Press, 2000), 56.

7. Gretchen Schafft, interviewed by author, Silver Spring, Md., 8 October 1999. All succeeding quotations are from this interview.

8. Conrad Christiano, interviewed by author, Washington, D.C., 16 November 1999. All succeeding quotations are from this interview.

9. Maija Hay, interviewed by author, Washington, D.C., 4 February 2000. All succeeding quotations are from this interview.

10. Pascoe, "Miscegenation Law."

11. Isobel (Peachy) Murray, interviewed by author, Washington, D.C., 26 October 1999. All succeeding quotations are from this interview.

12. Marilyn Christiano, interviewed by author, Washington, D.C., 16 November 1999. All succeeding quotations are from this interview.

13. Ben W. Gilbert, *Ten Blocks From the White House: Anatomy of the Washington Riots of 1968* (New York: Praeger, 1968), offers the immediate response of middle-class white Washingtonians to the events.

14. Barbara and Leonard Goodman, interviewed by author, Washington, D.C., 12 December 2001.

15. Marianne Meijer, interviewed by author, Washington, D.C., 14 December 1999. All succeeding quotations are from this interview.

16. *Report of the National Advisory Committee on Civil Disorders* summarized central causes of the riots as "pervasive discrimination and segregation in employment, education and housing, which have resulted in the continuing exclusion of great numbers of Negroes from the benefits of economic progress" (10).

17. Steven J. Diner, *Crisis of Confidence: The Reputation of Washington's Public Schools in the Twentieth Century* (Washington, D.C.: University of the District of Columbia Studies in D.C. History and Public Policy, 1982), offers a summary similar to mine and cites George D. Strayer, *The Report of a Survey of the Public Schools of the District of Columbia* (Washington, D.C.: Government Printing Office, 1949), which offered evidence that in 1948, eighth-grade white students were reading one year below the national norm, and black students were reading two and one-half years below the norm.

18. Adelaide Cromwell Hill, "Black Education in the Seventies: A Lesson from the Past," in *The Black Seventies*, ed. Floyd B. Barbour (Boston: Porter Sargent, 1970), 63, and Wolters, *The Burden of Brown*, 59.

19. *A Task Force on the Public School System in the District of Columbia as It Relates to the War on Poverty*, conducted by the Task Force on Antipoverty, the District of Columbia, Committee on Education and Labor, House of Representatives (Washington, D.C.: U.S. Government Printing Office, 1966), 59.

20. Wolters, *The Burden of Brown*, 13–14, citing *Investigation of Public School Conditions. Hearing before the Subcommittee of the Committee on the District of Columbia, House of Representatives*, 84th Cong., 2nd sess., 1956. Richter, *Integrating the Suburban Dream,* underlines the advantage Shaker Heights had in starting integration with schools ranked among the top thirty-eight in the nation, a school status quite

unlike that of the Neighbors Inc. schools (71). Rickie Solinger, in *Wake Up Little Susie: Single Pregnancy and Race before* Roe v. Wade, 2nd. ed. (New York: Routledge, 2000), argues that policy makers, physicians, and culture conceived black women as hypersexual during the postwar period and feared that white girls, whose rates of unwed pregnancy were converging with those of black girls, were susceptible, though white girls' sexual misbehavior was attributed to mental disturbance and not a racial propensity to sex. See esp. chaps. 2 and 3.

21. Carl F. Hansen, *Danger in Washington: The Story of My Twenty Years in the Public Schools in the Nation's Capital* (West Nyack, N.Y.: Parker, 1968), 56.

22. James G. Banks et al., "Civil Rights in Washington, D.C.: Status and Trends in Housing," and Irene Osborne, "The Public School System," both in *Civil Rights in the Nation's Capital: A Report on a Decade of Progress,* ed. Ben D. Segal, William Korey, and Charles N. Mason Jr. (New York: Association of Intergroup Relations Officials, 1959), 43, 66.

23. "Brief of North Washington Neighbors, Inc. ('Neighbors') *Amicus Curiae,* to United States District Court for the District of Columbia, *Julius W. Hobson et al. v. Carl F. Hansen et al.*," NIMSS, Box 8.

24. *Task Force on the Public School System,* 54.

25. Hansen, *Danger in Washington,* 66. In fall 1967, 7.8 percent of D.C. public school students were white (56). Richter, in *Integrating the Suburban Dream,* in striking contrast, reports that in the integration of the Shaker Heights schools, black students comprised 6 percent in 1964, 25 percent in 1970, and 40 percent in 1980 (69).

26. Diner, *Crisis of Confidence,* argues that the D.C. school debate confused issues of quality with those of the racial makeup of schools; for conservatives, the fact of a black majority explained the school failures, while for liberals, the persistence of racial segregation did. Neither group of whites in the debate had the knowledge about class differences among African Americans or the appreciation of middle-class black achievements that might have made possible more realistic assessments of the needs of poor students without implying that they needed to meet white standards to succeed. Gary Orfield concluded in the late 1970s in *Must We Bus? Segregated Schools and National Policy* (Washington: Brookings Institution, 1978): "During the mid-1970s [older] cities' school systems had to cope with unprecedented concentrations of low-income minority-group children, [and] tight money led to larger class sizes and shorter hours. . . . People in the older central cities could not keep up with the nation's rising income average" (52). The nationwide changes Orfield identifies with the 1970s occurred in Washington during the 1960s.

27. "Brief of North Washington Neighbors Inc.," 15.

28. District of Columbia Citizens for Better Public Education Inc., "Bulletin Boards," April 1968, summarized the effects of Wright's June 1967 ruling. "Statement of Neighbors, Inc. to the Board of Education," 19 February 1968, points out the need to take actions not realized by the Wright decision: "Judge Wright could not order that the schools be good; he could order only that they be equal." NIMSS, Box 16. Gary

Orfield and Susan E. Eaton, *Dismantling Desegregation: The Quiet Reversal of* Brown v. Board of Education (New York: New Press, 1996), notes that the Supreme Court's ruling against metropolitan responsibility for desegregation in *Milliken v. Bradley* (1973) "locked millions of schoolchildren into inferior, isolated schools" (13).

29. Caplan, *Farther Along,* 175–78.

30. Barbara Raskin, "Neighbors, Inc. No Longer Cares What Color the Neighbors Are," *Potomac Magazine,* 6 December 1970, 11.

31. Howard Wachtel, interviewed by author, Washington, D.C., 17 October 1995. All succeeding quotations are from this interview.

32. Barbara White, interviewed by author, Washington, D.C., 6 October 1999. All succeeding quotations are from this interview.

33. *Tifereth Israel Bulletin,* 15 July 1969, 1 March 1970, Tifereth Israel Synagogue Archives, Washington, D.C. Copies in author's possession. "Tifereth Israel Turns 75," *Washington Jewish Week,* 26 March 1992.

34. See Sandra Patton, *BirthMarks: Transracial Adoption in Contemporary America* (New York: New York University Press, 2000), 48–50, on the racial controversy over transracial adoption and the National Association of Black Social Workers 1972 statement. Patton argues that the white adoptions of black children in the 1960s "drew on racialized stories of salvation and rescue" (57) that absolved whites for continuing to enjoy the privileges of whiteness. Her argument applies to the 87 percent of adoptees raised in white neighborhoods, and she does not assess interracial living situations.

35. District of Columbia Government, *The People of the District of Columbia: A Demographic, Economic, and Physical Profile of the District of Columbia by Service Areas,* n.d., though the report analyzes 1970 Census Bureau data, 11.

36. Bert Landry, *Black Working Wives: Pioneers of the American Family Revolution* (Berkeley: University of California Press, 2000), 31. Landry demonstrates his thesis that ideology, not need, explains the racial difference in work patterns with data showing that, as married women's labor force participation increased after World War II, the earliest increase came among lower-middle-class white women and the latest among the upper middle class, at the same time that the highest rates for black families were among upper-middle-class wives. Even in the late 1970s, when upper-middle-class white women began to join the labor force in similar proportion to lower-middle-class white women and black women of all classes, only those without children raised their rates significantly. See esp. 89–111.

37. Milton Plesur, *Jewish Life in Twentieth-Century America: Challenge and Accommodation* (Chicago: Nelson-Hall, 1982), reports on studies of Jewish life during the 1970s and argues that Jewish synagogue affiliations rose as a result of the move to white suburbs, where Jews needed both a communal center to sustain identity and the religious affiliation required by white, Christian, suburban norms (186–87). Jonathan D. Sarna describes, in *American Judaism: A History* (New Haven: Yale University Press, 2004), the symbiosis of Conservative synagogues and suburban development in a new

appeal to suburban Jewish women who, "following middle-class cultural norms of the day, remained at home during the years that they bore and raised children, while their husbands spent long days commuting back and forth to jobs in the city" (285–86). Sarna does not mention the obvious, that the middle-class norms were also the white norms of racial segregation.

38. "Tifereth Israel Turns 75." Sarna, in *American Judaism*, describes what was felt to be revolutionary at TI as "virtually ubiquitous in Conservative synagogues . . . in the 1960s and 1970s" (287). At TI, the connections may have been made more directly between women's participation and other political movements toward equality.

39. Constance McLaughlin Green, in *The Secret City: A History of Race Relations in the Nation's Capital* (Princeton: Princeton University Press, 1967), states that by 1965 Shepherd Park was "the Negro 'Gold Coast' where colored and white families live side by side" (323).

40. Brenda Atkinson-Willoughby, interviewed by author, Washington, D.C., 24 May 2000. All succeeding quotations are from this interview.

41. Draft, *10th Annual Report, Neighbors Inc.*, September 1968, NIMSS, Box 27.

42. *Neighbors Ink,* December 1968.

43. Neighbors Inc., Board Minutes, September 1971, NIMSS, Box 27 (my italics).

44. *Neighbors Ink*, May 1973, February 1975.

45. Neighbors Inc., Board Minutes, 12 January 1972, NIMSS, Box 28; *Neighbors Ink*, September 1974.

46. *Neighbors Ink*, October 1975.

47. Neighbors Inc., Board Minutes, September 1972, NIMSS., Box 28.

48. Ibid.

49. Jenice View, interviewed by author, Washington, D.C., 18 May 2000. All succeeding quotations are from this interview.

50. Dan Meijer, interviewed by author, Silver Spring, Md., 5 October 1999. All succeeding quotations are from this interview.

51. Barbara Atkinson, interviewed by author, Washington, D.C., 16 December 1999. All succeeding quotations are from this interview.

52. Ruth Jordan, "Growing Up White in the D.C. Schools," *Civil Rights Digest*, Spring 1977, 35.

53. Gretchen Engle Schafft, *The Unexpected Minority: White Children in an Urban School and Neighborhood* (PhD diss, Catholic University of America, 1976).

54. *Neighbors: A Bi-Monthly Publication on Interracial Living*, June 1971. The founding conference of National Neighbors, held in Dayton, Ohio, in May 1970 with thirty-three neighborhood groups represented, grew out of the need of the Sponsors of Open Housing Investment, a religious group organized to fund integrated housing, to locate possible sites. National Neighbors, opening conference, minutes, NIMSS, Box 26. Saltman, *A Fragile Movement*, chap. 8, recounts the history of National Neighbors.

## Chapter 5

1. In response to Gus Garcia's argument in *Delgado v. Bastrop Independent School District* (1948), the federal district court declared unconstitutional segregation by classroom *within* an ostensibly integrated school. See Mario T. Garcia, *Mexican Americans: Leadership, Ideology, and Identity, 1930–1960* (New Haven: Yale University Press, 1989), 57–58. Gus Garcia had attended law school at the University of Texas in the 1930s, a privilege not available to aspiring African Americans until *Sweatt v. Painter* (1950) desegregated the state's premier law school.

2. I recovered this story as the result of an interview with Kathleen Voigt, one of the leaders of the Organized Voters League, San Antonio, 10 October 2000. This San Antonio section relies on the collections in the Catholic Archives of San Antonio, including the archdiocese's weekly newspaper, the *Alamo Messenger*, and oral history interviews with twenty-six people who were active in the Catholic Church, social justice work, labor organizing, Mexican American politics, and the formation of the Communities Organized for Public Service (COPS) and the Metro Alliance in the years between 1948 and 1988. The races, genders, and religions of those interviewed are: twelve white men, of whom seven are Catholic (including three priests), four Protestant, and one Jewish; seven white women, of whom two are Catholic sisters, four Protestant, and one Jewish; five Mexican American men, of whom four are Catholic and one Protestant; and two Mexican American women, both Catholic.

3. Montejano, in *Anglos and Mexicans*, argues that Mexican Americans were a "race" when "they were subjected to policies of discrimination and control" and implies that being Anglo, or white, was a central determinant of the ability to participate in public life (5). Control of political life was a substantial element of whiteness.

4. Amy Bridges, *Morning Glories: Municipal Reform in the Southwest* (Princeton: Princeton University Press, 1997), 111, 123, 126, and voting chart, 133; Rosales, *The Illusion of Inclusion*, 50.

5. See Booth and Johnson, "Community, Progress, and Power," esp. 19–27, for the history that follows.

6. George N. Green, *A Liberal's View of Texas Politics, 1820–1930s* (Boston: American Press, 1981), argues that by the 1920s Texan and Southern liberalism had "dwindled to 'business progressivism' that placed priority on service to industry, assumed that race relations were settled, and believed that tenants, factory workers, and the poor were not their problems" (40).

7. Neil Foley, *The White Scourge: Mexicans, Blacks, and Poor Whites in Texas Cotton Culture* (Berkeley: University of California Press, 1997), 5. Martha Menchaca argues in *Recovering History, Constructing Race: The Indian, Black, and White Roots of Mexican Americans* (Austin: University of Texas Press, 2001) that U.S. laws prohibiting citizenship standing for indigenous peoples and legal segregation of

peoples of African ancestry combined to penalize vast numbers of mestizo Mexican immigrants and Mexican Americans who could be disqualified under one or the other racial category. Only passage of the Nationality Act of 1940 "allowed indigenous immigrants from the Western hemisphere to obtain naturalization rights" (285).

8. Foley, *The White Scourge*, 8; Matthew Frye Jacobson, *Whiteness of a Different Color: European Immigrants and the Alchemy of Race* (Cambridge: Harvard University Press, 1998).

9. Mario Garcia, *Mexican Americans,* 43. Richard Garcia, in *Rise of the Mexican American Middle Class,* argues that the middle-class community sought to make itself loyally American while holding onto cultural practices and identity from Mexico, to become an accepted and nonracialized ethnic group like the Irish, for instance. See esp. chap. 9, "The Emerging Middle Class and LULAC." Thomas A. Guglielmo, "Fighting for Caucasian Rights: Mexicans, Mexican Americans, and the Transnational Struggle for Civil Rights in World War II Texas," *Journal of American History* 92 (March 2006), argues that middle-class Mexican Americans fought "for white rights for some, rather than equal rights for all," during the wartime era (1213). Many Mexican Americans identified as "white" and wanted to "distance themselves . . . from blackness," which a struggle for *equality* would imply (1234).

10. Zaragosa Vargas, in *Labor Rights Are Civil Rights: Mexican American Workers in Twentieth-Century America* (Princeton: Princeton University Press, 2005), reports that a 1943 San Antonio survey revealed "that the city's 100,000 Tejano [Texas Mexican American] residents had larger families, smaller houses, and less income than the city's blacks" (297).

11. Susan Lynn, "Gender and Progressive Politics: A Bridge to Social Activism of the 1960s," in *Not June Cleaver: Women and Gender in Postwar America, 1945–1960,* ed. Joanne Meyerowitz (Philadelphia: Temple University Press, 1994), points up the postwar activism of middle-class women and highlights especially the American Association of University Women, the League of Women Voters, the National Council of Jewish Women, the National Association for the Advancement of Colored People, and the Young Women's Christian Association (105).

12. Fay Sinkin, interviewed by author, San Antonio, 25 September 2000. All succeeding quotations are from this interview. Louise M. Young recounts in *In the Public Interest: The League of Women Voters, 1920–1970* (Westport, Conn.: Greenwood Press, 1989), an institutional history of the League, that the 1950s League adopted programs to "eradicate conditions of deprivation among all disadvantaged social groups" and to protect water within a broader environmental protection campaign (162). According to Heywood Sanders, longtime historian of San Antonio urban policy, the Chamber of Commerce was receiving "secret" reports in 1946 and then from its Public Health Committee in 1949 about the thousands of privies not connected with city water. It seems likely that the LWV survey contributed to the committee's work. Heywood Sanders, "Empty Taps, Missing Pipes, Water Policy, and Politics," in *On*

*the Border: An Environmental History of San Antonio,* ed. Char Miller (Pittsburgh: University of Pittsburgh Press, 2001), 145–46.

13. Sanders, "Empty Taps, Missing Pipes," 167.

14. Heywood T. Sanders describes the political battles over public financing for city services but doesn't connect these decisions to racializing the city's citizens. "Building a New Urban Infrastructure: The Creation of Postwar San Antonio," in *Urban Texas: Politics and Development,* eds. Char Miller and Heywood T. Sanders (College Station: Texas A & M University Press, 1990), 168.

15. Richard Lavine, "School Finance Reform in Texas, 1983–1995," in *Public Policy and Community: Activism and Governance in Texas,* ed. Robert H. Wilson (Austin: University of Texas Press, 1997), 119.

16. Richard A. Gambitta, Robert A. Milne, and Carol R. Davis, "The Politics of Unequal Educational Opportunity," in *The Politics of San Antonio: Community, Progress, and Power,* ed. David R. Johnson, John A. Booth, and Richard Harris (Lincoln: University of Nebraska Press, 1983), focuses on equalizing school finances in San Antonio, given the legal and political impossibility of reducing the number of districts to join poorer and richer schools in the same district. Guadalupe San Miguel Jr., *"Let All of Them Take Heed": Mexican Americans and the Campaign for Educational Equality in Texas, 1910–1981* (Austin: University of Texas Press, 1987). In chapter 7, San Miguel recounts Mexican Americans' legal fight to keep school districts from counting Mexican Americans as white for the purposes of school desegregation, which allowed authorities to integrate schools by sending black students to Mexican schools while Anglo schools remained racially exclusive, a struggle that ended only in 1973 when the Supreme Court ruled that Mexican Americans existed as an identifiable minority that had been systematically excluded from white schools, too. Chapter 8 examines battles for equalized school funding and bilingual programs that recognized Spanish as a legitimate language and the Mexican American cultural heritage as worthy of inclusion in the curriculum.

17. Bridges, *Morning Glories,* 169, 173.

18. Sanders, "Building a New Urban Infrastructure," 168.

19. Saul E. Bronder, *Social Justice and Church Authority: The Public Life of Archbishop Robert E. Lucey* (Philadelphia: Temple University Press, 1982), chaps. 1–3, provides the basic biographical information on Lucey.

20. William Murphy, "Rerum Novarum (1891)," and Thomas C. Kohler, "Quadragesimo Anno (1931)," in *A Century of Catholic Social Thought,* ed. George Weigel and Robert Royal (Washington, D.C.: Ethics and Public Policy Center, 1991), 20–22; 27.

21. Bronder, *Social Justice,* 72. Bronder's study of Archbishop Lucey's social justice interests overlaps mine on some particular events, though Bronder, writing at an earlier period, does not conceptualize race as constructed or Lucey's attitude toward Mexican Americans as Anglo benevolence.

22. Most Rev. Robert E. Lucey, "Are We Good Neighbors?" and "Reports," in *The Spanish Speaking of the Southwest and West: A Report of a Conference of Leaders, July 20–23, 1943* (Washington, D.C.: Social Action Department, National Catholic Welfare Conference), 14–17, 21–24.

23. Lucey, "Are We Good Neighbors?" 16.

24. Archbishop Robert E. Lucey, "Problems of Inter American Education," speech at Incarnate Word College, June 1944, Lucey MSS, (hereafter Lucey MSS), Catholic Archives of San Antonio (CASA), Social Problems: Race Relations, folder 1.

25. Stephen A. Privett, *The U.S. Catholic Church and Its Hispanic Members: The Pastoral Vision of Archbishop Robert E. Lucey* (San Antonio: Trinity University Press, 1988), 38, 144.

26. Fr. Sherrill Smith, Catholic Committee for Public Housing, to Reverend and dear Father, 21 May 1959, Lucey MSS, Social Problems: Poverty and Social Welfare, folder 2.

27. Fr. John Yanta, interviewed 1991, Bexar County History Collection, San Antonio Public Library; *Alamo Messenger*, 5 March and 21 May 1965.

28. *Alamo Messenger*, 18 June 1965.

29. Ed Foster, "Catholic Leader Rips Board," *San Antonio Light*, 22 January 1966.

30. Judge Charles Grace, interviewed by author, San Antonio, 30 November 2000. All succeeding quotations are from this interview.

31. "SANYO's Voter Drive," *Alamo Messenger*, 22 April 1966.

32. "Observers Agree It Will Take Years before Registrants Vote," *Alamo Messenger*, 21 May 1966.

33. Mary Beth Rogers, *Cold Anger: A Story of Faith and Power Politics* (Denton: University of North Texas Press, 1990), 67–69.

34. Juan A. Sepúlveda Jr., in *The Life and Times of Willie Velásquez: Su Voto es Su Voz* (Houston: Arte Publico Press, 2003), reports that late-1960s voter registration drives in Mexican American neighborhoods "typically resulted in higher registration rates in unorganized Anglo communities than in targeted Mexican American neighborhoods" (147), as Anglos responded to the perceived threat of Mexican American voting.

35. Daniel P. Moynihan, *Maximum Feasible Misunderstanding: Community Action in the War on Poverty* (New York: Free Press, 1969), 87.

36. Kemper Diehl, "Father Yanta and the S.A. Poverty War," *San Antonio Evening News*, 28 August 1967.

37. Vargas, in *Labor Rights Are Civil Rights*, cites complaints by Tejanos to the U.S. War Department on two grounds: first, that Mexican American farmworkers were being denied agricultural worker deferments because they were migrant and not stationary; and second, that Anglo draft boards preferred to send Mexican Americans and not Anglos into combat (208).

38. Everett Ross Clinchy Jr., *Equality of Opportunity for Latin Americans in Texas*

(New York: Arno Press, 1974), 76–79b. Rodolfo Acuña titles his survey of the bracero program "U.S. Capitalists Rent Their Mexican *Braceros,*" to indicate his evaluation of its transfer of labor power without labor protections, in *Occupied America: A History of Chicanos,* 4th ed. (New York: Longman, 2004), 285–89. Richard B. Craig, in *The Bracero Program* (Austin: University of Texas Press, 1971), offers a more neutral account. Ngai, in *Impossible Subjects,* 138–47, places the bracero program in a long history of manipulating Mexican workers' citizenship status to deny them bargaining protections and to enable employers to avoid U.S. labor regulations. Bronder discusses Archbishop Lucey's fight against the bracero program in *Social Justice,* 76–83.

39. Fr. John Wagner, interviewed by author, San Antonio, 20 September 2000. All succeeding quotations are from this interview.

40. J. Craig Jenkins, *The Politics of Insurgency: The Farm Worker Movement in the 1960s* (New York: Columbia University Press, 1985), describes the Delano strike and march and its civil rights associations, 144–56.

41. "'Huelga' Changes Hearts," *Alamo Messenger,* 4 March 1966.

42. "Hearts of People," *Alamo Messenger,* 8 April 1966; Susan Ferris and Ricardo Sandoval, *The Fight in the Fields: Cesar Chavez and the Farmworkers Movement* (New York: Harcourt Brace, 1997), 117–21.

43. "Pilgrimage of Penance," *Alamo Messenger,* 1 April 1966.

44. "Step after Step," *Alamo Messenger,* 15 April 1966.

45. Ernest Morgan, "Strike Puts Starr under Observation," *Corpus Christi Caller,* 6 July 1966.

46. Rev. Charles Grahmann to James E. Ryan, 9 September 1966; "Mass for Marchers," San Fernando Cathedral, 27 August 1966, Lucey MSS, Social Problems: Valley Farm Workers, folder 2 (1966) (my italics).

47. Most Rev. Robert E. Lucey to The Honorable John Connally, 30 August 1966, Lucey MSS, Social Problems: Valley Farm Workers, 2 (1966).

48. "The Confrontation," *Texas Observer,* 16 September 1966.

49. "The March: A Triumph, A Task"; Greg Olds, "Labor Day in Austin: A Bad Day for the Establishment"; "Politicians and the March," all in *Texas Observer,* 16 September 1966.

50. F. F. "Pancho" Medrano, interviewed Dallas, November 1971, Texas Labor Archives, University of Texas, Arlington.

51. "U.S. Would Ban Strike-Breaking by Alien Laborers," *Alamo Messenger,* 11 May 1967; "NLRA Coverage," editorial, *Alamo Messenger,* 18 May 1967, discusses the vulnerability of workers not protected by the National Labor Relations Act and concludes that "to deny this protection to these workers, we will be creating a class of second-class citizens, a class of untouchables in a land built on the belief that every man is created equal." "Rowdy Rangers," editorial, *Alamo Messenger,* 1 June 1967, concludes that the Rangers have a mythic history but are "now enforcing

a partial sense of justice and ignoring rights of unions, minority groups, and clergymen who defend unpopular causes."

52. Father Juraschek to the Archbishop, 12 September 1966, Lucey MSS, Social Problems: Valley Farm Workers, folder 2.

53. George N. Green, "Anti-Labor Politics in Texas, 1941–1957," in *American Labor in the Southwest: The First One Hundred Years,* ed. James C. Foster (Tucson: University of Arizona Press, 1982), 221–23; Robert H. Zieger and Gilbert J. Gall, *American Workers: American Unions,* 3rd ed. (Baltimore: Johns Hopkins University Press, 2002), 152–54, 179.

54. Archbishop Lucey to Rev. Sherrill Smith, 23 February 1959, Lucey MSS, Social Problems: Labor Relations, folder 2.

55. "Labor Mass, St. Mary's Church, Friday, April 15, 1953," Lucey MSS, Social Problems: Labor Relations, folder 2.

56. Most Rev. Robert E. Lucey, "Work, Wages, and Religion," *Texas State Federation of Labor 1953 Review,* 56, 59.

57. Ruth Harris, interviewed by author, San Antonio, 8 February 2001. All succeeding quotations are from this interview.

58. Paul Javior, interviewed by author, San Antonio, 8 January 2001. All succeeding quotations are from this interview.

59. Father Sherrill Smith to Dear Friend, 4 September 1962, Lucey MSS, Social Problems: Labor Relations, folder 3.

60. Most Rev. Robert E. Lucey to Mr. W. E. Thomas, 27 July 1964, Lucey MSS, Social Problems: Labor Unions, folder 3.

61. "Father Smith Leads March by Steves' Strikers," *Alamo Messenger,* 22 December 1966.

62. Kemper Diehl, "Poverty War: $17 Million Bexar Business," *San Antonio Express and News,* 26 August 1967.

63. "City Workers Get 10 Percent Pay Hike," *San Antonio Light,* 12 July 1967.

64. Christopher Newfield and Avery F. Gordon, "Multiculturalism's Unfinished Business," in *Mapping Multiculturalism,* ed. Avery F. Gordon and Christopher Newfield (Minneapolis: University of Minnesota Press, 1996), 80–81.

65. Andy Hernandez, interviewed by author, San Antonio, 18 January 2001. All succeeding quotations are from this interview.

66. Garcia, *Mexican Americans.*

67. "S. A. Solon Loses Minimum Wage Fight," *San Antonio Light,* 4 April 1967.

68. Joe Bernal, interviewed by author, San Antonio, 23 January 2001 and 7 February 2001. All succeeding quotations are from these interviews.

69. McGreevy, *Parish Boundaries,* 160.

70. Saul E. Bronder, in chap. 7, "Coming Apart," *Social Justice,* describes the tumultuous end to Lucey's career and blames it partly on the archbishop's unpopular defense of President Lyndon Johnson's Vietnam War policy.

## Chapter 6

The source of the epigraph is Virgil Elizondo, *The Future Is Mestizo: Life Where Cultures Meet*, rev. ed. (Boulder: University Press of Colorado, 2000).

1. Andy Hernandez, interviewed by author, San Antonio, 18 January 2001. All succeeding quotations are from this interview.

2. Armando Navarro, *Mexican American Youth Organization: Avant-Garde of the Chicano Movement in Texas* (Austin: University of Texas Press, 1995), 80–81. Navarro's book provides much of the background for my discussion of the MAYO/Chicano movement in San Antonio. "Los Cinco" also evoked the holiday of Cinco de Mayo, a commemoration of the day in 1862 when Mexican forces defeated an invading French army, which Mexican Americans were beginning to celebrate as proof of Mexican and Mexican American valor and independence.

3. See Isserman and Kazin, *America Divided*, 199–203, on the national decline of white sympathy for racial civil rights.

4. Ignacio Garcia, *United We Win: The Rise and Fall of La Raza Unida Party* (Tucson: Mexican American Studies, University of Arizona, 1989), 30, 31. Garcia was one of Lanier High School's striking students.

5. José Angel Gutiérrez, *The Making of a Chicano Militant: Lessons from Cristal* (Madison: University of Wisconsin Press, 1998); Sepúlveda, *Willie Velásquez*, 50. Sepúlveda's biography of Velásquez, the work of Armando Navarro, Ignacio Garcia, and José Angel Gutiérrez, are the central sources of information about the San Antonio Chicano leadership.

6. Sepúlveda, *Willie Velásquez*, 57. Ignacio Garcia, *United We Win*, argues that Velásquez did not move into the Raza Unida Party with José Angel Gutiérrez and other colleagues because "he believed in pluralistic participation rather than Chicano empowerment. . . . Velásquez later described himself as a Jeffersonian Democrat" (61–62).

7. Navarro, *Mexican American Youth Organization*, 227.

8. Kay Duarte, "Alinsky: Make Priests Shepherds," *Alamo Messenger*, 2 September 1966.

9. Arnold Flores, interviewed by author, San Antonio, 1 December 2000. All succeeding quotations are from this interview.

10. Texas Advisory Committee to the U.S. Commission on Civil Rights, *Status of Civil Rights in Texas, Vol. II: An Employment Profile of San Antonio, 1968–1978*, January 1980, 205–6, provides data that back up Flores's assessments about employment discrimination at Kelly Air Force Base.

11. Navarro, *Mexican American Youth Organization*, attributes some of the group's heightened masculinity to a need to appeal to barrio gang members (111) and tells how the MAYO participants he interviewed tended to rewrite the story in retrospect to include greater women's participation. Only in the early 1970s, according to Navarro's sources, did a generation of college-educated women begin to take on

the leadership roles held exclusively by men in the first few years of the movement (110–12). Vicki L. Ruiz, *From out of the Shadows: Mexican Women in Twentieth-Century America* (New York: Oxford University Press, 1998), argues that women's activism in the Chicano movement has been overlooked, possibly because Mexican American culture offered only two dichotomous conceptions of women: a protected virgin or a deceiving descendant of La Malinche, the traitorous Aztec mistress of the Spanish conqueror Cortez (106).

12. Navarro, *Mexican American Youth Organization*, 88

13. Ibid., 168–71.

14. Rosales, *The Illusion of Inclusion*, 100–101.

15. Jane Mansbridge argues in "Complicating Oppositional Consciousness," in *Oppositional Consciousness: The Subjective Roots of Social Protest*, ed. Jane Mansbridge and Aldon Morris (Chicago: University of Chicago Press, 2001), that oppositional consciousness may be essential to mobilize disempowered people; her assessment is more positive than mine (250–55).

16. Chela Sandoval, in *Methodology of the Oppressed* (Minneapolis: University of Minnesota Press, 2000), 57–63, lays out an idea of "differential consciousness" as a political position distinct from "oppositional consciousness." Her concept, which reflects developments among theorists from the late 1970s on regarding women of color, helped me understand the profound differences between opposition and assertiveness that I discern in San Antonio's Mexican American political approaches.

17. Michael Warner, *Changing Witness: Catholic Bishops and Public Policy, 1917–1994* (Washington, D.C.: Ethics and Public Policy Center, 1995), 59; George Weigel, "Pacem in Terris (1963)," in *A Century of Catholic Social Thought*, ed. George Weigel and Robert Royal (Washington, D.C.: Ethics and Public Policy Center, 1991); George Weigel, *Catholicism and the Renewal of American Democracy* (New York: Paulist Press, 1989).

18. *Commission of Mexican American Affairs, 1972 Annual Report*, Furey MSS, (hereafter, Furey MSS), Social Problems: Committee on Mexican American Affairs, CASA.

19. As part of his stand for desegregation, Lucey admitted black students to Central Catholic High School in 1953 and made the school a welcoming place for bright young Mexican American Catholic men. Many other activists of the 1960s and 1970s, including Willie Velásquez, graduated from Central Catholic, as did the city's first Hispanic mayor, Henry Cisneros. Sepúlveda, *Willie Velásquez*, 18–22.

20. Ernie Cortes, interviewed by author, Austin, 23 February 2001. Except where noted, all succeeding quotations are from this interview. Doug Rossinow, *The Politics of Authenticity: Liberalism, Christianity, and the New Left in America* (New York: Columbia University Press, 1998), recounts the importance of the UT YMCA-YWCA in the Austin civil rights scene from the 1930s through the early 1960s in chap. 3, "The Issues of Life: The University YMCA-YWCA and Christian Liberalism."

21. Saul D. Alinsky, *Reveille for Radicals* (New York: Vintage Books, 1989; reprint of Random House, 1969), xiii.

22. Sanford D. Horwitt recounts in *Let Them Call Me Rebel: Saul Alinsky—His Life and Legacy* (New York: Knopf, 1989) a correspondence between Alinsky and Jacques Maritain in which Maritain praised Alinsky for showing how to link moral engagement with the "elementary requirements of true political life," especially citizen participation (166). Harry C. Boyte, in *Common Wealth: A Return to Citizen Politics* (New York: Free Press, 1989), chap. 6, "Reconnecting Power and Vision," describes how Chambers and Cortes brought a theological basis to Alinsky's secular ideas to evoke a heritage of gathering people into communities able to claim a share of local "governance" (99).

23. Charles M. Payne argues in *I've Got the Light of Freedom: The Organizing Tradition and the Mississippi Freedom Struggle* (Berkeley: University of California Press, 1995) that taking time to develop competence and relationships was at the heart of a distinctly Southern black organizing tradition that made possible the brave actions of poor Mississippi African Americans who risked jobs, homes, and physical safety in the civil rights movement. The COPS/Metro organizing suggests that these steps can be consciously learned and transmitted to groups without such a heritage.

24. Charles Cottrell, interviewed by author, San Antonio, 28 February 2001. All succeeding quotations are from this interview.

25. Currin V. Shields, *Democracy and Catholicism in America* (New York: McGraw-Hill, 1958).

26. Kohler, "Quadragesimo Anno (1931)," 30–33.

27. Michelle Watkins and Ralph McInerny, "Jacques Maritain and the Rapprochement of Liberalism and Communitarianism," in *Catholicism, Liberalism, and Communitarianism: The Catholic Intellectual Tradition and the Moral Foundations of Democracy,* ed. Kenneth L. Grasso, Gerard V. Bradley, and Robert P. Hunt (Lanham, Md.: Rowman and Littlefield, 1995), 155–56; Ernie Cortes summarized this position years later in "Reflections on the Catholic Tradition of Family Rights," in *One Hundred Years of Catholic Social Thought*, ed. John A. Coleman (Maryknoll, N.Y.: Orbis Books, 1991), 160; Steinfels, in *A People Adrift*, recounts how Vatican II triggered a battle over the meaning of Roman Catholicism. For conservatives, particularly horrified at the diminution of hierarchical authority, the benefit and appropriate interpretation of the council's work is that it opened the Church from "a European-based to a genuinely global faith" (32), consolidated when Pope John Paul II reestablished papal authority and principles of hierarchy while also consolidating the global reach of the Church. For liberals, Vatican II "reversed the tendency to structure the church in ever more hierarchical, centralized and juridical terms" (34), a positive change unfortunately reversed by John Paul II's policies. Certainly in the late 1960s and early 1970s, many San Antonio Catholics, Mexican

American and Anglo, interpreted Vatican II as an encouragement of democracy within and outside the Church and found authorization for the freshly inspired congruence between their religious life and their political work.

28. Ernie Cortes, informally interviewed by author, Austin, 22 January 2001. Notes in possession of author.

29. Andres Sarabia, interviewed by author, San Antonio, 9 February 2001. Unless otherwise noted, all succeeding quotations are from this interview.

30. "Becker Orders Work on Drainage," *San Antonio Light,* 23 August 1974; editorial, "Our Capital Needs," *San Antonio Light,* 24 August 1974.

31. "Address of His Excellency, Most Reverend Francis J. Furey at the Convention of the San Antonio Organization Known as COPS (Communities Organized for Public Services), Thomas Jefferson High School Auditorium, November 23, 1974," Furey MSS, Organization, COPS, 1974–1975. Furey's slogan translates, "With COPS everything, without COPS nothing." The phrase was simple enough for Anglos to understand and a reminder that the Spanish language permeated life in South Texas.

32. Ruiz, *From out of the Shadows,* 138–41, credits COPS with providing a locus for women's organizing and public action and challenges Peter Skerry's dismissal in his *Mexican Americans: The Ambivalent Minority* (New York: Free Press, 1993) of COPS women as pliant followers of commanding organizers.

33. Beatrice Gallego, interviewed by author, San Antonio, 19 February 2001. All succeeding quotations are from this interview.

34. Rick Casey, "Church Plays Major Role in Community Group Forging Progress in San Antonio," *National Catholic Reporter,* 12 March 1976.

35. The Joske's and Frost Bank stories are part of the legend of COPS told in Warren, *Dry Bones Rattling,* at the opening of chap. 2, "A Theology of Organizing: From Alinsky to the Modern IAF," Warren's political sociology study of the IAF as a beacon for reviving citizen participation (40–41); and in Mary Beth Rogers, *Cold Anger: A Story of Faith and Power Politics* (Denton: University of North Texas Press, 1990), which examines COPS and IAF organizing through the late 1980s (114–15).

36. Warren, *Dry Bones Rattling,* 111. Without exception, every COPS person I interviewed quoted the Iron Rule, the principle of self-governance that distinguishes democratic organizing from charity work.

37. "COPS, EDF to Meet," *San Antonio Light,* 16 February 1978.

38. Don Politico, "COPS: Our Politico of the Year," *San Antonio Light,* 12 December 1975.

39. Heywood T. Sanders, "Communities Organized for Public Service and Neighborhood Revitalization in San Antonio," in *Public Policy and Community: Activism and Governance in Texas,* ed. Robert H. Wilson (Austin: University of Texas Press, 1997), 49.

40. John A. Booth, "Political Change in San Antonio, 1970–1982: Toward Decay or Democracy," in *The Politics of San Antonio: Community, Progress, and Power,*

ed. David R. Johnson, John A. Booth, and Richard J. Harris (Lincoln: University of Nebraska Press, 1983), 201.

41. Sanders, "Communities Organized for Public Service," 49 (my italics).

42. "Drainage Takes Bulk of Bonds," *San Antonio Express*, 26 February 1978. Skerry also tells the IAF/COPS story in *Mexican Americans*, but he sees the organizing as a successful campaign to increase nonracialized political power. He rejects the idea that Anglo interests racialized Mexican Americans and argues "that Mexican Americans are being seduced by the new American political system into adopting the not entirely appropriate, divisive, and counterproductive stance of a racial minority group" (367). Rejecting the premise of racialization, Skerry has no interest either in understanding the struggle of COPS members to retain their integrity as Mexican Americans without being treated as racial inferiors or in COPS's Anglo allies.

43. These headlines and some additional ones appeared in *San Antonio Light*, 12, 14, 15, 16, 23, 25, and 28 February 1978; *San Antonio Express*, 3 and 7 March 1978. Sanders, "Communities Organized for Public Service," also mentions this bond election "split along racial lines," though the bonds lost because only 72 percent approved in "predominantly Hispanic precincts" (51–52).

44. Sister Pearl Ceasar, interviewed by author, Dallas, 19 March 2001. All succeeding quotations are from this interview.

45. "N. Side 'COPS' Gearing Up," *San Antonio Light*, 19 February 1978.

46. Homer Bain, interviewed by author, San Antonio, 8 November 2002. All succeeding quotations are from this interview.

47. Sanders, in "Communities Organized for Public Service," argues that the city's business leaders struck a compromise with COPS. COPS neighborhoods controlled the federal Community Development Block Grant funds allocated to the city annually; the council evenly divided bond issue funds among every district; and the city staff issued "certificates of obligation" to cover downtown development projects (56–61).

48. *25th Anniversary, San Antonio Communities Organized for Public Service, 1974–1999*, 8–9, contains a brief "Metro Alliance History," as does *The Southwest IAF Network: 25 Years of Organizing* (Austin: Interfaith Education Fund, 1999). Copies in author's possession.

49. Jane Tuck, interviewed by author, San Antonio, 7 November 2002. All succeeding quotations are from this interview.

50. Although not officially segregated, the League of Women Voters had few black members in its Southern chapters (less than a hundred for the entire region in 1954), according to Young, *In the Public Interest*, 172. Young offers no data about Mexican American membership, but a League member's profile in the early 1970s—well educated and married to a professional man—made this a definitively white, middle-class group (156–57).

51. Rowena Rodgers, interviewed by author, San Antonio, 17 January 2001. All succeeding quotations are from this interview.

52. Marilyn Stavinoha, interviewed by author, San Antonio, 13 February 2001. All succeeding quotations are from this interview.

53. Robert Fisher, *Let the People Decide: Neighborhood Organizing in America* (New York: Twayne, 1994), distinguishes "social work" models of social change that emphasize charity from "political activist" models of change, such as in IAF, that focus on restructuring relationships of power (205–6).

54. David Semrad, interviewed by author, San Antonio, 16 June 2003. All succeeding quotations are from this interview.

55. Sanders, "Communities Organized for Public Service," 59, 61.

56. Henry Cisneros, "City Planning in the 1980s," speech to the American Planning Association annual meeting, 9 April 1984, in *Cisneros: Portrait of a New American,* by Kemper Diehl and Jan Jarboe (San Antonio: Corona, 1985), 148.

57. *The Cisneros Years: A Report.* San Antonio, 1989. No publisher is identified, and the author is "the People of San Antonio." This promotional catalogue of Cisneros's mayoral actions highlights the educational developments that Cisneros wanted to stress.

58. Swen Borg, interviewed by author, San Antonio, 15 February 2003. All succeeding quotations are from this interview.

59. Quoted in Rogers, *Cold Anger,* 126.

## Conclusion

The second epigraph is from Ernesto Cortes Jr., "Habits of Democracy," *Texas Observer,* 17 November 2006. Cortes continues as the executive director of the Southwest Region of the Industrial Areas Foundation.

1. Allen, *Talking to Strangers,* argues that when black Americans stood up for basic rights of citizenship, such as attending a desegregated Little Rock High School in 1957, the hostile white American response revealed the fundamental terms of citizenship that were being altered: white dominance and black acquiescence (18). Allen's inspiring book focuses on relationships of black and white, but her analysis is provocative for rethinking the relationships between white Americans and other groups racialized as nonwhite: interned Japanese, excluded Chinese, exploited Mexican American farmworkers, colonized Puerto Ricans, and marginalized American Indians.

2. *Eyes on the Prize: America's Civil Rights Years, 1954–1965,* produced by Blackside, 1987, PBS; *Eyes on the Prize, II: America at the Racial Crossroads, 1965–1985,* produced by Blackside, 1989, PBS.

3. *www.allencol.edu/default.aspx?pageid=143* (accessed 25 June 2007).

4. Joan Wallach with Michael Wallach, *The Enemy Has a Face: The Seeds of Peace Experience* (Washington, D.C.: United States Institute of Peace Press, 2000), 7–8, 32, 59.

5. Ibid., 115.

6. The site for Neve Shalom/Wahat al-Salam, the bilingual village, is *www.nswas.net* (accessed 25 June 2007).

7. Douglas Stone, *Difficult Conversations: How to Discuss What Matters Most* (New York: Penguin Books, 2000).

8. Among the most vehement defenders of racial improvement are Dinesh D'Souza, *The End of Racism* (New York: Free Press, 1995), and Abigail Thernstrom and Stephan Thernstrom, *America in Black and White: One Nation, Indivisible* (New York: Simon and Schuster, 1997). Among the opponents, see Brown et al., *Whitewashing Race*, the collaborative project of seven sociologists from the University of California at Berkeley and at Santa Cruz. Both positions emphasize the black-white split as the measure for racial change. Oddly, given the University of California authors' pairing of "black and Latino" throughout the text, they, too, assess racial division with primarily "black" and "white" statistics.

9. Gary Orfield states in "Commentary," in *Latinos Remaking America*, ed. Marcelo N. Suarez-Orozco and Mariela M. Paez (Berkeley: University of California Press and David Rockefeller Center for Latin American Studies, Harvard University, 2002): "Latino students . . . are by far the least successful group of students in finishing high school and their access to college is declining" at the very moment that high school and college degrees are essential to good adult incomes (390).

10. Michael B. Katz, Mark J. Stern, and Jamie J. Fader, in "The New African American Inequality," *Journal of American History* 92 (June 2005), state that by the 2000 census, "post-World War II configurations of spatial segregation and inequality remained mostly in place." Even though black families followed the trajectory of white families into suburbs, these quickly segregated, so that in 1990 and 2000, the roughly one-third of black families in suburbs lived in neighborhoods that were 46 percent black (79). This means, of course, that substantial numbers of white families were living outside white enclaves.

11. Setha Low, in *Behind the Gates: Life, Security, and the Pursuit of Happiness in Fortress America* (New York: Routledge, 2003), reports the number of people living in gated communities in the United States as four million in 1995, eight million in 1997, and sixteen million in 1998. The 2001 American Housing Survey found 5.9 percent of households living in areas surrounded by walls or fences and another 3.4 percent in communities with "access by entry codes, key cards, or security guard approval" (15).

12. Lani Guinier and Gerald Torres point out in *The Miner's Canary: Enlisting Race, Resisting Power, Transforming Democracy* (Cambridge: Harvard University Press, 2002), 72–74, that research carried out during the political battle to keep students of color on campus after the University of Texas's affirmative action plan was declared unconstitutional found that "some counties in [rural] West Texas had *never* sent a high school graduate to the University of Texas" (73). All rural students suffered from not living in white middle-class areas.

13. Martin P. Wattenberg, *Where Have All the Voters Gone?* (Cambridge: Harvard

University Press, 2002), 11. Wattenberg goes on to say that turnout is declining in all established democracies but argues that the U.S. case is extreme and that the decline represents a failure in democracy if we assume that the standard of success is that "all voices are heard and all interests represented" (81).

14. *To Assure Pride and Confidence in the Electoral Process: Report of the National Commission on Federal Election Reform,* cochairs Jimmy Carter, Gerald R. Ford, Lloyd N. Cutler, and Robert H. Michel (Washington, D.C.: Brookings Institution Press, 2002), 45–46.

15. In the introductory chapter of his study about the IAF in Texas, *Dry Bones Rattling,* Warren "argues that the key to reinvigorating democracy in the United States can be found in efforts to engage people in politics through their participation in the stable institutions of community life" (15).

16. Stewart Kwoh, "Improving Race Relations: What Have We Learned in the Past 15 Years?" Pat Brown Institute of Public Affairs, Policy Paper No. 5 (November 2006), laments the loss of NCCJ to Los Angeles human relations work. *www. patbrowninstitute.org/educationprograms/documents/NovemberWhitePaper.pdf* (accessed 25 June 2007). The California Conference for Equality and Justice site is *www.cacej.org* (accessed 25 June 2007).

17. The information is on the Web site *www.nccjsocal.org* (accessed 25 October 2005).

18. Cashin, *The Failures of Integration,* 5, 14.

19. Interviews with Rabbi Ethan Seidel, 27 April 2004, and Shepherd Park resident Susan Cotter, 28 June 2004.

20. "Network of Texas IAF Organizations. Draft Standing for Families Agenda of Issues (9/7/06)." Copy in author's possession.

21. Allen, *Talking to Strangers,* 19.

22. Ibid., 157.

23. As I was finishing this book, two sermons held out a promise of the greater security that may come from loving relationships. On 10 July 2005, just days after the London subway bombings of civilians, Rev. Lib McGregor Simmons at University Presbyterian Church in San Antonio took her message from a sermon Rev. Martin Luther King Jr. delivered in the harshest days of the civil rights battles of the early 1960s. Citing King, Simmons reminded listeners of two requirements for Christians in the present fearful moment: to be "tough-minded" in analyzing the sources of human cruelty, despair, and hate, and, even as we push against evil, to be "tender-hearted" and remember the requirement of love for all God's creation. The next week, Rev. Paul Abernathy, rector of St. Mark's Episcopal Church in Washington, D.C., refined my sense of "justice," which he defined as "dealing fairly with others. Being in honest and balanced relationship with others and myself and with all of creation and the Creator." These Protestant Christian leaders—a white, Southern-born woman and a black, border state–born man—continue to inspire their predominantly white congregations to expand their relationships.

# Index